CENTER OF DREAMS

UNIVERSITY PRESS OF FLORIDA

Florida A&M University, Tallahassee
Florida Atlantic University, Boca Raton
Florida Gulf Coast University, Ft. Myers
Florida International University, Miami
Florida State University, Tallahassee
New College of Florida, Sarasota
University of Central Florida, Orlando
University of Florida, Gainesville
University of North Florida, Jacksonville
University of South Florida, Tampa
University of West Florida, Pensacola

CENTER OF DREAMS

BUILDING A WORLD-CLASS PERFORMING ARTS
COMPLEX IN MIAMI

LES STANDIFORD

University Press of Florida

Gainesville · Tallahassee · Tampa · Boca Raton

Pensacola · Orlando · Miami · Jacksonville · Ft. Myers · Sarasota

This book may be available in an electronic edition.

23 22 21 20 19 18   6 5 4 3 2 1

Library of Congress Control Number: 2017947595
ISBN 978-0-8130-5672-2

The University Press of Florida is the scholarly publishing agency for the State University System of
Florida, comprising Florida A&M University, Florida Atlantic University, Florida Gulf Coast University,
Florida International University, Florida State University, New College of Florida, University of Central
Florida, University of Florida, University of North Florida, University of South Florida, and University
of West Florida.

University Press of Florida
15 Northwest 15th Street
Gainesville, FL 32611-2079
http://upress.ufl.edu

This book is dedicated to the many individuals who labored
long and hard in service of what was often called impossible—
the building of a world-class center for the performing arts in Miami.

In memory of Parker D. Thomson, 1932–2017

CONTENTS

CENTER OF DREAMS

Introduction

More Than Just a Building

As this manuscript neared its completion in 2016, one of the more spirited presidential contests in the nation's history was taking place. While no overt cultural question dominated that race, it easily might have, for the issues that were debated concerning immigration, taxation, the state of the economy, and the proper distribution of government resources are tied directly to the larger implications behind the narrative shaping this book. Scarcely a quarter of a century ago, staunch conservative and influential North Carolina Senator Jesse Helms expended unprecedented political capital in attempts to abolish the National Endowment for the Arts. While the agency managed to survive, Helms's efforts diminished the NEA's budget and its workings significantly and ensured that questions regarding government support for the arts would hover ever after in the country's political consciousness.

The story of the long fight to establish a world-class county-owned performing arts center in Miami is a compelling tale of political intrigue in and of itself, offering insights into the social realities of a place whose largely immigrant makeup has been termed a bellwether for the United States. But at bedrock, the questions at the heart of this story go to the very core of what is deemed the proper role of our government and its responsibility to its citizens. It is not the intent here to provide definitive answers to such questions, but this account will hopefully lay out with clarity the manner in which one often fractious community found its own solutions.

On its most immediate level, the story of the decades-long struggle played out in an emerging city to create a dual-theater performing arts center meant to rival the Kennedy Center and the Lincoln Center in scope and quality contains all the necessary elements of the mythic story paradigm described by noted anthropologist and social commentator Joseph Campbell. As Campbell explains, in every effective story across all cultures, an individual, motivated by the need to make his community whole in some fashion, is called to a journey toward a goal deemed impossible by many.

This individual—just like Dorothy in Oz—attracts a cadre of like-minded and able helpers to help navigate the journey, solve ensuing problems, and fight a series of battles ever-escalating in their intensity. Though there is a moment when all seems irrevocably lost, the seeker eventually prevails and sets out to return home with the prize. There will be a moment in the final stages of this journey, Campbell says, when the forces arrayed against the mission make a final attempt to crush it. In the balance hangs the answer to the question whether all effort will be for naught or if indeed the struggle will be successful and productive, not only for the seeker but for the seeker's society as a whole.

Such a structure—common to comedy, romance, and tragedy alike— has an appeal unto itself, and the presence of that timeless pattern in this material is what drew this writer to the task. However, the substance behind the structure is what determines whether the story is a mere diversion or has something to offer thoughtful readers beyond its particulars.

One goal here, of course, is to recreate the drama of the long journey toward the creation of a center for the performing arts in Miami, for this is about as unlikely a place imaginable to set about building what would become the most costly and ambitious cultural arts complex since the Kennedy Center. And Miami's performing arts center is certainly one of the most demanding and most significant public building projects ever undertaken in South Florida. In the end, the cost of what we know today as the Adrienne Arsht Center for the Performing Arts of Miami-Dade County was more than ten times that of Henry Flagler's fabled Oversea Railway from Miami to Key West, completed just short of a century earlier.

Furthermore, while Flagler's project took about twenty years to complete, from its original conception to the driving of the final spike, Miami's performing arts center was nearly thirty-five years in the making, spanning the years from the germ of its conception in 1972 to its opening in 2006. There were a number of times, in fact, when the latter project, its costs soaring to unimaginable heights, seemed doomed. Despite its glamorous image as a tropical tourist destination, Miami, a retiree and snowbird haven for most of its existence when the performing arts center was first imagined, has never enjoyed the benefits of a broad-based economy with a cadre of philanthropically inclined corporate partners ready to be touched for such undertakings.

It also might be supposed that the diversity that has come to characterize modern Miami would have only worked against any accord on the need for such a center. How on earth could there be a "cultural center" for a place that had become so culturally divided? In the 1960s the Cuban revolution unleashed a flood tide of immigration unexperienced in the United States since hordes were overwhelming Ellis Island. And for more than half a century since, millions of immigrants from every country and dependency in the Caribbean and Latin America have poured into Miami in pursuit of the American dream, despite the region's limited economic base.

Additionally, these new arrivals only compounded the difficulties faced by Miami's substantial African American population, who formed the traditional backbone of a principally service-based economy. Topping off the fractiousness were the complaints of many longtime white residents who found the Spanish suddenly being spoken on "their" streets distasteful and threatening. One of the bumper stickers favored by disgruntled crackers of the 1980s was, "Will the last American leaving Miami please bring the flag?"

Those who fought for the establishment of the performing arts center were undaunted by such divisiveness, however, believing that the project constituted the very antidote to bigoted thinking and that it was a necessary investment on the part of civic leaders truly interested in the well-being of a citizenry. Such dedication requires the long view, of course, and flies in the face of political expediency.

Given all this backdrop, it should be no surprise that the creation in Miami of a world-class performing arts center should have been so difficult to pull off, nor to hear that even after the roof was on and the doors were opened, the performing arts center teetered precariously on the verge of financial collapse before its eleventh-hour salvation.

Obviously, this story embodies a political and social history of a most unusual place. But just as clearly, there is an even more significant theme, a question at the heart of the quest itself. At a time in our nation when it seems almost impossible to keep roads paved and bridges standing, police and first responders adequately trained and fully equipped, the less fortunate fed and housed, to what extent is government everywhere obligated to attend as well to the cultural needs of its citizens?

God forbid that this question had come up during the presidential debates of 2016, for there was more than enough on the candidates' plates already, but it is nonetheless an issue at the heart of this story, and it is also a question that every governmental body will inevitably debate in the years to come, for there will always be a significant number of citizens who will demand that it be.

Nor can this narrative be discounted as one singular to a strange and distant place, for as any number of commentators including Joan Didion, T. D. Allman, David Reiff, and many more have pointed out, the social and political changes that have taken place in Miami since the initial Cuban diaspora of the early 1960s are but bellwethers for every city of size in the United States. Political rhetoric aside, immigration—and all the change that comes with it—is a fact of American life, and as cities of the future debate the question at the heart of this book, the voices weighing in will be as intense and as disparate as they were during the long path to the establishment of the Arsht Center.

Michael Spring, today director of the Miami-Dade County Department of Cultural Affairs, an agency with a budget of more than $30 million, is unequivocal in his assertion that government support for parks, libraries, museums, and the arts is essential. "These things make people's lives better," he says, flatly. "Donors from the private sector bear a responsibility as well, of course, but it is simply a citizen's right to have affordable access to libraries, museums, and cultural performances."

Furthermore, for Spring, it goes beyond rights. "Exposure to the arts can change kids' lives," he says. "It can make them aspire to become artists, sure, but it can also simply suggest that there is more to life than simply surviving. A play or a song can make the difference to a young person between giving up and deciding to work hard. Government contribution to the arts is not a gift; it is an investment."

An allied perspective is evidenced in the work of Judith Rodin, former provost of the University of Pennsylvania and author of *The University and Urban Revival: Out of the Ivory Tower and into the Streets*. During her tenure at Penn (1994–2004), Rodin led what some have termed an "urban revolution," casting her institution as the leader in revitalizing the severely distressed inner-city neighborhood of West Philadelphia, not so much through educational outreach, but by investment in retail, real estate, and cultural activity, guided by the belief that "town and gown" could develop into a rich and diverse community. Rodin's efforts helped to redefine the traditional role of a public university and have since been cited by those who would broaden the responsibility of government institutions to include the enhancement of the quality of a citizenry's lives.

Parker Thomson, Harvard-educated attorney and the individual who is generally credited with leading the long fight to bring a performing arts center into being in Miami, concurs that government bears a responsibility for support of things cultural, though in the case of a massive project such as the Arsht, he says, "There's a huge responsibility on the private sector as well. In the end, something such as that has to be a full-fledged collaboration between government and the private sector. That was always our vision in Miami."

Adrienne Arsht, the former banking executive who made the gift that Thomson and Spring call "the tipping point" in the history of Miami's performing arts center, agrees with Thomson. "Government cannot be put in the role of an enabler of projects that would be doomed without endless bailouts of public money," she says. But she also points out the practical benefits that government investment in arts centers can bring. "Look at what happened in New York with the Lincoln Center. It was built on land that nobody was interested in at the time. It wouldn't have been donated otherwise, just like the land in Miami. But—all other benefits aside—take a look at how land values and tax revenues have risen in both cases."

This book, then, is an attempt to tell a story that is at once arresting, significant, and valuable as an object lesson far beyond Miami and South Florida. There are any number of colorful characters who both collaborated on and opposed the making of the Arsht, but the individual at the center of this narrative is Thomson. In one way or another, he was from the beginning at the center of nearly every crucial battle fought concerning the project's future, and in his deft and intricate navigation of Miami's halls of powers lies a glimpse of the true nature of a complex city's makeup. Today's readers know that the Arsht has become a glittering reality, but they may not fully appreciate how fraught its road to actuality was, just as they may not realize the significance of its impact on what has become a major American city.

Though no story wants to get too far ahead of itself, it might be noted at the outset that in the opinions of both Thomson and Spring, one thing is inarguable: "Culturally, the Arsht has changed everything here." What follows intends to demonstrate just how.

PART I

. . . .

A SNOWBALL'S CHANCE
IN MIAMI

Finding Consensus on the Performing Arts Center,
November 1972 to December 1988

I

. . . .

NEWS ITEM:

On October 21, 2010, a reception was held to honor the Miami Performing Arts Center Trust's Founding Chair Parker Thomson, who retired from the Board of Directors after more than 20 years of service. Mr. Thomson was the first Chairman of the Center Trust's Board of Directors. Among the accolades bestowed upon Mr. Thomson were a Certificate of Congressional Recognition from Senator Bill Nelson, a congratulatory letter from Governor Charlie Crist and a resolution by the Miami-Dade County Board of Commissioners declaring September 28, 2010 "Parker Thomson Day." "Due to his leadership, the cultural landscape of Miami-Dade County has been forever transformed," stated Valerie Riles, the Center's Vice President of Board and Government Relations.

Point of View: A Week in Review at the Adrienne Arsht Center for
the Performing Arts of Miami-Dade County

Parker Thomson Day in the city of Miami came and went the way so many street-namings, keys-to-the-city-presentations, and civic proclamations do. In this case the event passed without so much as a mention in the *Miami Herald,* an omission made ironic by the fact that over a large part of the two decades that preceded the ceremony, that newspaper had published innumerable stories, editorials, and letters devoted to the controversy surrounding the seemingly endless struggle to build a performing arts center in a city long on glitter but often short on hard-dollar support for its cultural institutions. In fact, the words of Valerie Riles constitute a model of understatement, for were it not for the maneuvering, statesmanship, and savvy of Thomson, Harvard Law graduate and longtime champion of the Florida environment, the $480 million facility known today as the Arsht Center might well remain the stuff of dreams.

By the mid-1980s, and despite or perhaps in part owing to the cultural cacophony on its streets, Miami had become world famous as a destination for artists, fashion designers, filmmakers, and immigrants of every world region, cultural persuasion, and political stripe. The year 1987 saw major publications by three of America's most-noted social commentators analyzing the cultural appeal and widespread influence of the city: Joan Didion's *Miami*; T. D. Allman's *Miami: City of the Future*; and David Reiff's *Going to Miami: Exiles, Tourists, and Refugees in the New America*.

The city's various cultural institutions had grown by that time from a handful to more than one thousand. Yet beyond the aging Gleason Theater on distant Miami Beach and a few woefully outdated auditoriums in the city proper, including downtown Miami's Gusman Theater and the far-flung Dade County Auditorium, there existed no venue truly suitable for the presentation of serious music, drama, or dance. As Edward Villella, artistic director of the bright new Miami City Ballet put it, "the community simply hasn't been able to match in support what we have been able to achieve artistically." Without an up-to-date center suited for the presentation of ambitious modern productions—in the mold of the Lincoln or Kennedy Centers—cultural leaders feared that the promising artistic development that had gained a foothold in South Florida would soon be stalled.

And the stakes seemed to go beyond mere support of arts interests. As Villella put it, "There are very few cities in history that can be called major without making significant cultural comment." It was the kind of statement that resonated at many levels in a city just becoming aware of its vast potential, for it had been fewer than twenty years since the Kennedy Center (1971) had opened, and many could recall John F. Kennedy's resolute support of that endeavor and the arts as a whole. As Kennedy Center Founding Trustee Ralph Becker reminds readers in his *Miracle on the Potomac: The Kennedy Center from the Beginning* (1990), Dwight Eisenhower may have signed the legislation authorizing a national cultural center in 1958, but it was Kennedy who was the project's prime mover, calling it a "disgrace" for the richest nation in the world not to have proper facilities to display its performing arts.

In late 1988 the Dade County Commission took the first substantial step toward the creation of a performing arts center when it voted to form a public trust chaired by Thomson to develop a workable proposal for the building of a performing arts center. Leaders of the Concert Association of Florida, the Florida Grand Opera, the Florida Philharmonic, the Miami City Ballet, and the New World Symphony began meeting with a number of sympathetic philanthropists in the community, and by 1990 these five organizations had ushered into being a Performing Arts Center Foundation to raise $40 million from the private sector to supplement another $169.7 million in public financing for an arts center approved that same year by Dade County Commissioners. In October 1992 the PAC Trust recommended a downtown site for a Miami performing arts center on 5.9 acres of land offered up by Sears, Roebuck & Co. and Knight-Ridder, the media conglomerate and publisher of the *Miami Herald*. Finally, it seemed, a center would be built where the city's leading artistic groups would be resident companies, and an unmistakable signal of cultural commitment beamed out forever.

By 1993 the County Commission had given its approval for the site, signed off on a $1.5 million escalation in costs, and authorized a search for an architect, thereby sealing the deal on a project that became the largest public-private partnership ever undertaken in the county. In March 1996 the noted architect Cesar Pelli was chosen to design the center, and by 1999 the design phase of the project was completed. In April 2000, after seemingly endless debate on how much of the original seven-story, Art Deco–inspired Sears Tower still standing on the chosen site might be saved, work began with the demolition of the remainder of the surrounding and long-abandoned retail building. Construction on the center itself began in 2001, and after more than five arduous years and at more than $200 million over the bottom line of an ever-escalating budget, the center opened, featuring the 2,400-seat Ziff Ballet Opera House, the 2,200-seat Knight Concert Hall, and a pair of smaller venues where more-modest productions could be presented.

The October 2006 grand-opening ceremonies of what was initially called the Carnival Center drew the likes of Gloria Estefan, Andy Garcia, and Bernadette Peters, and critics applauded both the beauty of the 570,000-square-foot structure and initial presentations of the Miami Opera and the Miami City Ballet (the Florida Philharmonic disbanded in 2003). But the center ended its first year with a $2.5 million operating deficit, leading to renewed criticism from those who had opposed the undertaking from the beginning. Only a gift of $30 million from Miami philanthropist Adrienne Arsht was able to return the center to financial stability and silence the ever-present critics. Today, the Arsht Center remains an architectural gem as well as a cultural beacon, an unmistakable source of pride for a rich and diverse populace.

Arsht, for whom the center was renamed, was indeed an angel to the city's beleaguered cultural leaders, but had it not been for the nearly two decades of work by the unsung Thomson, there likely would have been nothing there for her to save. In truth, Thomson's work as a driving force for culture in Miami began long before his appointment as chair of the Performing Arts Center Trust, and the implications of all that he contended with over the years go far beyond the struggle to bring a bricks-and-mortar project into being. In fact, in this process is embodied the social history of one of the nation's singular cities, and in order to fully understand it, we must drop back a few years.

2

. . . .

Even given the timeline above, it is difficult to pin down a true start date for the establishment of a performing arts center in Miami, if for no other reason than the number of times the notion of such a center of culture in the city was previously born, only to die as the victim of various combinations of political wrangling, indifference, and lack of funding. Certainly, there were any number of times when proponents and opponents of such a concept might have considered the idea dead, once and for all. Then again, what is a phoenix for, if not to rise from the ashes?

To begin at one beginning, an observer might point to November 7, 1972, when Dade County voters passed an historic referendum authorizing the issuance of a series of public improvement bonds, known as the Decade of Progress Bonds, in the then-astronomical amount of $553.1 million to provide funds for a number of worthy projects meant to upgrade the quality of life in the Magic City. Some $50 million was approved for an enhancement of the sewage system, and another $50 million was dedicated to the enlargement of trash collection and landfill operations. Another $132.5 million was budgeted for an upgrade of rapid-transit facilities, including the groundwork for what has become today's Metrorail system. The public Jackson Memorial Hospital Complex received $88.6 million for modernization and improvement of buildings and facilities, and another $34.7 million was slated for improvements to the county's library system.

Streets, bridges, railway crossings, and sidewalks were slated for improvement to the tune of $113.5 million. Another $8 million was set aside for the creation of a significant "zoological park," with "animal exhibit areas," and attendant educational and support facilities, an undertaking that would eventually morph into today's Zoo Miami, a sprawling and popular free-range-styled attraction in South Dade.

Also approved was question number 8, where 183,000 voters, or about 60 percent of the total turnout, overcame the disinclination of 122,000 of their counterparts to issue nearly $76 million in bonds for "recreational and cultural improvement and facilities," which were to include the improvement of parks, athletic and recreational facilities, improvements to the county's beaches and marinas, the enhancement of public landscaping, the creation of bicycle paths, improvements to Vizcaya Museum, including the construction of a new Arts Building, a makeover for the Museum of Science and Natural History, and major upgrades to the Miami-Dade County Auditorium.

Just over half of the electorate of some 600,000 had turned out, but it was an ambitious, even an auspicious, milestone for Miami, which in the early 1970s was in no way the edgy, hipster-laden, gateway city that it would one day become. South Florida writer James W. Hall has quipped that there are three periods in Miami history: before Miami Vice, during Miami Vice, and after Miami Vice, and while it may be something of an exaggeration, the truth is that in 1972, and even though Miami Beach had attracted the 1968 Republican Convention and that of both the Republicans and the Democrats in 1972, the city much more resembled the relatively quiescent tourist mecca that it had lived as for most of its seventy-six-year history than the headline-grabbing leader in finance, culture, media, entertainment, sports, arts, and international banking that it is recognized as today.

There were no Miami Marlins, Florida Panthers, or Miami Heat, and the Dolphins were still a relatively new phenomenon with a recently acquired head coach named Shula, who claimed to have no magic formula for winning. Miami Beach had its glitter, attracting high-rolling tourists to such hotels as the Eden Roc and Fontainebleau, where Sinatra and the Rat Pack entertained and cavorted; and in the mid-1960s Jackie Gleason had brought his popular variety show to film at the Miami Beach Auditorium that would later bear his name, but just how "cultural" such offerings were is open to debate. As for South Beach, that was nothing more than a strip of sand backed by a string of run-down hotels sharing an outmoded and little-discussed "deco" architectural style from the 1920s and 1930s.

In fact, given the prominence that Miami occupies in the present world consciousness, with fashion shoots clogging the streets and such phenomena as Art Basel and the music festival Ultra bringing the discerning and the droves flocking from around the world, it may be difficult to comprehend that scarcely more than three-quarters of a century prior to 1972, there literally had been no such place. In 1896 there was an area population of about three hundred hardy pioneers, most clustered about the mouth of the limpid Miami River in a community known as Fort Dallas, named after the remote Army outpost built in 1836 to help root out recalcitrant Seminole Indians. A Cleveland, Ohio, native named Julia Tuttle is generally credited with the vision that would create a city where virtually nothing had existed before. At 41, after the death of her industrialist husband, Tuttle pulled up stakes in Ohio and risked everything on a 640-acre homestead allotment she purchased from a development company, moving herself and her two children to the shores of Biscayne Bay to the spot where the old fort had once stood.

Tuttle refurbished one of the fort's original crumbling buildings as a home for herself and her children, and then set off on her next order of business: given that the only way to reach her newly adopted community was by boat, she intended to convince someone to create a land route to Fort Dallas so that commerce could be conducted and the value of her property be enhanced. First, she appealed to Tampa railroad magnate Henry Plant to consider building a railway the 250 or so coast-to-coast miles southeastward across the Everglades, and Plant actually gave the matter some thought, dispatching his chief of operations with a team to check out the route. James Ingraham had orders to make his way to Fort Dallas, meet with Tuttle, and report back on the prospects. The trip across the soggy, uncharted Everglades turned into a near-death march for Ingraham and his men, however, and when Plant heard the hair-raising details of Ingraham's account, he quickly dismissed the notion of a Tampa to Miami railway.

Undaunted, Tuttle next approached Florida's other great turn-of-the-century railway tycoon, Henry Flagler, who had by 1894 brought his own Florida East Coast Railway as far southward as Palm Beach, only eighty miles from Fort Dallas. Though Flagler was not initially enthusiastic about pushing the FEC a single mile further down the peninsula, a hard freeze that winter virtually wiped out the Florida citrus crop all the way to Palm Beach. It is a staple of Miami lore that the indefatigable Tuttle sent Flagler an armload of fragrant orange blossoms to prove that southerly Fort Dallas was indeed a frost-proof paradise and that a railway servicing the settlement would have an endless cornucopia of fruits and vegetables to haul off north to market.

Whether or not Flagler found himself intoxicated by the scent of fresh-cut citrus blossoms or simply believed the word of James Ingraham, now hired away from Plant, that Fort Dallas was indeed worth a closer look, the legendary railroader was soon on his way from Palm Beach to meet with Tuttle. With a promise of 420 of Tuttle's acres to do with as he pleased, along with a grant of another 100 acres on the south bank of the Miami River pledged by the Brickell family, Flagler promised to bring his railroad to Fort Dallas, and by late April of 1896, he had done just that.

It was a prescient move. Within three months of the railroad's arrival, the town's population had quintupled to fifteen hundred, and grateful citizens applied to reincorporate as Flagler City. The modest Flagler gently steered the citizens to choose instead the name of the river about which the settlement was clustered, and thus out of a virtual airy nothingness had become a permanent habitation and a name.

Finally connected to the rest of civilization (the FEC still links the 351 miles from Jacksonville to the Port of Miami), Miami would boom greatly over the ensuing thirty years, attracting the likes of George Merrick, who created Coral Gables where only his family's farms and groves had stretched before, and Carl Fisher, who developed an uninhabited barrier island into the mecca of Miami Beach during the Florida boom of the early 1920s. However, exacerbated by the practices of far less-principled men than Fisher and Merrick, the Florida boom had already begun to cool, when the Great Hurricane of 1926 swept in shortly after midnight on September 18.

The winds of that storm had reached 128 miles per hour when the last gauges were ripped away, and most experts theorize the storm likely topped out at around 140 miles per hour, a category 4 leviathan in contemporary terms. Storms of course were not named nor categorized in those days, nor were they greatly understood. Survivors had scarcely staggered out to survey the catastrophic damage wrought upon homes and buildings when the lulling eye of the storm passed on, and the winds began to climb to maximum force again. Before it was over, every pane of glass in the splendid new Biltmore Hotel in Coral Gables was blown out, and Miami Beach was literally washed away. One hundred and fourteen people were killed, and every building in downtown Miami suffered major damage. "Miami Is Wiped Out," headlines blared from coast to coast, and if there was exaggeration in the reports, it was not by much.

In the wake of the storm, and for the first time in its history, more people were leaving Miami than were coming to settle there. Even Carl Fisher, instrumental in bringing "Dixie Highway" (US 1) to Miami in 1916, decamped from Florida to begin anew in Montauk, but others stuck it out. The University of Miami opened its doors (albeit they were doors in hastily acquired and much less grand buildings than the flattened Old Main) less than a month after the storm, and George Merrick labored tirelessly to rebuild the prospects of his City Beautiful. What the storm did not wipe away, however, was soon battered by an even greater force. The stock market crash of 1929 and the ensuing Great Depression would put an emphatic end to the first great era of Miami's development. Nearly three thousand homes were built in the first ten years of Coral Gables development; in 1932 all of three were completed.

The doldrums would persist for nearly two decades, until after World War II, when a sizable number of the hundreds of thousands of veterans who had passed through the many military training camps established in South Florida began to return to a place that had captivated them. "Once you get sand in your shoes . . ." was the common refrain for many Midwesterners explaining why they'd moved south, so far from home. With a renewed surge in the nation's economy, tourists were once again flocking to Miami Beach, and Pan American Airways and Eastern Airlines, having established headquarters in Miami during the troubled 1930s, were now thriving.

A 1946 article published in the journal Tequesta pointed out that despite hard times the population of Dade County had grown from 267,000 just before the war to 315,000 in 1945. (There had been about 140,000 in 1930 and only about 40,000 in 1920, before the boom began.) The way things were going, the article's author ventured, Dade County might count half a million citizens by the 1960s.

In fact, the county reached the half-million milestone by the time the 1950 census was taken. Certainly, by the mid-twentieth century it seemed that indeed things were looking up for Miami. And then, before that promising decade closed, matters took a completely unexpected turn, one that would redefine Miami in a way that no other American city has ever been.

There had always been a fair amount of Cuban immigration to the United States, and to Florida in particular. Cigar-makers and other skilled laborers as well as dissidents and other refugees had long favored Key West, only ninety miles across the Florida Straits, as an idyllic home away from an often politically troubled home, and the Ybor City neighborhood of Tampa had been attracting its share of Cuban, Spanish, and Italian immigrants since the 1870s, shortly after Cuban cigar manufacturer Vicente Ybor moved his operations to that area during one of the periodic upheavals in his native country.

But in 1959, when Fidel Castro toppled the Batista regime in Cuba and seized control of the country, a wave of emigration ensued that would change Miami and South Florida (not to mention the very political landscape of the United States) in an unprecedented manner. Over the next dozen years, as many as two hundred thousand Cuban citizens, many of them business owners, intellectuals, and professionals, fled Castro's regime. A number of these individuals had initially fought alongside with and supported Castro's efforts to oust the corrupt Batista, only to discover that the new regime was even more despicable. As part of a program dubbed Operation Peter Pan, as many as fifteen thousand Cuban children were spirited off to the United States by themselves between 1960 and 1962 by parents fearful that their sons and daughters would be relocated, "reeducated," pressed into Cuban military service, or worse.

By 1970 the population of Dade County stood at around one and a quarter million, but in terms of its traditional makeup—an amalgam of longtime merchants and service-oriented businessmen, independent-minded "crackers," and transplants from America's Midwest and Northeast looking to put that fabled sand in their shoes—matters would never be the same again. For one thing, all these newly arrived immigrants pouring into the neighborhoods of Hialeah and Westchester and West Miami had not come because they wanted to. Furthermore, the vast majority saw this enforced removal to foreign shores as decidedly temporary in nature. The Communist dictator would be deposed, order would be restored, and they would quickly return from this temporary asylum to homes, lives, and loved ones left behind in Cuba.

After all, the U.S. government had as early as 1960 been funding a secret CIA-backed operation for an invasion of Cuba by a force of some fourteen hundred, composed primarily of Cuban nationals intent on the overthrow of the Castro regime. The Bay of Pigs invasion, originally bankrolled by President Eisenhower, and later signed off on by President Kennedy, turned into a fiasco, however, one that irrevocably depicted the United States in an imperialist light with most Latin American governments. In the Cuban American community, outrage was directed at a U.S. government that had failed to live up to its commitments and its capabilities as the most powerful nation on earth. For a significant portion of those Cubans who had been forced to give up homes, livelihoods, and family members for fear of political reprisal, imprisonment, and death, the Bay of Pigs would stand not only as a betrayal but as a portent: indeed their stay in a place where they had never wished to be in the first place might never come to an end.

Evidence of this initial compartmentalization of communities is seen in the county's voter registration statistics of the period. In 1973, the first time "Spanish" voters were ever tallied, only 38,542 were counted among the county's 610,000 voters, about 6 percent of the total. By 1988, when the question of whether government should fund a performing arts center had coalesced into a serious possibility, the elections bureau stipulated that Spanish voters (albeit from many different nations) numbered about 185,000 out of roughly 700,000, well more than 25 percent. In 2013 elections officials counted 1,277,112 voters, identifying nearly 700,000 as "Hispanic," some 55 percent of the total.

Certainly, it is not the aim of this volume to serve as the definitive version of Miami's colorful history, relatively brief as that history may be. Nor could any writer hope to easily untangle the intricacies of a political landscape that is second to no other on the continent in terms of its complexities. But on the other hand, even as brief a thumbnail sketch as this seems necessary in order to appreciate what those civic leaders in 1972 Miami had to contend with when they proposed and fought for voter approval of that comprehensive set of bond proposals, that blueprint for "A Decade of Promise" ahead.

3

. . . .

Asked what drew him to Miami in the first place, Parker Thomson does not hesitate. "I wanted to live in a place where I thought I could make a difference," he says. From this vantage point in time, it seems that he could have scarcely made a more propitious choice.

Before coming to Florida in 1961, Thomson, a graduate of the Harvard School of Law, had been living in Boston, working at the old-line firm of Ropes, Gray, Best, Coolidge, and Rugg, the largest in Boston at that time. Ropes had been the historian for the North of the Civil War, and Gray was a noted early professor at Harvard Law School. It was the kind of setting where men could speak without their lips appearing to move—in Thomson's words, "A very, very proper place."

"There was an old joke that went around back then," he says. "A young lawyer like I was goes to the barber, who asks where he works. The young lawyer responds, giving the whole name of the firm. The barber nods knowingly. 'Oh, all six of you in there together.'"

Thomson shrugs. "Jokes in the then-Boston were like that," he says, adding that the firm is now called Ropes and Gray and is still based in Boston, though it has expanded to other U.S. cities as well. He lasted two and a half years at Ropes and Gray, learning the craft of his trade. "It was a very good firm," he recalls, "even if the pay was not so good."

But even more difficult for Thomson was the rigid social structure of Boston as a whole. He'd grown up the son of a college professor of modern European history, with the family dividing its time between Troy, New York, and Camden, Maine. He went to Princeton as an undergraduate, where as a student in the liberally designed Woodrow Wilson School of International and Public Affairs, he'd been able to indulge interests as diverse as Chinese art and Russian history. After graduation, he served a stint in the service, had married, and by the time he was out of law school, was the father of two. He was something of his own man by the time he took the job at Ropes and Gray, not so much a blank ready to be stamped in the corporate mold.

"I was thinking about Southern California," Thomson says, and he had received some interest from a couple of small firms in Los Angeles. Then, through a mutual friend, he met Dan Paul, a young, upcoming lawyer with a firm of his own in Miami. "I liked Dan," Thomson says, "and besides, he offered me a raise of 40 percent over what I was making at Ropes and Gray. By that time I had three children [he and his wife, Vann, would eventually become the parents of five]. I thought about it, but I didn't think too long."

Eventually, he and Paul would form Paul and Thomson and would together make it into a significant Miami entity named as one of the nation's top twelve small firms by the mid-1970s. "But the best part," Thomson insists, "is that I got to take part in the formation of what has become a defining city. Surely Miami is a defining city for the state of Florida, and likely for the U.S. as well."

He remembers the campaign for the Decade of Progress bonds issue in 1972 and his accompanying sense that the implications of the vote were clear. He had chosen well. Miami was a city on the move with intentions to better itself, and he intended to be a part of that civic development.

The $76 million authorized by item number 8 among the Decade of the Progress initiatives included spending on cultural improvements, including upgrades to the Dade County Auditorium, the Museum of Science and Natural History, and Vizcaya, the architectural gem and former estate of International Harvester tycoon James Deering, occupying fifty acres of tropical gardens on Biscayne Bay. And while the measure seemed to echo the sentiment expressed by Edward Villella that no city could aspire to significance without a commitment to supporting serious cultural endeavor, there was no clear mission statement included as to just how to proceed and no agency within local government with the expertise or the authority to make important decisions in such matters. A multimillion-dollar upgrade to a crumbling sewer system might be a snap for a civil servant, but when it comes to parceling out monies for the support of diverse artistic enterprise, another order of expertise is required.

Jack Orr, the former crusading prosecutor elected as Dade County mayor in 1972, is credited by Parker Thomson for including a significant commitment to cultural improvements within the Decade of Progress agenda. "If it hadn't been for Jack's continuing pressure and his political clout, culture wouldn't have been part of the equation," Thomson says. Though the wording of the 1972 bond issue referendum made no mention of the construction of any new cultural center, it was part of Orr's vision that the $35 million earmarked for library improvements could be combined with monies set aside for "cultural improvements" mentioned in item 8, and a fine arts complex could be built in downtown Miami that would serve as a cultural focal point.

The Main Library then located at Flagler Street and Biscayne Boulevard would be one pillar of the new complex; the Historical Museum of South Florida would be another; and a museum for the fine arts would constitute the third. Orr, who gained notoriety in 1956 as the only member of the Florida House to vote against a measure to maintain segregation in the state's schools, died while still in office in 1974. But by then, the concept of a cultural center for downtown Miami had gained traction.

Stephen Clark, who had preceded Orr in office, assumed Orr's unfinished term (and would continue on as metro mayor until 1993). Though Clark's reputation was as more of a folksy peacemaker than a hard-driving policy-maker—he often offered up Harry Truman as his political idol—one of his strongest suits was his ability to judge whom within his constituency was worth listening to. When Dan Paul and Bill Frates, a highly successful personal injury attorney, assured him that Jack Orr had been right in wanting to plant the flag for culture in Miami, Clark took note.

"This was a time when the cultural community had real influence," Parker Thomson says. "Most of the people on the Orange Bowl Committee [responsible for South Florida's venerable holiday college football classic], for instance, saw the value there, and when people like Dan Paul and Bill Frates told Steve Clark there should be an arm of county government dedicated to the support of the arts, Clark took them at their word." In the end, Clark supported the formation of the forerunner of today's County Department of Cultural Affairs in 1976, the Council of Arts and Sciences, at the time an all-volunteer board that would advise country government on matters pertaining to culture and the arts in

Dade County. Today, that advisory panel is known as the Cultural Affairs Council. Appointed as the council's first chair was Thomson.

"I just wanted to make sure that some things got done correctly," Thomson says. "I worried that the county would end up doling out a bunch of grants willy-nilly, with no guiding policies in mind, and that would be a disaster." As it turned out, Thomson's decision to accept the post had long-lasting implications, beginning a partnership of public and personal interests that would span more than thirty-five years.

During the long struggle to find accord on a site for the performing arts center years later, Thomson would sometimes be identified by reporters as the man who had seen to it that the Dade Cultural Center (the first of any such project undertaken by the county since the building of the Dade County Auditorium at 2901 West Flagler Street in 1951) was to be built on its downtown Flagler site. "But that site [a square block next to the county courthouse, formerly home to a rescue mission and a number of long-abandoned retail storefronts] had already been decided by the time I came on board the Council of Arts and Sciences," Thomson says. Shortly after the passage of the bond issues, in fact, University of Miami professor Howard Malt led a three-year study that resulted in the recommendation of the downtown site over locations proposed at Vizcaya, Dinner Key, Watson Island, and on Brickell Avenue.

Also determined before the council had much to say about it was the choice of architect for the center—namely, Philip Johnson, one of the country's leading architects, founder of the Department of Architecture and Design at New York's Museum of Modern Art and well-known for his Glass House (1949) in New Canaan. Johnson had also worked with Mies van der Rohe to design New York's thirty-nine-story bronze and glass Seagram Building in 1956. But perhaps the most persuasive factor was that Johnson had been in charge of development for New York's Lincoln Center during the 1960s and as part of that project had designed the home of the New York City Opera/New York City Ballet Company, the 2,713-seat New York State Theater, now known as the David H. Koch Theater.

Those familiar with Johnson's work and his championing of the so-called international style of architecture likely expected something along the lines of the sleek, glass-sheathed structures that Johnson had promoted since the 1930s. But they were in for a surprise. "When we finally saw the drawings," Thomson says, "all I could think of was 'Biltmore North.'"

The reference is to the iconic Coral Gables hotel, done in the highly decorative Mediterranean style that characterized much of the building during the Merrick era and elsewhere in boom-time South Florida of the 1920s, about as far from the minimalist international approach as one might get. Other than Freedom Tower, the former home of the *Miami News*, constructed in 1925 and modeled after the bell tower of the Cathedral of Seville, Johnson's design seemed connected to little else in downtown Miami and certainly not to the typically skyscraping bank towers of downtown nor the County Administration Building standing now just across the street.

Johnson described the Dade Cultural Center, the first of his designs to break with the international style, as "neotraditional" and explained that he had been influenced by the Italian Renaissance–styled work of Addison Mizner in Palm Beach, Deering's Vizcaya, Merrick's many fairy-tale structures in Coral Gables, and, of course, by the nearby Freedom Tower. "I got sick of modern architecture 20 years ago," Johnson told a reporter. "I see no sense in perpetrating more of those flat, slick, un-topped— Frank Lloyd Wright called them flat-chested—no-headed buildings." He went so far as to dub his approach Florida Regional Architecture, and when heckled by a persistent audience member during a talk in Miami, he peered out from behind his trademark owlish spectacles to quip, "I hadn't realized so many of you here *cared* about architecture."

Despite surprise and debate, Johnson's design was ultimately approved. Johnson, whose similarly iconoclastic AT&T building would be completed in New York City the following year, argued to commissioners that even if his design seemed out of keeping with what was already there, that was not necessarily a bad thing. "Some of the buildings you see in downtown Miami today, I find extraordinarily painful," he said. And besides, as county manager Ray Goode told reporters, Miami had a different kind of image to think about. How was it going to look to the rest of the world, Goode explained, "if we selected a nationally famous architect and rejected his work."

Construction began in 1980, with a budget of just under $25 million. It was dedicated just before Christmas in 1983, though the two museums would not actually open until the following year, largely because of a year or more delay caused when a last-minute inspection by the fire department revealed that the center's smoke exhaust systems were faulty. Entire walls and ceilings would have to be removed, at a cost of $16 million, two-thirds the cost of the entire project. Though most of the costs were borne by insurance policies taken out by the architect and engineers, politicians were aghast and voters outraged. Still, there was little to be done but forge ahead.

"We had nothing, really, to do with the error," said architect Johnson's partner on the project, Jon Burgee. "It was an engineering error made by the local engineer down there. He made a big one. It's a most unpleasant subject." Eventually, the repairs were made, and the Center for the Fine Arts opened early in 1984, with the history museum debuting soon after (the library would not open until 1985).

Despite all, the cultural center's opening was much celebrated in the community. A tuxedoed Johnson was described as "ebullient" at a VIP party held on the center's central plaza the evening before the dedication. The seventy-seven-year-old architect described the expanse flanked by the buildings of the still-to-be-opened museums and library as a great urban space in the tradition of the Italian piazza, America's answer to St. Mark's Place in Venice. "This may be the first place in America where you will be able to get a decent Campari and soda," he told reporters.

More than two thousand turned out for the public ceremony the following evening as a brass band played Christmas carols and hundreds waited in line at the Metrorail platform catty-corner from the plaza for free rides that featured dramatic views of the downtown skyline and the Miami River. "This is going to be the great meeting place in Dade County," declared Commissioner Ruth Shack, gesturing about the near-acre of tiled space where citizens, celebrities, and architecture critics mingled, sampling hors d'oeuvres and sharing opinions.

While there was general agreement on the visual appeal of the plaza, at least one visitor wondered if it wasn't going to be a bit hot on a summer's day without awnings and umbrellas. And there was no shortage of perplexity about a piece of sculpture unveiled that evening as a part of the county's Art in Public Places program. When Center Director Jan van der Marck whisked off a cloth that had draped Raymond Duchamp-Villon's highly impressionistic 1914 work *The Horse*, there was applause, of course, but also some confused murmuring. "It looks like they went out to the junkyard and put it together," said one onlooker, a retired school teacher.

"It looks like that masked man on TV," another visitor ventured. But Patricia Fuller, then administrator of the Art in Public Places program, was unfazed. "When you see it from one side, it's a remarkable essence of horse," she said, providing a counterpoint for the enduring battle of taste.

There would be no such controversy surrounding future acquisitions for the soon-to-be opened art museum, however, for, as Parker Thomson recalls, the advisory panel had been won over during the planning process for the center by the reasoning of Thomas Hoving, the former director of the Metropolitan Museum hired as a consultant for the project in 1979. Hoving counseled against any attempt to create a permanent collection in the new center, arguing that Miamians would be better served if the available resources were devoted to mounting a series of traveling shows and pieces borrowed from other museums.

"The Treasures of Tutankhamen [1976–79] exhibit had just toured the U.S.," Thomson says. "There were only seven stops, and it was a blockbuster everywhere it went. New Orleans was the only Southern city that got it, for the simple reason that there was nowhere in Miami with enough space to put it at the time. When Hoving reminded people here of what could happen if we focused our efforts that way, it was persuasive."

Certainly it was a practical decision, even if those who envisioned a "real" museum of fine art in the city were disappointed. And of course, with no auditoriums, this cultural center did little to address the needs of the performing arts. Delma Iles, then artistic director of Momentum Dance Company, attended the dedication ceremonies and was asked by a reporter if possibly the plaza itself might be used in some way to showcase dance or music. Iles glanced about the vast plaza. The Council of Arts and Sciences had recently financed a sophisticated portable dance stage with the aid of a grant from Humana. "With that, we could probably do something here," Iles said, but it was hardly a stirring endorsement.

To Mayor Clark, however, the opening of the cultural center was but a first step, "evidence of the maturation of a city and its peoples," as he told the *New York Times*. Clark went on to enumerate. Miami now had a strong arts council in place with a 2 percent bed tax set aside for its funding, a functioning art-in-public-places program, a new arts center and historical museum in place, and the city was moving forward on "improvements to theaters and concert halls, and the possibility of a 'world-class' performing-arts facility."

The response of critics outside Miami was generally favorable to the very fact that such a center had come to be, and since New Yorkers knew what was coming in Johnson's Chippendale-styled AT&T building scheduled for completion in 1984, there was no great sense of surprise in the *Times* story covering the opening. The design of the three-building complex, "designed in a Spanish mission style as a way of evoking the area's past" was misleading, the writer said, pointing out that it more accurately evoked the aping of the 1920s "than the real age of the Spaniards in Florida."

But the real concern of the piece was a more practical one. Johnson's work had usually been noted for its care to encourage pedestrian activity, it was pointed out, but this time, in the writer's opinion, Johnson had "struck an odd tone." For all the talk about Piazza San Marcos and the declarations that this would be a great meeting place for Miamians, the center was set on a high platform a full story above the street, the writer pointed out, "and the complex sets itself off from the rest of the city with high travertine walls."

In fact, the buildings and the plaza—reached by climbing a gently sloping, colonnaded ramp from Flagler Street alongside a splashing fountain—were constructed for practical reasons atop a parking garage, and Johnson intended the walls that face outward to serve as a buffer from surrounding street noise. However, that does not alter the effect that to the casual pedestrian at street level, the building, with its steep stone-sheeted walls and steel-grated windows, appears intimidating. Some commissioners griped early on that the place resembled "an old Italian prison," and, given the comments by one of the construction supervisors on the project, one might wonder if it really were noise that Johnson intended to keep out of his plaza.

"Because of all the bums around here, I couldn't even go out on the corner when we started building," a foreman for the electrical contractors told *Herald* reporters covering the dedication. Though he allowed in 1983 that "this area's really been cleaned up since then," the fact is that the city's homeless continue to find Johnson's piazza as much "the great meeting place in Dade County" as do tourists, culture seekers, and office workers on break. There is sometimes a sandwich cart to be found, but Johnson's dream of finding the only good Campari and soda on the piazza remains just that. As *Herald* architecture critic Beth Dunlop noted early on, a plaza needs people, and people need a reason to populate one. "In an Italian town the piazza is the heart, the center around which everything else has grown," she wrote, underscoring the truth that neither visitors to nor residents of Venice *go to* St. Mark's Plaza; one simply arrives there, inexorably.

In contrast, the Dade Cultural Center was not set at the organic nexus of a city, but was placed at just about the outermost edge from anything resembling a downtown hub. Furthermore, Dunlop theorized, even as the center was being dedicated, "Johnson found downtown Miami a bit bedraggled and a bit boring, so he set his plaza on a pedestal, above and away from the rest of the city."

"One cannot see history," was Johnson's reply. "It is very hard to prognosticate how the citizens of Miami are going to use it." Still, even he seemed open to the question: "Will it be one of those sun-drenched emptinesses, the moonlit desertions that you find even in some Italian towns?" Miami, and history, would eventually decide.

4

· · · · · · · ·

Regardless of how the hopes and dreams surrounding the Dade Cultural Center would turn out, the mood of cultural leaders in Miami in the wake of the center's opening was decidedly upbeat. The very fact that such a cultural center had opened its doors seemed an extremely significant step forward for cultural leaders. As Maurice Ferre, mayor of Miami, told the *New York Times* early in 1984, the center was nothing short of a miracle, looming immense "in a fairly unsophisticated city like Miami that doesn't have cultural facilities in abundance. It reminds me of the scene from *Alice in Wonderland*," Ferre said, "when the Mad Hatter asks Alice how she can give him more tea when he didn't have any to begin with."

Lessons had been learned about how to facilitate such public-private undertakings, and just as important, the dream of a "world-class" performing arts center to complement the cultural center was alive and well—if County Mayor Stephen Clark was willing to say so to the *New York Times*, how could anyone doubt the possibility that it could indeed happen?

As for Parker Thomson, he had left the Council of Arts and Sciences in 1982, though he still retained a place on the board of the Art in Public Places program, the agency that had placed that bewildering Duchamp horse at the cultural center. Any controversy surrounding that decision was small potatoes to Thomson, though, who by then was a veteran of the "Flying Bacon" controversy that had swirled about a proposed installation at the Miami International Airport in 1982.

The program was another offshoot of the Decade of Promise agenda, founded in 1973, and requiring that 1.5 percent of any county construction budget be devoted to art installations connected thereto. In the early years much of the money went for the addition of unremarkable sculpture dropped somewhere in a fountain, courtyard, or green space associated with a public building, but as the advisory board matured, a more venturesome spirit developed. Just possibly, it might be a good thing to install artwork that people actually noticed. Of course, drawing attention to any expenditure made on behalf of taxpayers has its drawbacks.

In 1982 the board of Art in Public Places acquired for $285,000 an immense, 17-by-46-foot painting entitled *Star Thief*, by noted pop-artist and former billboard painter James Rosenquist, whose work is sometimes linked with that of Andy Warhol and Roy Lichtenstein. The board intended that the visually arresting, if highly impressionistic, rendering of space exploration would be hung in Concourse B of Miami International Airport, then the home of Eastern Airlines. However, Frank Borman, the airline's CEO, took one look at the painting and put his own critical foot down. As a former Apollo astronaut, Borman pointed out that he had actually traveled into outer space and at no time while there had he ever witnessed any giant strips of bacon floating there.

Rosenquist's own explanation that the intent of the painting had very little to do with depicting space travel in the literal sense, but was instead a metaphor for creative exploration in the larger sense, is interesting, of course. But attempts to explain the piece had about as much effect as would have an apparition by Duchamp-Villon to explain that his sculpture on the Dade Cultural Center plaza was about the "essence of horse" more than a horse itself.

Even Dick Judy, airport director at the time, was doubtful about hanging the work. Judy confided that he actually liked the painting but saw little benefit in carrying on the fight. Judy doubted that as a practical matter most travelers would pause for so much as a moment to ponder Rosenquist's work—or any other painting, for that matter. Airports were all about getting on a plane and going places, not appreciating art. "Put the paintings in a museum somewhere" was his take on the matter. In any case, the idea was scotched, and the painting was returned to the artist.

"I think Rosenquist eventually sold it for about $1.5 million," Parker Thomson says, recalling the incident. "It just shows you what you are dealing with when you expend taxpayer monies for cultural purposes." *Star Thief* now hangs at the Museum Ludvig, in Cologne.

While something of an embarrassment, the incident was no major setback for cultural endeavor in Miami. The truth is that if it hadn't been for the quirk of fate that Frank Borman had traveled into space without seeing any bacon there, Rosenquist's painting might well have gone up, and travelers might have been unable to keep from wondering about that strange, arresting image they'd passed by. In fact, the Art in Public Places program would continue to thrive, with a Professional Advisory Committee of practicing artists added to the mix, and any number of challenging works by Claes Oldenburg and others would be placed for taxpayers to encounter without significant objection.

Meanwhile, cultural activists continued to fight for the construction of a performing arts center that would complement Miami's new cultural center, a concept that had been floated from the earliest meetings of the Council of Arts and Sciences chaired by Parker Thomson in 1976. By the summer of 1982, a new penny tax tri-county bond referendum for the construction of new sports and performing arts facilities in Palm Beach, Broward, and Dade Counties was announced, including a $100–110 million arts center arena on the docket for Miami.

Voters were to decide on the matter in the November elections, and speculation immediately began as to just where Miami's new center would be placed. The smart money was on city-owned Watson Island, a man-made spit of sand lying in Biscayne Bay a few hundred yards east of downtown, offering spectacular views of the city's skyline, and connected to the city and Miami Beach by the MacArthur Causeway. From its very inception, developers had been seeking a use for Watson Island, and the number and nature of suggestions over the years—World's Fair site, Disney-esque amusement park, underpinning for massive electronic billboards to be visible from twenty miles away—would stagger the imagination of P. T. Barnum.

This time, however, backers were buoyed by the undeniable substance of a performing arts center for the island and were surely influenced by worldwide acclaim for the Sydney Opera House, the stunning complex constructed at the mouth to the Australian city's port in 1973. Undeterred by the fact that residents and tourists could actually walk from Sydney's adjacent business center or the popular Royal Botanic Gardens to enjoy music, dance, or theater offerings at the Sydney Opera House center, supporters of the referendum played up the cultural, tourist-drawing benefits to all residents sure to devolve from the project.

Voters, however, were not convinced. The 1982 penny tax bond referendum failed in all three counties, and Miami's performing arts center supporters were back to square one.

Though that 1982 vote was a stinging defeat, a number of things had taken place in Miami that had distracted voters from cultural concerns. There were economic practicalities, of course. After Castro seized control of Cuba in 1959, and Miami became the refuge for a large part of Cuba's business and professional community, a few families managed to transplant substantial interests in sugar, distilling, and construction, but the vast majority were forced to begin anew, in a place where white-collar work was hard to come by. Successful attorneys became car salesmen, and physicians were waiting tables. Many endured years of hardship, nursing dreams of returning home once the hated dictator was overthrown. And even if one had been able to gain an economic foothold here, the idea of participating in building a cultural center in a temporary home had little appeal.

Furthermore, there had been the aftershock of a more recent wave of immigration from Cuba. In 1980, in the middle of a serious depression in the island's economy, as many as ten thousand Cubans sought asylum in the Peruvian embassy grounds in Havana, intending it as a temporary haven during their efforts to leave the country. Ultimately, the Cuban government announced that anyone who wished to leave the country could do so, and that boats from any nation wishing to transport emigrants elsewhere were welcome to dock at Mariel Harbor.

As might have been expected, Castro's announcement unleashed a veritable flotilla of seacraft—most seaworthy, many not so much—from Miami, across the ninety-three-mile-wide Florida Straits. Most estimates suggest that between April 15 and October 31 of 1980, more than 125,000 Cubans took advantage of the opportunity to flee their homeland as part of the Mariel boatlift for South Florida. And soon it became apparent that among the new wave of immigrants was a significant number of prisoners and mental patients (estimated variously as anywhere from seven thousand to forty thousand) that Castro had freed and salted among the hordes jamming the docks at Mariel. What had once been Cuba's problem became that of Miami, with crime suddenly on the upswing and social service agencies overwhelmed with the sudden influx of those in need. Many old-timers, outraged by this "invasion," slapped bumper stickers on their pickups promising summary justice by .45 for lawbreakers, and a coalition that called themselves Citizens of Dade United was able to force a measure on the ballot in the fall of 1980, requiring that the county refrain from conducting its business in any language other than English. The English Only law remained in place until repealed in 1993.

In addition, there had also been upheaval within Miami's African American community. Their treatment by fellow citizens might have been shabby enough, but it was further aggrieved by that of many Cuban émigrés. On the island, those who considered themselves descendants of the Spanish had a history of prejudicial attitudes toward those of dark skin or "native" heritage, and they brought this baggage along to the United States. In December of 1979, the situation began a march toward catastrophe when six Miami police officers (two of them Latino) pulled over thirty-three-year-old Arthur McDuffie after the black salesman and former Marine had led them on a high-speed chase on his motorcycle.

McDuffie was beaten to death during an ensuing scuffle with the officers, who fabricated a cover-up of the incident, claiming that McDuffie had resisted arrest. Four of the officers were brought to trial in May 1980 and were acquitted, a verdict that touched off three days of rioting in the black enclaves of Overtown and Liberty City, the first such disturbances in the United States since the assassination of Martin Luther King in 1968. More than thirty-five hundred National Guardsmen were brought in to quell a wave of destruction so severe that Miami was declared a disaster area by the federal government, at the same time that the masses were clambering ashore from Mariel.

Yet this very cacophony was a reminder to those who championed the creation of a cultural center of significance that the project was an essential part of creating a community, not an undertaking incidental to that community. As banker and new Arts Council Chairman Raul Masvidal told reporters, "Is there any doubt that we need these things? If you're in the middle of a desert thirsting for water, is there any doubt?"

By September of 1983, shortly before the dedication of the Dade Cultural Center, the Miami Beach City Commission announced a ballot measure that would authorize $22 million to rebuild the outdated Theater of the Performing Arts. Judy Drucker, longtime arts impresario and founder of the Concert Association of Florida, appeared before the commission to argue on behalf of the measure. Calling the theater a "white elephant," Drucker told stories of having to bring in a trailer for Mikhail Baryshnikov to use for a dressing room during a recent appearance at TOPA, and when she'd invited Zubin Mehta to conduct there, he flatly refused because of the hall's faulty acoustics.

The lack of a theater capable of presenting top-caliber dance and orchestral productions was "an embarrassment to the whole world," said Drucker, a Beach High graduate who studied at Julliard and performed on Broadway and with the Greater Miami Opera. The plan would nearly double the theater's size, but was touted as a bargain, given that the city of Miami Beach owned the existing building and land. Estimates to acquire a site and build from scratch ran anywhere from $75 to $125 million. Furthermore, boosters said, pointing to how New York's Lincoln Center had revitalized a shabby neighborhood, such a center would attract new hotel building and other tourism-related development. Opponents countered that the $66.25 per year that the measure would cost the average homeowner was simply too steep.

Also in 1983, across Biscayne Bay, the findings of a $50,000 study commissioned by the Greater Miami Chamber of Commerce had just been released. If the city's cultural growth was to keep pace with its economic growth, the report by New York's Artec Consultants concluded, a new performing arts center would have to be built. "Performing arts facilities that enjoy world-class status have acoustic and staging features worthy of the world's most demanding performers," the report stated, adding that these should be: "facilities which will stand out as exemplary additions to the world's top-ranking cities."

The study suggested that such a center should have at least two major halls: one for symphonic concerts and one of a somewhat different nature better suited for presentations of dance, opera, and musical theater. The consultants also recommended that a number of smaller spaces be provided for more intimate theater, chamber music, and the like, and they also stressed the need for resident companies to be housed in the complex. At the time, none of the county's dance or music companies had a permanent home.

The consultants had evaluated the possibility of renovating the existing venues, including the Coconut Grove Playhouse, the Gusman Theater, the Dade County Auditorium, and the Theater of the Performing Arts on Miami Beach, but concluded that none could be converted into the type of cutting-edge facility needed. "The absence of 'properly scaled' halls and the presence of layout and technical problems preclude converting any of these into a 'world-class' facility," the consultants explained.

The very thought of raising Miami into the ranks of America's first-class cities seemed effrontery to some ("audacious," *Herald* columnist Charles Whited called the consultants' concept), but, said noted Miami surgeon Philip George, chair of a performing arts center committee commissioned by the Dade Council of the Arts and Sciences, "If we really want to move forward as a city, let's do it on all fronts. The arts are just as important as industry, tourism and commerce; they are all interrelated."

The consultants did not delve into issues of cost or site selection, pointing out that such were beyond the scope of what they were hired to do. However, as we look back from the present day's end of the historical telescope, one aspect of that 1983 report does stand out: the consultants were confident that all the necessary committees could be formed, a site chosen, and an architect chosen in less than a year.

5

. . . .

To some, championing the drive to build a performing arts center of nearly unprecedented scope in a community where ethnic tensions blazed and economic opportunity was limited might seem an easy political target. But the truth is far more complex. For those whose aim lay squarely upon the betterment of the city, the effort to lift the quality of citizens' lives was no inconsequential matter. To this day, the panoply of foods, music, and arts available in Miami constitutes one of the city's principal lures. In most any purview, pleasure is synonymous with tropical living, and the attempt to create a performing arts space of unparalleled quality in such a place only dovetails with that perception. Transforming Miami into a manufacturing hub or a second Silicon Valley might in fact have seemed a tall order in 1983, but besting the Kennedy or the Lincoln Center seemed quite possible to proponents.

In any case, buoyed by passage of the Theater of the Performing Arts bond issue on Miami Beach as well as by Broward County's decision to move forward on a $20 million downtown theater and concert hall of its own, Miami's Downtown Development Authority wasted little time in the wake of the Artec study's release. Within two months, late in 1983, that agency appeared before the Council of Arts and Sciences to present an analysis of three possible sites for a Miami performing arts center.

One possibility, of course, was Watson Island. The second, called the Government Center site, was adjacent to the about-to-be-completed Dade Cultural Center and Metro-Dade Administration Building. The third, and most controversial, was known as the FEC or Bicentennial Park site, on the water and just north of the newly announced Bayside Marketplace development. While the Bicentennial Park site would conceivably allow for a Sydney-style signature structure for the Miami skyline, many people were vehemently opposed to the use of what little remained of public waterfront lands for any building purposes. In fact, the city had in 1981 passed an ordinance barring the placement of any permanent structure on park land.

Roy Kenzie, director of the Downtown Development Authority, and Kenneth Kahn, executive director of the Council of Arts and Sciences (one of the uses of bed tax monies was the creation of that paid position and a staff), favored the Government Center site despite the dubious nature of the surrounding neighborhood. Kenzie argued that the area where Lincoln Center was built had little appeal originally, and that furthermore, the main concern should be for the beauty and character of the spaces within any new facility, not the space outside it.

Following Kenzie's presentation, the Council of Arts and Sciences approved the Government Center site, with five of the nine members present in favor. They cited the fact that public transportation, in the form of the new Metrorail line, was already in place (with Metromover soon to come), and that nearby parking garages and utility facilities were already in place, advantages that could cut as much as $20 million off a still-to-be-determined budget. Three members held for the Bicentennial Park site, arguing that the "signature" aspect of such a building would be a priceless asset for the city. Architect Hilario Candela saw a bayside installation as "a front door to the community," featuring sea and sky assets that few other communities could boast, but the DDA's Kenzie likely carried the day when he pointed out that the choice of the Bicentennial Park site would mean an immediate delay, given the legal obstacles facing such a choice. Only one of the council members present voted in favor of the Watson Island site.

Though the matter might have seemed settled and the prognostication of the Artec consultants confirmed that preliminary matters involving the center's planning might be settled in jig time, another meeting of the Council of Arts and Sciences was convened a month later, on December 21, 1983, to reconsider the question. The matter was complicated by the fact that prior to the opening of the meeting, members listened to a report from its own Performing Arts Center Steering Subcommittee and architect Candela stipulating that the Government Center site was inadequate.

The steering subcommittee was endorsing the bayside (Bicentennial Park) site by a vote of 7–2. Proponents of that site, including Philip George, implored fellow council members to reconsider the "humanistic considerations" of a waterfront location and questioned whether the limited amount of land available at the Government Center site would be sufficient for a single full-sized opera house, let alone the two- or three-theater configuration that the Artec report had suggested. After much debate, the eleven council members resolved, by a vote of 6–5, to submit a series of recommendations to the county commissioners. They rated the three proposed sites in order, with the Government Center site first, the bayside parcel second, and the Watson Island site third.

Along with the rankings, the council asked the commission to appropriate funds for a feasibility study that would more specifically lay out the nature and space needs for the construction of the center, and they also asked that the county consider the need for a bond issue to finance it; prophetically enough, the council also suggested that commissioners might want to invite Miami city officials to suggest any other possible downtown sites. And in a backdoor move of sorts, the council also asked commissioners to inquire if the city might be open to reconsidering its recent ordinance banning future construction on Bicentennial Park property. The council also agreed that it would be a good idea to name a panel of independent architects to research the question of whether there was indeed enough space on the Government Center parcel for a center of substantial size, and with that action the meeting concluded.

Things simmered for the next couple of months, until word came in mid-February of 1984 that the panel of architects had concluded that indeed there would be plenty of room for a formidable performing arts complex at the Government Center site. Charles Pawley, chairperson of the panel that used Washington, D.C.'s Kennedy Center as a model, said in the report that there was sufficient room at the Government Center site for a 2,500-seat opera house, a 1,000-seat theater for Broadway-style shows, and a 500-seat theater for more modest events.

Instead of settling anything, however, the Pawley report simply precipitated an apparent step back. Robert Herman, director of the Greater Miami Opera Association, immediately protested that while the opera theater conceived of by the Pawley group might indeed have 2,500 seats, other aspects of its design did not provide enough space for the company's needs. The following day, the Council of Arts and Sciences abruptly reversed field and withdrew the resolutions it had forwarded to county commissioners in December. The council asked commissioners to disregard all recommendations previously discussed and requested that the commissioners appropriate funds for a comprehensive feasibility study that would first pinpoint the needs of various companies, *then* survey possible sites. The study would also include a marketing survey, suggest a proposed management plan for the center, and research potential funding sources for the project. Kenneth Kahn, the council's executive director, announced that it would take a bit of time to put a price tag on the cost of the study, but he was going to see that it happened.

Meantime, it appeared that the council was making every effort to avoid any appearance of a rush to judgment on the site, an issue that had divided the body nearly evenly. Perhaps this delay made it less likely that preliminary matters might be wrapped up by the fall of 1984, as the Artec consultants had projected, but it is doubtful that anyone else was thinking along the same lines as Kahn, who, at the time the Artec findings were announced, warned that the process was not as simple as some might assume. "This may take six, or even ten, years," Kahn had remarked.

It was mid-June of 1984 before that feasibility study's price tag had taken shape, and by then, other ideas as to the nature of the drive to build a performing arts center had begun to develop. A *Herald* story offered new details of a concept that the Council of Arts and Sciences had developed in the wake of the site controversy: a proposal for a dedicated arts district stretching four blocks eastward from the newly opened Dade Cultural Center all the way to the new Bayside Marketplace, including the new downtown campus of Miami-Dade Community College along the way. Somewhere in that swath of property would be built a performing arts center, proponents said, and City of Miami officials would be asked to alter zoning requirements within the district to encourage developers to include galleries, dance studios, and small theaters in their plans. The idea was to create a kind of oasis for the arts in the middle of downtown, one modeled upon a similar twenty-square-block arts district in Dallas.

It was certainly a bold idea, but it was also freighted with any number of practical impediments that threatened to dissipate the energies that had so recently seemed coalesced. At Metro Mayor Stephen Clark's urging, the pragmatic-leaning attorney Parker Thomson had gotten involved in putting together ideas for a comprehensive feasibility study for the performing arts center project. The study would cost $120,000, Thomson estimated, and he would soon appear before Miami and county commissioners to try to get them to approve sharing the expenditure. Then-Mayor of Miami Maurice Ferre was already on record as supporting the concept of putting the horse in front of the cart. "I think that it's long overdue that we stop arguing about who and where and start arguing about what," Ferre said. "Once you know what you are going to do, where is almost secondary."

Eventually, both Miami and Metro Dade commissioners agreed to share the cost of such a study, but it would be nearly two and a half years until a consulting team was assembled and its results were made known.

Part of the delay can be attributed to the social upheaval that marked the period. At the same time that civic leaders were celebrating the opening of the cultural center as a showpiece for the area's more worthy side, movie audiences around the United States were flocking to see *Scarface*, director Brian De Palma's 1983 remake of the 1932 crime classic, with the Al Capone figure from the original recast as brutal Mariel émigré Tony Montana (Robert De Niro). In 1984 *Miami Vice* debuted, with Metro Dade Vice Squad detectives Sonny Crockett (Don Johnson) and Rico Tubbs (Philip Michael Thomas) chasing down a never-ending cavalcade of drug-running criminals and other miscreants, beginning with the pilot episode's "Trini de Soto," who identified himself as having been "among the Marielito riffraff." The television show, cited as one of the most influential ever, became a worldwide sensation during its five-year run and is still syndicated in overseas markets.

Nonetheless, proponents of culture in South Florida persevered. The $22 million renovation of the Theater of the Performing Arts would begin in 1985, and Broward County was to announce plans for a $33 million multipurpose performing arts center near downtown, with construction to begin in 1987. Palm Beach County announced that it too would build a 2,000-seat arts complex with a target date for completion sometime in 1988.

In Miami, on May 2, 1985, Metro Mayor Stephen Clark announced the appointment of an independent blue-ribbon committee with a single stated purpose: to make sure that Dade County would build a new performing arts center. "I don't know where it's going to be built at," Clark said, "or how much it will cost. But I intend to see a top-notch facility in this town."

To lead the committee, Clark picked a man with a reputation for getting things done, a champion of the arts with whom he had consulted on such matters since the 1970s: Parker Thomson. "It's time to stop talking and make sure this thing happens," Thomson told reporters. As a sign that indeed it might just, Dade's representatives to the state legislature were able to secure $200,000 for planning the center in the new budget.

Ultimately, the consulting team included the accounting firm of Touche Ross; the New York architectural firm of Hardy, Holzman, and Pfeiffer; theater consultants Jules Fisher Associates of New York; acousticians Peter George Associates; and fund-raising specialists Benz Whaley Flessner Associates. Unveiled on December 17, 1986, the study, which came in at a cost of $140,000, had as its lynchpin the immediate renovation of the Gusman Theater. In addition, the plan called for the creation of a performing arts district and the building of up to seven separate performing arts facilities over time within an area bordered by Biscayne Boulevard, Northeast First and Sixth Streets, and Northeast Second Avenue. The plan suggested that the area could be designated as a redevelopment district that would allow for the acquisition of necessary land by the county and the use of taxes to pay off any associated bond issues.

While the report concluded that the Biscayne Boulevard site would be ideal in helping to develop a synergy with Bayside Marketplace, the outdoor amphitheater at Bayfront Park, the Miami-Dade Community College campus, and the nearby Gusman Theater, consultants were agreed upon the Government Center site as a workable alternate. Since most of the necessary land there was already owned by the county, and utilities were in place, using Government Center could trim nearly $25 million off a cost projected at somewhere between $156 and $163 million. The money would come from a bond issue of up to $100 million, the panel suggested, with the rest to come from grants, taxes, and donations. The first step, however, was to be the immediate $16.9 million renovation of the Gusman into an up-to-date 1,700-seat facility. The first step in that process was to seek initial funding from the state legislature for the historic theater's remodeling.

"This is different," said Parker Thomson, still chairing the advisory panel Mayor Clark appointed back in May of 1985. "It calls for immediate action. It calls for turning Gusman, which everyone who has ever been in loves, into a real, working, first-class facility now."

"*Now*," alas, turned out to be an elusive concept. While the study endorsed only two sites as practical, the group had actually evaluated eight conceivable sites in all, including the seemingly indefatigable possibility on Watson Island. Mayor of Miami Xavier Suarez remained a champion of the city-owned island site, and by April of 1986 the County Council of Arts and Sciences was calling for construction of a $60 million two-theater performing arts center there. Though a *Herald* editorial supported the notion—"Of all the uses proposed for Watson Island, none has made more sense than a performing-arts facility"—the paper's architecture critic Beth Dunlop disagreed. She told readers that while such a site might provide visual appeal to the casual passer-by, it would likely prove useless as a true "center" for the community. Such a center should be integral to the life of the city, Dunlop argued, "linked up with schools, museums, restaurants, shops, offices, apartments." An in-town center could be a boon to the city, she said, adding that "the city still needs all the help it can get."

In the end, the county's Cultural Affairs Council appointed a subcommittee to once again review the potential sites and issue a report. In November, a year after the unveiling of the much-ballyhooed Touche Ross report, the subcommittee rejected the notion of placing the center on Watson Island. As panel member and architect Hilario Candela said, "I don't believe we should look at Watson Island just because it is empty and just because it belongs to the city." The longtime veteran of many a site-discussion debate agreed with many others that the real show at a performing arts center was to be found *inside* the walls. And after the show was over, he pointed out, "There would be nothing on Watson Island to hold you. We have to consider the overall value to the city." The panel's recommendations were taken up by the full council on November 24, 1987, which firmly rejected the Watson Island site, presumably once and for all. Instead, the council said, it was recommending a site on Biscayne Boulevard somewhere between Northeast Third and Tenth Streets, "depending on the availability of land."

The vote was viewed as a positive step by many, though architecture critic Dunlop seemed ready to pull her hair at the continual dithering. There needed to be a full-time director and staff committed to planning and fund-raising and construction, she pleaded, not endless debate.

By the following February, it seemed that someone had taken note. At a press conference, Miami Mayor Xavier Suarez announced the formation of a private-public sector committee with the power "to make decisions" about the building of a performing arts center, and he added that the City of Miami would put up $25 million of the costs to build a permanent home for ballet, opera, symphony, and theater companies. The group was to be chaired by CenTrust Savings Bank CEO David Paul and included City Commissioner Rosario Kennedy; County Commissioner Sherman Winn; Cultural Affairs Council Chairman Luis Laredo; Alvah Chapman, chairman of Knight-Ridder; Garth Reeves, publisher of the *Miami Times*; and Parker Thomson. David Paul said that the private sector would match the $25 million pledged by the city, and Metro Mayor Stephen Clark said that the county would kick in $25 million more, though Suarez groused that the county's share should be much more. "It has five times the tax base of the city," he pointed out.

There was no announcement as to where the center would be built, though it appeared that Suarez had finally conceded on the idea that Watson Island would be the site. "It's unlikely that voters would approve," he said. When he was asked about a site, Paul was evasive. "We're not going to do any more studies. We certainly have enough information on a site," he said, pledging to kick-start the project. "We intend to move it along relatively rapidly."

Unfortunately, Paul's determination to break the logjam seems to have planted along with it the seeds of trouble. At the committee's first meeting on February 12, just four days after the press conference announcing its formation, the group quickly reached a consensus on a site. Following along with Alvah Chapman's strong preference for Bicentennial Park (which the Touche Ross report had faulted for its distance from other facilities, among other things), the others concurred, though Commissioner Kennedy had her doubts that voters would concur with the plan. Even though the park was run down and little used except by the homeless, there was the bugaboo of the city ordinance prohibiting construction there and the difficulty of securing approval of a city giveaway of land for such a purpose.

Still, Mayor Suarez felt it an acceptable compromise given the waterfront location, and Chapman, as chairman of the paper's parent company, was confident that he could secure the editorial backing of the *Herald*. While Parker Thomson leaned toward a site west of Biscayne Boulevard, he was willing to go along if it meant that matters could move forward. The committee met again a month later and confirmed its earlier decision, then met twice more on March 22 and 24 to discuss strategies for taking their plans public and securing broad-based community support. It seemed as though something might actually get done at long last. And then it all abruptly unraveled.

On April 28 *Miami Today*, a business-affairs newspaper, published substantial portions of the notes of the blue-ribbon committee's meetings, igniting a firestorm of criticism that the discussions had violated the Florida Sunshine Law, requiring that any group formed to make policy suggestions to government agencies must give public notice of its meetings. While no one suggested that any of the committee members had ulterior motives for their decisions, the fact that it had settled on a site that was opposed by a number of city and county commissioners as well as the Touche Ross panel and the Cultural Affairs Council proved disastrous.

On May 18, 1988, less than three weeks after the *Miami Today* story had run, and following a number of critical articles on the matter in the *Herald*, Chairman David Paul disbanded the committee. "I think most of the committee feels that it is not in the best interest to continue," Paul said. "Personally, I am pretty disgusted with the process," he added. It was rumored that Paul had identified someone on the committee too timid to voice objections to the choice of Bicentennial Park as the tipster who had gone to *Miami Today*, but he never voiced his suspicions publically.

The latest setback seemed to crystallize the essential problem with Miami's approach to the issue of building a performing arts center: a direct grappling with the issue of how any center would be paid for. The underlying theme in all the previous site scenarios had always been money, but it was little discussed, likely for fear that voter sticker-shock would put a practical end to the prospect. Sites at Bayfront Park, Watson Island, Government Center, and Bicentennial Park had drawn their share of supporters for one important reason: they would be free and shave as much as $25 million in land-acquisition costs from the bottom line, but the endless wrangling over a site seemed to preclude any substantive consideration about where the millions necessary to build it—even at a discount—would come from. "It's as though we could consider site apart from financing," said Rita Bornstein, a member of the Chamber of Commerce.

Though the Touche Ross report predicted that a performing arts center would create as much as $200 million in direct benefits within its first ten years of operation, even as stout a proponent of the undertaking as Xavier Suarez doubted that voters would approve a $100 million bond issue to finance it. Lack of public funds would require a substantial donation from the private sector to make it happen, though discussions by the recently disbanded blue-ribbon panel had identified only $12 million or so from likely sources.

In the wake of the panel's dissolution, Miami Beach civic leaders floated a $47 million plan to build a new symphony hall and opera theater in proximity to the Theater of the Performing Arts and were busy lining up private developers to share the costs. Meantime, in Miami, Rita Bornstein, chair of a Chamber of Commerce subcommittee, called a meeting of opera, ballet, and symphony leaders together to cull their suggestions on any new center. Parker Thomson was dour about the concept of more suggestions, however. There had been more than enough suggestions already, he said. "People need to understand that these facilities require M-O-N-E-Y."

At a November 14, 1988, meeting of the Cultural Affairs Council, a number of audience members stood to proclaim the need for a performing arts center in Miami, many citing the fact that Ft. Lauderdale, West Palm Beach, and Tampa were far ahead of the city on such projects and lamenting that Miami seemed to be running dead last in the cultural race among Florida cities. Finally, then Vice Chair of the Council Pauline Winnick (and a Miami Heat vice president) stood to make a point. "There are ten men in this town to whom a symphony hall is important," she said. "We cannot take this matter to the voters. It would never fly."

Winnick's advice to supporters: go to the next Dade County commissioners' meeting on December 6 and let them know "what's on your mind."

If it seemed a somewhat quixotic notion, Winnick's words did have their prophetic import. It is not clear how many of the one hundred or so community members present at the council meeting heeded her advice, but at that December 6 meeting, county commissioners were in fact to take action that would finally set the matter of a performing arts center in Dade County on track, at long last.

Along with raising fees for taxicab licenses and making it illegal to carry spray paint cans and magic markers with "an intent to deface property," commissioners also voted that day to establish a twenty-four-member Performing Arts Center Trust, with the charge to decide whether a center should be built in Dade County and, if so, how it should be financed. Those who heard the news at the time might have been forgiven for feeling that it was simply one more in a series of a dozen or so groups formed to study and recommend. But this was no mere mayor's advisory group, but a county-level panel established by ordinance. And there was another indication that this time around, things might proceed differently: named as chair of the group was a man who had long held the trust of Metro Mayor Stephen Clark when it came to cultural matters: Parker Thomson.

Of course, why Thomson would agree to subject himself to another round of committee debate and public scrutiny is yet another story. Meantime, for the sake of the arts in Dade County, it turned out to be a very good thing that he did.

PART II

. . . .

FIRM HAND AT THE WHEEL

Finding the Money and Finding a Site, December 1988 to July 1993

6

. . . .

In naming Parker Thomson as chair of the newly created Performing Arts Center Trust on December 6, 1988, Mayor Clark was taking a pragmatic step. Thomson was no politician, no architect or designer, no representative of any special interest group. He had practiced law in Miami for more than a quarter of a century, however, successfully arguing cases involving penalties for stalking and hate crimes before the Florida Supreme Court and winning a number of reapportionment cases before the U.S. Supreme Court, earning a reputation for an ability to cut to the quick in the most complicated proceedings. It was, of course, valuable preparation for finding a way to build consensus among a fractious array of those uninterested, divided, and outright opposed to the notion of public funding for a costly performing arts center in Miami. Thomson believed to his core that not only could such a center be built, but that it should be. It would change the quality of life in his city for the better.

On January 13, 1989, Thomson called the first meeting of his newly formed panel and told *Miami Herald* cultural affairs columnist Gail Meadows that he intended to proceed expeditiously and openly. The first meeting brought "all the camels inside the tent," he said, and lasted one hour and ten minutes, "ten minutes longer than it should have." He also told Meadows that he projected that the group would wrap up its work in the three months to follow. "You don't accomplish anything in more than three months that you can't accomplish in less," he said.

Thomson also vowed to avoid one of the recurring mistakes of preceding panels, that of exclusion and any appearance of backroom dealing. He had already scheduled a meeting for January 30 and told Meadows the call was out for "anyone who has a valid proposal to make" to appear before the group on that day. Previous panels had been accused of ignoring the very organizations that would make use of such a center—musical, dance, and theater companies—but this group would not make that error. "You don't accomplish anything on a policy of exclusion."

Indeed, that January 30 meeting did take place, but at the end of three mind-numbing hours, columnist Meadows suggested that too much "inclusion" might not necessarily be a good thing. Among those appearing before the trust was developer Allen Morris, who presented a slide show the veteran reporter described as "dazzling," in support of building a $500 million complex on property he owned between Northeast Third and Fifth Streets, to include "one or two" forty-five-story office towers, a hotel, and retail space, all of which could be completed by 1992 or 1993. Morris's plan for financing the project would require commitments from as-yet-unidentified investors as well as $25 million from taxpayers, but when questioned by Miami Beach City Manager Rob Parkins on the details of the tax plan, Morris gave an answer that no one in attendance seemed able to comprehend.

Also appearing before the group was Phillip Yaffa, an executive with Florida East Coast Properties, to outline a plan for building a center on a six-acre site in the Omni area, east of Biscayne Boulevard between Thirteenth and Fifteenth Streets. Yaffa admitted that there was no agreement among the various owners of the property parcels (including the *Miami Herald*) and had little to offer in terms of financing details, lamenting that he had had only five days to work on the proposal. Returning to a theme he had long espoused, an unimpressed Thomson responded by telling Yaffa that "a site without financing won't go very far."

At the end of it all, Meadows had heard little to convince her that progress was under way. "After a decade of discussion," she opined, "Dade may not get a performing arts center until Miami's 100th birthday in 1996—if then." She complained that all the proposals seemed to rely too heavily on tax revenues from a county that could scarcely keep its beleaguered public hospital—Jackson Memorial—in operation, and she furthermore suggested that the trust needed to find the funds to hire a full-time executive director with practical experience in building such centers elsewhere.

Thomson's intentions might be laudable, Meadows implied, but the process of bringing a performing arts center into being was a full-time job unto itself. She also called into question the very need to pursue such a mammoth undertaking in the first place. Pointing to the Touche-Ross study that suggested improvements at existing venues such as the Dade

County Auditorium and downtown's Gusman Theater might stave off the need for a glittering new center for the foreseeable future, and passing along the stated intention of Carnival Cruise Line CEO Ted Arison to build a new symphony hall on Miami Beach, Meadows theorized that listening to a parade of self-serving proposals from developers was an exercise in futility.

The only immediate development in the wake of the January 30 meeting was for Mayor Clark to increase the size of the trust from twenty-four to thirty-one members, in an effort to increase representation from more sectors of the county, though it is arguable whether that many camels could fit inside the same tent. On February 9 the *Miami Herald* noted signs of accord, however, reporting that the Miami Beach City Commission had unanimously endorsed Miami's plan to build a first-class opera house somewhere along Biscayne Boulevard. The piece also said that Miami had in turn agreed to support Miami Beach's effort to build its long-rumored symphony hall across the street from the Gleason Theater of the Performing Arts. There was also accord among all on a Miami-Dade Community College proposal to build a drama-dance theater near its downtown campus, and all were agreed that the Dade County Auditorium would be renovated for the Greater Miami Opera until the new opera hall was built.

Herald dance critic Laurie Horn was quoted in the piece as having written a letter to Santa Claus, pleading for "a way out of the deadlock on the Performing Arts Center." Horn said that with the ongoing centers in Ft. Lauderdale and Palm Beach, "Miami soon will be in the embarrassing position of being the only city in South Florida without a major performing arts center—but the only city in South Florida with a nationally recognized ballet company, opera troupe, and symphony orchestra." Space was inadequate for the Miami City Ballet to produce large-scale works at the Gusman, Horn pointed out, lauding the cooperative spirit evidenced between the cities of Miami and Miami Beach. Such peacemaking made the prospect of significant State of Florida contributions for projects likely to total as much as $100 million, she said.

Still, Parker Thomson vowed to press on. In early March of 1989, he told *Herald* columnist Meadows that he hoped to have the trust's recommendations ready for presentation to the Miami-Dade Commission on

March 21, prior to the opening of the state legislature's session in April. By the time of its March 6 meeting, the trust had resolved its intentions to pursue a three-venue complex to include a symphony hall, a major theater, and a smaller space for dance and drama in one location, along with rehearsal and office space. Now, Thomson said, and in contrast to site-selection squabbles that had paralyzed progress on the performing arts center for a decade or more, the trust members had moved along to discussion of costs and funding. He hoped that the state might contribute up to a quarter of the necessary funds, but they would likely be "last dollars," he said, "not first." Though there were now thirty-two members of the trust, at no meeting had all camels yet crowded inside the tent, it might be noted.

It appeared that Thomson might actually make good on his promise to wrap up the work of the trust within three months, but then, just as he prepared for a meeting with county commissioners where he intended to lay out the committee's recommendations and seek funding to hire professional consultants to carry on with the details, a bombshell dropped. Miami Beach City Manager Rob Parkins sent Thomson a letter on March 20, announcing that Miami Beach had decided to proceed on its long-bandied plan to build a 2,200-seat, $67.5 million hall at Washington Avenue and Seventeenth Street, across from the Gleason Theater of the Performing Arts, where the New World Symphony would be housed. The project would be funded by a $20 million bond issue, a similar amount to be raised from private donors, and a $22.5 million "last-dollar" 1:2 match by the State of Florida.

The announcement threw some trust members into a tizzy, with Seth Gordon, also chairman of the board of downtown Miami's New World School of the Arts, opining that the state legislature was not likely to fund more than one major building project in the same metropolitan area. And Miami City Manager Cesar Odio seemed ready to throw in the towel when he opined that if Miami Beach were to actually go forward with its proposal, it would make all the work of the trust to date a waste. But Thomson was not so pessimistic. In all the time that the possibility of a performing arts center in Dade County had been discussed, he pointed out, the proposal from Miami Beach was the first to include a feasible financing plan. Perhaps they could all learn from that.

Logic dictated to most that a full-fledged performing arts center belonged somewhere in downtown Miami (the *Miami Herald* had editorialized several times on that score), and in an April 2 interview with *Herald* editor Jim Hampton, Thomson said as much. "This is a countywide project, and it should be built and financed by the county." However, Thomson added, if the county government was going to dither forever, "who are we to criticize Miami Beach for going ahead?" Then the plain-speaking Thomson fired a last shot. "The county ought to put its money where its mouth is. If it has no money [for a center], it shouldn't have a mouth."

The *Herald* weighed in forcefully—it would be "insane" to place a performing arts center on Miami Beach, far from the population center and the newly announced Metromover transit line that would circle downtown, one editorial stated—and pleaded for some individual in government to take the lead in guaranteeing public funding for such a project. Nor was everyone on Miami Beach overwhelmingly in favor of placing a performing arts center in an already densely packed area. Some merchants on Lincoln Road feared that parking garage spaces lost to the needs of so much as a lone new symphony hall would kill business. But Thomson remained unflappable. The center could end up on Miami Beach if for no other reason than "They're the only people who have put their money where their mouth is."

To this day, Thomson claims no gamesmanship was involved in his public comments. The central question regarding the feasibility of a performing arts center had always been funding. If only one community was willing to commit funding to such a project, then all else was secondary.

Meantime, some county and City of Miami leaders urged their counterparts to action. Metro Dade Commissioner Charles Dusseau proposed the formation of a special taxation district for a thirty-four-acre parcel he identified on the north side of the Miami River close by the I-95 freeway. His concept included aspects of developer Morris's calling for the encouragement of commercial development that would surround the center and provide seed money for a $60 million bond issue to help build it. The county "did not have $25 million to give away," for the building of a performing arts center, Dusseau said. Such a plan as he proposed was the only viable source of public funding. City Commissioners Victor De Yurre and Rosario Kennedy, a member of the Performing Arts Center

Trust, announced that they would pursue a resolution to create a special tax district in a downtown area across from Bayside Marketplace, favored by Morris, to help raise the necessary funds.

All of that was encouraging, Thomson noted, but the near-term prospects for the creation of special tax districts and the ready solidification of private-sector development plans seemed dim. In essence, the creation of tax-incentive districts meant that the city or county would agree to return taxes generated by new development in an area in the form of tax breaks or infrastructure relief to developers, not exactly an incentive to commissioners already desperate to find new sources of revenue. Furthermore, in order to make the center a reality, state funds would have to be forthcoming, and he had already been assured, he told the *Herald* on April 10, that the state first wanted to see a comprehensive proposal including all components of a fully functioning performing arts center on one site, along with a detailed plan for private support and local government contributions.

While all of this was being tossed about, Miami Beach City Manager Parkins stepped forward to announce what seemed the final blow to Miami's hopes. Mindful of what Thomson said about the preferences of the state legislature, Miami Beach would in fact expand its announced plans for a symphony hall and was proposing instead a full-fledged performing arts center at a cost of $153 million. Key to Miami Beach's plan was that city's intention to donate two city-owned blocks occupied by municipal parking garages and valued at as much as $30 million. Beyond that, City Manager Parkins said, Miami Beach would issue about $100 million in bonds backed by its hotel and tourist taxes, and the city had commitments of $20 million fund-raising efforts from both the New World Symphony and a joint effort from the Miami Opera and Miami City Ballet.

Many who had fought long and hard for a performing arts center in metropolitan Miami seemed resigned that momentum for the choice of the center's site had shifted to Miami Beach. An April 21 *Herald* story quoted Miami City Commissioner Kennedy as saying, "If they have the money, so be it. I guess it will have to be there." And Parker Thomson seemed in agreement: "If they do have the financing, then clearly it is going to be built on the Beach."

Trust members were scheduled to meet on May 15, 1989, to consider the details of the Miami Beach proposal, but encountered something of a snag. A little-known provision of regulations applying to the 1984 3-percent convention development bed tax revenues—monies that Miami Beach officials were planning to tap as part of their new performing arts center proposal—stipulates that any excess in such funds can be claimed by any municipality in Dade County. As it was reported in a May 21 story in the *Sun-Sentinel*, several months previously the city of Homestead, in far south Dade, claimed $12 million sitting in the fund for their own uses for a baseball stadium that would attract the Cleveland Indians to hold their spring training sessions there. Though a settlement had been proposed, the Miami Beach city commission rejected the proposal, and a sizable hole had suddenly appeared in the formerly airtight budget of the Miami Beach performing arts center proposal. Beach Manager Parkins asked the trust for an extension for his proposal while it was all being sorted out.

The delay encouraged Metro Commissioner Charles Dusseau and other politicians on the mainland to renew their efforts toward a counterproposal. Dusseau rallied his fellow commissioners for a resolution directing County Manager Joaquin Avino to come up with a plan to finance construction and operation of a performing arts center somewhere in the downtown area. At a meeting of the trust on May 31, Avino told panel members that he intended to comply with the directive from his supervisors but indicated it would not be an easy task. "It may mean cutting back on other services," he said, prompting Commissioner Barbara Carey, also a member of the trust, to interject, "We don't plan to cut back on services, I can tell you that. We'll find another pool of money or create one." Miami City Manager Odio also appeared before the trust to pledge the city's intentions to work with the county to come up with viable alternatives to the Miami Beach proposal, though he reiterated his long-held belief that the Gusman Theater should be part of the alternative plan.

Odio concluded by contending that the directive to Avino meant that there was at last an alternative to the proposal put forward by Miami Beach, but Thomson reminded the city manager of the realities: "There is only one proposal before us at this moment," he said. "There is a number 1 plan, but there is no number 2."

Miami Beach City Manager Rob Parkins told the trust that the county commissioner's efforts were well intentioned, but added, "I think we showed we are perhaps somewhat better prepared to get it done. We have the land available at no cost. We have financial resources at the Beach's control or discretion. And we now see a strong sense of support by Beach citizens." In the end, the panel voted to announce a thirty-day window during which any new proposals could be submitted for its consideration. An independent consultant would be retained to evaluate the formal proposal from Miami Beach and any others received, and a final decision would be made in early August.

"There were any number of such pauses along the way," Parker Thomson recalls, "and a number of sites were being bandied about at the time, but the constant in my mind was the need for the site to be free. I did not believe that the County Commission would ever approve the purchase of land for a project many people doubted could ever come to fruition."

Alyce Robertson, who would become the director of the Downtown Development Authority, was working for one of County Manager Avino's deputies at the time, and she remembers hearing Avino weigh in on the future of the performing arts center. "That thing will never be built here," was his refrain.

Matters simmered until July 21, 1989, the deadline set by the panel for receipt of alternative proposals, when it was announced in a *Herald* story that its parent company, Knight-Ridder, Inc., had the previous January secretly purchased a parcel of land between the *Herald* building on Biscayne Bay and Biscayne Boulevard to the west. The story said that the parcel would be identified as the site for a new performing arts center proposal to be submitted to the trust that day by the Miami Downtown Development Authority.

The implications were significant. In contrast to the mainland sites previously proposed by Commissioner Dusseau and developer Morris, the Knight-Ridder parcel was in the control of a single entity and furthermore was adjacent to the planned Metromover extension and part of an already existing tax-increment financing district. The news suggested that Knight-Ridder would be a willing partner in efforts to secure a downtown site for the proposed performing arts center, a stance long supported by the *Miami Herald*.

As reported the following day, six proposals were received by County

Manager Avino by the 4 p.m. deadline: that of Miami Beach to build a performing arts complex near the Gleason Theater for $141.5 million; developer Morris's proposal to build two theaters for $99.77 million on Biscayne Boulevard between Third and Fourth Streets; the Dusseau proposal for a $127.5 million complex on forty acres north of the Miami River; another proposal for Bicentennial Park, facing Biscayne Bay south of the Rickenbacker Causeway, from developer Bernard Jacobson, for a center to cost $175 million "or less," with $20 million in funding to come from annual user fees levied on cruise ship operators; a fifth for a $136.5 million center on a site at Biscayne Boulevard between Fifteenth and Sixteenth streets from an agent for property-holders Montgomery Ward and the Transportation Communications International Union; and finally, from Knight-Ridder, for a $109.5 million center to be built in the Omni area, on Biscayne Boulevard between Thirteenth and Fourteenth Terraces.

A seventh proposal, to build a center at the site of the long-shuttered Sears building between Thirteenth and Fourteenth Streets near the offices of the Dade County school board, was later added to the list, but as *Herald* columnist Gail Meadows noted, the $13.5 million price tag on the cost of the property there effectively eliminated that proposal from serious consideration.

The proposals were to be evaluated by Touche-Ross, the consulting firm that completed the 1986 performing arts center feasibility study, and by September 8, 1989, Thomson said, the trust would vote on which proposal it would recommend to the county commission at its September 19 meeting. Hopes were high that one of the proposals would be endorsed and, after more than thirteen years of study and debate, progress could at last begin on actual building. Jacobson's notion for Bicentennial Park had the backing of Alvah Chapman, Knight-Ridder chairman, and the well-tuned Miami Beach proposal had been endorsed by Carnival Cruise Line CEO Ted Arison, along with a $10 million pledge from his own coffers. Additionally, and while Knight-Ridder was not enthusiastic about the Omni site, it was understood that the company would likely donate the $6.5 million parcel in return for tax incentives for developers already in place at that site.

7

· · · · · · · · ·

It might have seemed that approval of the plan submitted by Miami Beach was a foregone conclusion, particularly given Trust Chairman Thomson's wish that anyone with serious intentions for a performing arts center "show him the money." The Miami Beach plan laid out the intended sources for $136.5 of the $141.5 million price tag for the center in its final draft, leaving only $5 million to be sought from the state, and the seven acres of land was owned by the city, thus removing another obstacle unresolved in the other proposals. In addition, Miami Beach enjoyed a reputation as an already flourishing arts center, with the Miami City Ballet and New World Symphony headquartered there, along with the established presence of the Gleason Theater, the Colony Theater, and the burgeoning bevy of nightclubs and associated glitter sprinkled about the streets.

However, as anyone who has ever braved Miami Beach's nighttime traffic or sought a parking place there on a weekend can attest, ease of access was not among the selling points. Nor, as *Herald* editorial writers had often pointed out, was it necessarily logical to build a metropolitan area's grand and primary cultural center on its furthest fringes, glittering as they might be.

On August 23, 1989, as cultural leaders and politicians on both sides of Biscayne Bay waited for the September 8 meeting of the trust that would determine the matter, surprising news came from Miami Beach City Manager Rob Parkins. Miami Beach was no longer waiting, but was actively soliciting proposals to build its long-discussed concert hall atop one of the city-owned parking garages at the site also proposed for the Miami Beach performing arts center. To a number of members of the trust, Parkins's announcement was astounding. It seemed outright sabotage of the selection process, if not near blackmail, for if indeed Miami Beach were to proceed with the plan to build the music hall, it would threaten the chances of receiving state support for a full-fledged performing arts center anywhere else in Dade County. Questioned about the propriety of such an action, Parkins seemed unconcerned. "We always said we're building a symphony hall," he told a *Herald* reporter. "We meant what we said."

If that were not enough, other trust members were dismayed by the apparent foot-dragging of Touche-Ross, the consulting firm hired to evaluate the proposals. The firm might not be able to meet its agreed-upon September 1 deadline, an August 31 *Herald* story said. A Touche-Ross spokesperson claimed that the firm was working as fast as it could, but that it had not received all of the proposals from the trust in a timely fashion. For her part, trust member Rita Bornstein, University of Miami vice president for development, dismissed such cavils: "Did they work last weekend? I did." Bornstein went on to say, "I'd like that report at least a week before our September 8 meeting, and I'd like to see no surprises."

Jeffrey Babcock from the New World Symphony echoed uncertainty about the rigor and expertise of the Touche-Ross process, wondering why proposals calling for a concert hall of only two-thirds the necessary size, or under-bid at two-thirds the generally understood costs of construction ($300 or so per square foot), were even being considered. Babcock recounted horror stories of mistakes made by bureaucrats in the design of other facilities, including the brand-new Paris Opera, where he said the balcony steps were four inches from front to back. "To go down them, you have to walk sideways," he said. "Try doing that in high heels. There are no railings." At the Dorothy Chandler Pavilion in Los Angeles, where he worked for a decade, a pleasant mezzanine space was set aside for informal concerts. However, Babcock said, the elevators serving that area were designed with doors two inches too narrow to get a grand piano through. "So you have to budget an extra $1,200 to hire men to drag the Steinway up the stairs every time you want to have a concert there."

As the day for the trust's decision approached, leaders of some groups tried to take matters into their own hands. The day before the meeting scheduled for September 8, a *Herald* story announced the news that a consortium representing the Greater Miami Opera, the Miami City Ballet, the New World Symphony, the Florida Philharmonic Orchestra, and the Concert Association of Florida had issued a statement endorsing the Miami Beach plan and urging that all others under consideration be scrapped. As Robert Heuer, manager of the Greater Miami Opera, put it, the other proposals were pie-in-the-sky fantasies, the best of which "would take so long to happen that it will hurt the community." Heuer said the group dismissed developer Morris's site across from Bayside Marketplace because it was too small to allow for the construction of both a major concert hall and a theater, and never mind the political opposition to locating the complex outside downtown Miami. In relation to the others, the proposal submitted by Miami Beach, with its ample free land and financing in place, said trust member Rita Bornstein, "there's no comparison."

In response, a *Herald* editorial published on the morning of the trust meeting argued that the position of the cultural groups was "shortsighted." Placing the center anywhere away from the reach of the new Metromover system would be illogical, the piece said, reiterating the importance of situating a cultural center in the urban core where citizens and cultural groups from all the county's communities would enjoy easier access. Miami Beach was simply not the place to build a cultural center meant to serve the entire greater Miami area, the writer concluded.

The trust meeting itself began with a showdown between Miami Beach City Manager Parkins and his City of Miami counterpart Cesar Odio, both trust members. Odio lambasted Parkins for his audacity in announcing Miami Beach's intentions to go forward with the building of a symphony hall without regard for all of the trust's work. "The trust has been meeting since January," Odio told Parkins. "You have no respect for this process."

Parkins shot back, "We've never made any secret of our intention to build a symphony hall."

There followed an avalanche of commentary from various downtown site supporters, including representatives of the Miami Sports and Exhibition Authority and the Greater Miami Chamber of Commerce, with most of the talk focused on development and financing and very little having to with the needs of potential users, according to *Herald* columnist Meadows.

Finally, County Commissioner Barbara Carey rose to put an end to the debate. The commission had been on vacation for the month of August, she said, waving a copy of the consultant's report meant to shed light on the matter. "We just got this Friday. We haven't had time to talk to our county manager," Carey said, then moved that the agenda be post-poned.

Opera Manager Heuer protested. "We don't mind waiting if there's $90 or $100 million to be found. But we're leery of putting a great deal of faith in something that's only wished for. We'd just like to see it built during our lifetimes," he concluded. Still, the members of the trust voted in favor of tabling the matter until September 22, 1989.

There was much furor in the days that intervened, with *Herald* film writer Bill Cosford weighing in to deride downtown politicians for ob-structing the inevitable and using the Metromover argument as its prin-cipal practical objection to the Miami Beach site. Even if Miami Beach didn't have a Metromover stop, Cosford said, "If recent experience is any guide, they'll find a way to do valet parking."

When the September 22 meeting rolled around, County Commis-sioner Carey stood to tell the trust, "No matter what you do, the County Commission has to be intimately involved with the funding. Let's not have chaos." County Manager Joaquin Avino then rose to introduce a ten-point memo outlining possible sources of county funding for a per-forming arts center, including the use of the same county-wide conven-tion development tax raided by the City of Homestead and key to the Miami Beach proposal, which Avino contended could support a con-struction fund of "approximately $117.8 million."

Trust Chairman Thomson's response might have been expected: "If the County Commission says build it on the mainland, I say *find the money*. Otherwise, my position is that we endorse the Beach. It is a sound proposal." In the end, trust members voted to give the county commis-sion a month to come up with a firm plan to fund the building of a down-town complex—otherwise, it would endorse the Miami Beach proposal.

Though the vote might have been interpreted as a half-victory, the Mi-ami Beach city manager's response was also predictable. "Why do they treat us as if we're in Georgia?" he said to *Herald* columnist Meadows in a story of October 15, 1989. Parkins had just come from an emergency meeting of his own city commission called to reaffirm commitment to building the performing arts center, and he was heartened by an appear-ance by Parker Thomson and a 6–1 vote in favor. Still, activity on the mainland had heated up. County Commissioner Dusseau had presented a report to a subcommittee on culture and recreation saying that a $40 million surplus could be recovered from the current budget and that he would be recommending a vote in favor of building the center downtown to the full commission in the upcoming week. In addition, Downtown Development Authority Director Matthew Schwartz announced that both the Miami River site and the Morris/Bayfront site would offer land to the project "at no cost up front."

Furthermore, as Meadows reported, support was growing for the 3.5-acre site further north on Biscayne Boulevard purchased by Knight-Ridder earlier in the year. The company had let it be known that a ninety-nine-year lease would be available on the land for one dollar, and, in fact, the tax-increment financing incentives already in place on the parcel were the source of the "$40 million surplus" announced by Dusseau. "I think [the project] is moving west," was the assessment of Seth Gordon, New World School board chair.

A *Herald* editorial called on the county commission to commit funding to a downtown performing arts center, pointing to arguments made by the lone dissenting Miami Beach commissioner during that body's recent emergency meeting. William Shockett had complained that commitment to the $141.5 million performing arts center would exhaust that city's revenues from its resort bed tax, the convention development bed tax, and its parking revenues, essentially stifling any capability to underwrite bonds for other projects well into the foreseeable future. Furthermore, the piece contended, free land was now being offered for a downtown site at both the Miami River and Knight-Ridder sites. Using the convention development tax proceeds would require an agreement between the Cities of Miami and Miami Beach, but the writer suggested that such a deal could be struck if it included a promise to cover the Miami Beach Convention Center's long-standing operating deficit.

In fact, on Tuesday, October 17, 1989, the Metro Dade county commission settled the matter with little debate. The key decision, of course, had to do with how to engineer the financing of a downtown performing arts center, and that issue was solved with a vote to retake control of the county-wide convention development tax, a 3-percent surcharge on every hotel bill in the county. Control of the proceeds, which had previously been delegated to the City of Miami Beach, would revert to the county, and $76 million would be taken from that fund to finance the building of the downtown performing arts center, along with $40 million in private donations and $25 million in state grants. It meant, in essence, that no taxpayer monies would be necessary. The proposal, assuming that one of the two free-land sites available would be chosen by the Performing Arts Center Trust on the ensuing Friday, carried by a vote of 5–4. "Wherever it goes," a *Herald* story announcing the decision said, "the arts center is almost certain to encourage urban rejuvenation, increase land values and give impetus to plans for private development."

The front page of Saturday's issue of the *Herald* carried news of a decision that seemed to put an end to years of indecision and bickering. With little discussion, the Performing Arts Center Trust voted unanimously to approve the construction of a $159 million complex south of the struggling Omni International Mall on land owned by Knight-Ridder, Inc. The tide essentially swung toward that site because of the fact that its lone owner had agreed to make the necessary land available at no cost in return for favorable tax and zoning concessions on the surrounding property that would remain under its control. In fact, according to the proposed arrangement, the center itself would not be constructed on the newly acquired two-block parcel fronting Biscayne Boulevard, but rather on essentially vacant land between the street and the *Herald* building to the east, at the spot where employee parking was then located.

As suggested during the county commission meeting earlier in the week, principal funding for the project would come from the county convention development tax and presumed a state contribution of $25 million. "These numbers are reasonable," said County Finance Director Ed Marquez, "but they are not solid." Nonetheless, the vote took place, and at long last, it seemed, the process to build a performing arts center in metropolitan Miami could begin. The trust and Knight-Ridder agreed to begin immediate negotiations on a contract for transfer of the property, and the trust set a meeting for November 6 for a report on the progress of those talks and discussion of how construction and operation of the facility would be handled. Philip Blumberg, development consultant for Knight-Ridder, suggested at the time that the county would have to agree to finance parking garages that could be used by both the company and the performing arts center, and that the company would want input in the exterior design of the center as well.

Though the mood among most trust members and Miami politicians was upbeat in the aftermath of the vote, there was a nearly immediate skirmish to attend to when the Miami city commission was asked to approve a recommendation of its Heritage Conservation Board that the Art Deco–themed Boulevard Shops Building, part of the recently acquired Knight-Ridder parcel on Biscayne Boulevard, be designated as an historic site. Under city code, such a designation would have given the Heritage Conservation Board the power to delay any planned demolition of the building—designed by well-regarded Miami architect Robert Law Reed and built in 1930—for up to six months and also would require the board's approval for any alterations to protected structures. City historic planner Sarah Eaton called the building, formerly known as the Shrine Building, "the city's finest Art Deco building," but Knight-Ridder attorney Robert Traurig countered that the city could scarcely ask the company to donate millions of dollars' worth of land for the building of the performing arts center and then place restrictions on its development of adjoining property. As might have been predicted, the commission agreed unanimously not to grant the designation.

Meanwhile, as negotiations with Knight-Ridder continued, troubling word came from Palm Beach County, where work was about to begin on the building of the Kravis Center for the Performing Arts. As a *Herald* story of November 3, 1989, pointed out, the Palm Beach County project was far more modestly scaled at $55 million, with $8 million of the total budget to come from state grants. However, state regulations prohibited the start of construction on projects receiving such grants until all stipulated private contributions were in hand. In response, directors of the Kravis Center voted to move the proposed site of the project to a West Palm Beach redevelopment area where that city pledged $5 million to offset the loss of state funding, with no strings attached. In order to proceed with construction, however, Palm Beach County commissioners had recently voted to issue $17 million in industrial-revenue bonds secured by the Kravis Center itself. It meant that the county's performing arts center could be seized by creditors in the event of a default on the bond payments. While no one expected that such would ever come to be, the crisis pointed out that even the most "iron-clad" funding proposals could founder in the real world.

As if to underscore the nettlesome aspects of "agreements in principle," shortly after the news from Palm Beach came, Trust Chairperson Thomson sent word to trust members that the November 6 meeting set to discuss issues concerning the performing arts center's operating structure would be postponed until November 20 to allow the subcommittee in charge of those matters more time to propose specifics. Additionally, a separate subcommittee meeting on contract negotiations was set for December 6, 1989.

At that November 20 meeting, general accord was reached that the performing arts center would be directed by a fifteen-member board including representatives from the Cities of Miami and Miami Beach, Dade County, the five principal users of the facility (Miami Opera, New World Symphony, Miami City Ballet, the Philharmonic Orchestra of Florida, and the Concert Association of Florida), six community members selected for their abilities and interest in fund-raising, and one additional representative from a future tenant to be named. The group would be responsible for raising the endowment fund for the center and for the formulation of the construction and operating budgets, and among its first priorities would be the hiring of an executive director.

Next would come the selection of developers, architects, and acoustics and design experts to ensure that the sorts of gaffes detailed by the New World Symphony's Babcock were avoided. A minimum rental fee of $3,500 per night was floated, and the question of setting limits on annual deficits also was kicked about. More specific discussion followed on the issue of hiring an executive director, including the suggestion of various local prospects, but Thomson weighed in strongly on that matter. "If I have anything to do with it," he said, "we'll do a nationwide search. You need experience in booking these things, and above and beyond all, you need to be a very, very good diplomat." Thomson also pointed out that formal bylaws would need to be drafted and a clear understanding reached as to the relationship between the nonprofit entity formed to run the center and the county, including the question of whether or not the county would assume any responsibility for the costs of running and maintaining the facility after it was built. The principal issue there, Thomson said, was the need to establish a dedicated source of county funding. "If you rely on the county's general fund to meet the operating deficit," he said, "that guarantees the government's not going to go away."

As for construction financing issues, there was much discussion of just exactly what sources of state funding might be pursued. It would indeed be possible to secure as much as $25 million from the state's Public Education Capital Outlay (PECO) fund, trust member Seth Gordon said, but others pointed out that those monies came with significant strings attached. Thomson pointed out that while Ft. Lauderdale's Broward Center received nearly $8 million of its $50 million construction budget from PECO, it was required to allow use of its small theater for school use up to 50 percent of the time. Furthermore, working through the New World School of the Arts, the natural conduit for a PECO application from the trust, would mean involving the New World's governing structure, which included the Dade County School Board, Miami-Dade Community College, and Florida International University.

There would be another meeting on December 15, 1989, where the focus would be on the negotiations with Knight-Ridder, Thomson announced, but meantime, one thing was becoming increasingly clear: what might have seemed the end of a long process was truly only the beginning.

Q

. . . .

Discussion at the trust meeting of late November 1989 had implied that the group was ready to conclude its mission and turn the guidance of the project over to a full-time director. Trust member and attorney John Schulte theorized that Miami being the star-struck town that it was, perhaps someone on the order of Rudolph Bing (who had managed the New York Metropolitan Opera for twenty-two years) was appropriate; "someone who will command respect," Schulte said. Bing had retired in 1972 and, suffering from Alzheimer's, had recently been admitted to the Hebrew Home for the Aged in New York, but a number of trust members were in sympathy with Schulte's general point.

Before that proposed hire took place, other matters would have to be resolved, however, including the details of the transfer of land from Knight-Ridder to be used for the site. At their December 8 meeting observed by *Herald* arts columnist Gail Meadows, trust finance negotiating committee members received a presentation from the company that surprised many. For one thing, Knight-Ridder was offering a fifty-year lease on two acres of its property, not the ninety-nine-year term that had previously been floated. For another, architect Hilario Candela, sixty-five-year old former Cuban immigrant and designer of the much-admired Miami Marine Stadium (1963), rose to present a series of slides embodying his vision for an arts complex on the site. The complex, to be built a block east of Biscayne Boulevard, would include an opera house on the northeast corner of the property with a symphony hall diagonally opposite. In between, Candela proposed a grand plaza reminiscent of New York's Lincoln Center Plaza, where traffic could circulate and passengers might disembark. Candela explained that he had been hired by Knight-Ridder to prepare a site plan and that he attempted to come up with a plan with the "whole to be greater than the sum of its parts."

Some subcommittee members were taken with the design, including Opera General Manager Heuer, who enthused, "The idea of creating a place with a great deal of activity is something I've always wanted." Not all were as smitten, however, including the subcommittee's chairman, Bernard Jacobson, who wondered why the length of the lease had suddenly been sliced by half. And Miami Beach Commissioner Stanley Arkin pointed out that the proposed third, smaller theater for theater and dance seemed nowhere to be found in Candela's plan. "It's a mandate of the trust," Arkin protested. "We're committed to building it." Other committee members theorized that perhaps the Gusman Theater or the theater proposed by Miami-Dade Community College at its nearby downtown campus could fulfill that obligation. In the end, Jacobson called for the proposal to be turned over to Touche-Ross consultants, who would review it in advance of the meeting of the full trust scheduled for December 15. That meeting was subsequently canceled, however, with the recess to last until after the first of the year.

If some thought that "after the first of the year" meant sometime in early January, however, they were mistaken. For one thing, Philip Blumberg, the site design consultant retained by Knight-Ridder, had taken seriously the need to incorporate the smaller dance and theater space into the preliminary plans, and it was no easy matter to design those changes. Then, when new drawings were submitted to subcommittee chairman Jacobson, he turned them over to the trust's own design consultant, Donnell and Associates, who deemed the symphony hall "too small."

Suddenly, longtime trust members were grumbling that the ironic catch-phrase "In Our Lifetime" had regained its meaning. "It depends on how old you are," quipped trust member Grant Beglarian, president of the National Foundation for the Advancement of the Arts to a *Herald* reporter early in February. It might take another fifteen years at the present rate, Beglarian added. Meantime, Blumberg reminded the trust that the proposed site was a valuable asset that Knight-Ridder would not let lie idle for long. "It will not be available indefinitely," he said. Trust member Arkin shifted the blame back to the politicians. "Until the county determines if the site is a go or a no go, we're just standing by," he said.

Indeed there were concerns within county government, but the issue was not so much a question of site but of finances, the age-old bugaboo of the project. As a February 5, 1990, *Herald* story detailed, about half of the $158.7 million estimated cost of the performing arts center was projected to come from convention tax proceeds. But spokespersons for Miami Beach and for the Miami Sports and Exhibition Authority, agencies dependent upon that same source of funds for previously authorized projects, questioned whether there would indeed be enough money forthcoming to support everything. Miami Beach was using two-thirds of the presently available convention tax funds to pay off the costs of construction and maintenance of its convention center, and the City of Homestead had claimed $12 million for the building of a baseball stadium meant for a major-league spring training site. The Sports and Exhibition Authority used the other third of the revenue flow to pay off and operate the Miami Arena, home of the Heat. County projections that there would be enough added income in the future to pay off nearly $80 million in bonds were unrealistic, these entities claimed.

But Trust Chair Thomson dismissed such assertions. "The problem is that the sports authority, whose money it is not, would like it to be," he said. "To a lesser extent it's the same for Miami Beach." The county was in fact basing its more optimistic figures according to projections made in 1987 by the accounting firm of Laventhol and Horvath that the convention tax income would increase by approximately 90 percent by 1995. Though critics were not convinced, County Finance Director Ed Marquez pointed to the fact that the accountants' projections had proven correct for 1988 and 1989, and there was no reason not to believe their projections for 1995 were sound. For his part, Thomson was resolute. "I have no reason to doubt what they're saying," he told the Herald.

An attempt to broker a compromise on use of the convention tax funds resulted in a delay on bond issuance discussions by county commissioners in early March of 1990, and when Hilario Candela presented an alternative design on March 7 that included a small dance and drama hall, site committee chairman Jacobson said that he would recommend the trust hire its own architectural consultant to review the new plans. "We need some expertise to guide us," Jacobson said, "to help us understand what we can and cannot do."

Parker Thomson did not contest Jacobson's action, but he seemed less than certain that adding a third component to the design would prove feasible. "It's doubtful to me you can build more than two world-class facilities," he told the Herald. In the meantime, questions regarding the lease agreement with Knight-Ridder, realignment of streets at the site, and questions regarding the tax status of the property also remained unresolved.

As delays stretched on and an April 2 meeting of the trust had to be scratched when a quorum failed to show up, some wondered if members truly cared about moving the process forward. Bernard Jacobson, site committee chair, dismissed such fears. "There is no time schedule," Jacobson told the *Herald*. "Our focus is getting the job done right. It'll take several years to do all the things necessary." Thomson chimed in that it was scheduling conflicts and not lack of interest that was to blame. "Some of us have to earn a living," he pointed out.

Finally, on April 23, 1990, the trust reconvened and after reelecting Thomson as its chair, voted to hire its own architects to design the center. As site negotiations chair Jacobson pointed out, they could hardly rely on the recommendations of Knight-Ridder, the company with whom they were negotiating for the land, as to what was and was not feasible to build there. "We don't know if we have a workable site," he told the group. "We need professional guidance." However, he warned, the selection process could take as long as six months. In the meantime, Thomson said, talks would be renewed with Knight-Ridder on the issue of the term of the lease—sources within the financial world were suggesting that a fifty-year term would prove to be an impediment to investors.

Some trust members were concerned that the move to hire an architect for the center was premature, however, and at a June 9 meeting, the trust voted to call off preparations for such a competition and instead to hire consultants to review the very concept that had guided the trust from its beginnings. The essence of what a performing arts center should comprise dated from 1986, site negotiations committee chair Jacobson explained. Since that time, the Miami City Ballet had developed into a national player, as had the New World Symphony. Even the question of whether or not sufficient support and office space had been prepared for was uncertain, and all of the questions had bearing on the adequacy of the site proposed by Knight-Ridder.

It might have seemed yet one more unnecessary delay in the process, but as Parker Thomson said, "If we stop rethinking issues, we're dead." Without greater clarity about what was literally needed within a vast, comprehensive facility, even the most able architect could scarcely design a serviceable structure, Thomson said. Or to put it another way, what good would a Maserati roadster be to a soccer mom on game day?

In other matters, the group also voted to hire a professional search firm to find an executive director and ratified the formation of a fifteen-person board to operate the performing arts center—five to be appointed by county commissioners, five to be named by the principal arts group users, and five more selected by the first ten. The trust also heard a heated letter from New World Symphony President Jeffrey Babcock, questioning the feasibility of garnering $40 million in donations from private donors. "I don't know under which rocks we expect to find $40 to $50 million," Babcock said, also adding that he feared that annual operating deficits—which he estimated at as much as $2.5 million—could quickly put the center out of business. As a result, and while he believed that $40 million in private donations had been the long-accepted assumption, Thomson appointed committees to study both issues.

The most pressing concern, however, remained that of securing an agreement on financing from the county, which in turn required an end to the impasse that had formed when the Miami Sports and Exhibition Authority (MSEA) refused to cede any incursion into its share of the convention tax proceeds. Cost estimates on the center had already risen to $160 million, and the trust now had a target of $174 million, with any excess pegged for an endowment fund. Miami Beach had agreed to give up $58 million in future tax revenues (the county wanted $76 million), and the City of Miami was being asked to relinquish $42 million, though that figure required the cooperation of MSEA. Another $12 million would come from Omni District Tax Increment bonds and $4 million from interest earnings. The remaining $40 million would come from the private sector. In order to break the impasse with MSEA, Thomson said, commissioners would need to vote in support of the budget as proposed by the trust.

Thomson did offer the heartening news that Knight-Ridder had agreed to expand the original 1.8-acre parcel into 3.45 acres, however, and also asked the commission to approve the reorganization of the trust into a fifteen-member private, nonprofit board of directors so that future fund-raising meetings with individuals could take place in private. Otherwise, in accordance with Florida Sunshine Laws, as Opera Manager

Heuer explained, any time two trust members wished to meet with an individual to solicit a donation, it would need to be publicized in advance, with an agenda, including the size of the gift to be sought. By this point, there could scarcely be a soul still laboring under the assumption that building a public performing arts center in Miami was going to be a simple, straightforward process.

At the trust's next meeting on July 13, 1990, Miami City Manager Cesar Odio stood to protest the makeup of the proposed new performing arts center board of directors. Odio complained that while both the Cities of Miami and Miami Beach were being asked to contribute substantial tax dollars to the building of the center, they would have no representatives on the board that would govern its operations. Given the stakes involved, there was little objection to Odio's request, and the trust agreed to place formal discussion of the matter on the next agenda.

Another question regarding the realities of operating the center was highlighted in a *Herald* editorial of July 16, where the writer opined that it seemed a stretch to constitute the new board as a private entity, thus exempting the operations of a facility built with $130 million or more of taxpayers' money from public scrutiny. The answer, the piece suggested, lay in establishing one governing body to oversee day-to-day operations, while creating a separate private trust or foundation for fund-raising, the latter group to understandably be exempt from the so-called Sunshine Laws. "This was the trust's position from day one," says Parker Thomson. "But until we got to the point where private fund-raising would begin, there really was no need to create a separate 501(c)(3) nonprofit."

The matter lingered without resolution throughout the rest of the summer and well into the fall, while the Broward Center struggled to come up with cash to break ground on its project, and news of general economic doldrums cast a shadow over the prospect of raising $40 million in private funds for the performing arts center. An October 15 column by *Herald* columnist Meadows noted the difficulties many organizations dependent on private donations were having: the last fund-raising gala held by the New World School of the Arts had netted only $30,000, and that was without taking into account staff and volunteers' time. And the Metro-Dade Library was pleading with county commissioners to wave the $1,000 security fee for its $100-per-person fund-raising event set for the cultural center plaza.

It was an issue that many had raised from the earliest days of the Performing Arts Center Trust's existence. In an earlier, February 26, 1989, article by Meadows, a number of spokespersons from established South Florida arts and donor organizations talked about the difficulties particular to such fund-raising in the region. "We're not a community with a large number of Fortune 500 companies to underwrite what we're trying to do," said Maurice Weiner, chairman of the Coconut Grove Playhouse. "We may need to scale back across the board."

Meadows's story pointed out another feature unique to South Florida's makeup: given that many of the area's wealthy were snowbirds, their loyalties to cultural organizations "back home" often took precedence over the needs of what many considered vacation homes. It was a problem that extended beyond individuals, Meadows pointed out, given that many of the corporations with offices in the region were headquartered elsewhere. "If Pratt and Whitney has a bad year," said Will Ray, then the director of the Palm Beach County Arts Council, "Hartford tells Palm Beach to cut back on local contributions by 90 percent."

Meantime, in late October of 1990, Tampa opened its own $140 million new convention center after a ten-year process of planning and building, along with reports that the price tag amounted to a $48-a-year bill for every member of the city's populace for the next fifteen years. The announcement came at the same time that a consortium of the five major arts user groups sent out fifty thousand letters to Miami-area residents, urging support of a proposal detailing the final funding formula for the performing arts center, set to come before the county commission on November 6. No "personal tax dollars" would be paying for the center, the letter reminded recipients, only the proceeds from the existing convention development tax and proceeds from the Omni development district tax.

The funding proposal, little changed since it was outlined back in February, earmarked $109 million of convention tax monies, calling on the City of Miami to give up its grip on about $26 million in future revenues, with Miami Beach tapped for about $58 million. At that time, County

Commissioner Joe Gersten (whose later activities would rock the South Florida political landscape) was the chairman of that group's finance committee and had been working diligently behind the scenes to hammer out an agreement among the parties. He had wrested a grudging commitment from Miami Beach leaders, but complicating negotiations with the City of Miami was the position of that entity's Sports and Exhibition Authority, with two-thirds of its operating budget of nearly $1 million coming from the convention tax. The authority's public position was that projections for increases in tax revenues were inflated and that operations at the arena might be threatened if those projections did not pan out. But others suspected that the authority had been planning to tap into those funds to subsidize efforts to bring a professional baseball team to Miami and realized that the performing arts center funding formula would prevent any such activities for the foreseeable future.

Gersten was confident that his committee would approve the plan and that commissioners would concur on November 6, for as he put it, the majority of his colleagues were "sensitive to the need for Dade County to have and be a world-class arts center." Trust member Seth Gordon opined to a *Herald* reporter on October 31, the eve of the finance committee's vote, that he hoped Gersten was right. "If not," Gordon said, "it's back to the drawing board."

Gersten's proposal sailed through the preliminary vote, prompting a jubilant *Herald* editorial the following day, likening the project to the centuries-long communal efforts to build the great cathedrals of Europe, lauding Gersten for securing the agreement of Miami and Miami Beach officials, and calling upon his colleagues on the full commission to follow suit the next week. And follow suit they did on November 6, 1990, in a 9–0 vote that approved a $169 million package to build the performing arts center on the Knight-Ridder site. Gersten told the *Herald* it was a "cornerstone" moment, and Mayor Steve Clark called it the culmination of a "decade-long dream." Added Opera Director Robert Heuer, "For 11 years we've talked about having a performing arts center. I feel like 11 years of work has finally paid off." As for Gersten's influence on the matter, Parker Thomson is succinct. "Joe Gersten understood power very well. To call him the 'chair' of the commission's finance committee understates his basic total control of such matters."

All involved conceded that there remained much work to be done, including the pesky matter of wresting $40 million from private donors. That was a matter for another day, Gersten opined, however. "It is a lot of money," he said. "But I have to accept the protestations of the leaders in the arts community that the money is going to be there." The issue of whether fund-raising would be undertaken by a private nonprofit group was still undecided, complicating the prospect of a 1994 completion date for the performing arts center. Plans could be drawn and other preparations made, but construction work was unlikely to proceed until donations were in hand and state funding thus assured. It would indeed be expecting a great deal for all of that to coalesce within four years.

9

· · · · · · · · ·

It did not take long for that late-1990 sense of euphoria among Performing Arts Center Trust members to dissipate, for scarcely a week had
passed after the historic commission vote when prominent trust member
Seth Gordon sent a letter to a number of his colleagues announcing that
he intended to ask at the next meeting that about half of the proposed
project be scrapped. They should do away entirely with the concept of
a symphony hall, Gordon said, and build just an opera and ballet house
instead.

"Our plans are too big," Gordon said in his letter, predicting that the
center could end up being a veritable monster, a "gigantic black hole,
sucking every dime of arts money in the community into its maw." The
opera and ballet house could be designed to accommodate symphony
and theatrical presentations, Gordon said, and the money saved could
be used to refurbish the Gusman Theater on Flagler Street several blocks
south, thereby helping to revitalize that area. He had waited until now to
bring the matter up, Gordon said, because he didn't want to muddy the
waters around the commissioners' funding deliberations.

Commissioner Gersten seemed perplexed, telling *Herald* reporters
on November 16 that if the trust were to revise the proposal in any significant way, the matter would have to be brought back before the commission. "Nobody who appeared before us discussed this issue," he said.
Trust Chair Thomson reacted mildly, saying that there were probably
other trust members who shared Gordon's concerns. "I'm never sorry
to revisit things," he told reporters. Privately, however, Thomson had
no intention of second-guessing the need for separate theaters. "From
the outset, one of the principal purposes of a PAC was to provide a real
home for all of the major performing arts organizations in Miami," he
said recently. "There was never any serious possibility we would back off
from that." As for whether or not Gersten had sought him out for advice
on Gordon's assertions, Thomson is sure about one thing. "Joe may have

called me," Thomson says, "but if he did, I would have told him to relax and go back to sleep."

Others on the trust board were not as diplomatic as Chairman Thomson. "[Gordon's declaration] is only going to confuse people and make our job harder," the Miami Opera's Robert Heuer said in an interview with *Herald* columnist Meadows, November 18, 1990. And, said New World Symphony head Jeffrey Babcock—who had himself wondered "under what rock" fund-raisers were going to find the needed $40 million—"Take the symphony hall out now, and it will never get built. We're not thinking about what will be needed tomorrow, we're trying to think 15 years down the road."

Heuer fumed that Gordon had not shared his thoughts with him or opera leaders and that furthermore Gordon essentially didn't know what he was talking about: "He's not privy to our consultants' information on the viability of private funds. Why would we start confusing the public now?" When Meadows finally got in touch with Gersten, it seemed the commissioner had revised his earlier stance. "Mr. Gordon is certainly entitled to his opinion," Gersten said, "but I would have preferred he expressed it sooner, because our present position is etched pretty deeply in stone."

As might have been supposed, and following pleas from representatives from the New World Symphony and the Philharmonic Orchestra of Florida, Gordon's motion at the trust's meeting of November 19 that the group amend its proposal and include funding for the Gusman Theater and other venues died for lack of a second. As trust member Bernard Jacobson observed, "We finally have it in our grasp, and now is not the time to shoot ourselves in the foot."

Herald columnist Meadows attended the meeting, noting that while Chair Thomson had little to say, it was apparent that he had prepared his colleagues for what might take place. Gordon's proposal was dismissed with much ado, but he was not the only squeaking wheel to be dealt with. Miami City Manager Cesar Odio was well into a harangue about the need for the trust to hire an executive director as soon as possible when he was reminded that the trust had already voted to hire a search firm for that very purpose.

Shortly after a somewhat chastened Odio sat down, attorney John Schulte rose to complain that the proposed reorganization of the trust board omitted representatives from the Cities of Miami and Miami Beach. Another trust member cut in to remind Schulte that he was the chairman of the governance committee who had asked the full panel for the approval of that very proposal. Schulte then took his seat. And Meadows noted that new County Commissioner Mary Collins also stepped before the trust as the recently appointed chair of the commission's Culture and Recreation Committee. She was there, she said, to ask the trust's help in responding to the "many questions about the performing arts center" that she had received from Latin radio commentators in Miami, reminding everyone of what a hot political potato the project was in this community.

There had of course been two years of debate among trust members and city and county politicians concerning the intricacies of the performing arts center proposal, but it seemed a brand new constituency had sprung up once the commission had actually passed a resolution approving that vast sums be spent to build it. It was as if a giant Las Vegas casino marquee had appeared in the ether over downtown Miami: "$170,000,000 available HERE!"

First among the new petitioners was former Miami City Attorney George Knox (1976–82), intent on jackhammering the proposed center from the Knight-Ridder site and moving it to Bicentennial Park (today's Museum Park), a tract on Biscayne Bay just to the south of the *Herald* building, walled off by the entrance to the MacArthur Causeway. That parcel was purchased by the city from the Florida East Coast Railway during Knox's tenure for $23 million. When Knox announced to Trust Chair Thomson that he intended to make a formal proposal involving the use of that land to the trust at its first meeting in January 1991, Thomson put his head in his hands. Did Knox realize, Thomson wondered, that the city had never offered the site, which had been ruled off-limits for any use other than a park? To Knox, those were inconsequential details. Building the center at Bicentennial Park would spur development in the nearby predominantly African American Overtown neighborhood, he responded, and he intended to see that it happened.

And though the trust agreed to include one representative from

Miami and another from Miami Beach on the proposed new governance board, that action seemed only to open the door to more demands. At a workshop on the performing arts center called by new Commissioner Mary Collins just before Christmas, attended by arts columnist Meadows (*Herald*, December 26, 1990), Collins—who had thrown in with Knox, saying, "I love the idea of [the performing arts center] being on the water"—announced that each of the nine county commissioners now wanted to name a person to serve. Lawyer and trust member Schulte pointed out that the composition of the board was not meant to be a political matter. "We need people who can devote time, business expertise, and influence to this, who have great standing in the community, an ability to raise cash," he said. That might be all well and good, Collins responded, but she pointed out that commissioners hadn't fully comprehended the matter when they approved the formula back in November. "I know you've put a lot of work into this, but I also know that the commission wants some changes in the governance," she said.

At that workshop Collins also passed along one of the complaints whirling around the previously mentioned Latino talk-radio waves. In response to what they'd heard on air, the Hialeah City Commission passed a resolution that the Knight-Ridder site should not be accepted, because of the fact that a clause in the negotiated contract with the county called for the reversion of the property to the company after thirty years. The company's site consultant Blumberg replied that no such clause existed and that there had only been mere mention of a requirement that the land be used only for the performing arts center. The company didn't want to see the complex, "at some point down the road, be turned into a county office building," he said. As for how the rumor had gotten started, he hadn't a clue. Perhaps the confusion stemmed from the fact that the construction bonds would have to be repaid within thirty years, but that was a common restriction in such matters.

It all pointed back to Parker Thomson's comment about the years-old feud over the purchase of the "Flying Bacon" piece under the Art in Public Places aegis. "That's what happens when you talk about spending public money on culture." And in this case, the amount of public money seemed immense.

In an interview for a *Herald* story of February 24, 1991, Commissioner

Collins admitted to columnist Meadows that prior to her election the previous October, she had not even heard of the plan to build a performing arts center. It was only after she was blasted by callers during a series of appearances on "Cuban radio" that she became aware of the project and of the concerns of her constituents. Part of the problem could be attributed to misunderstandings regarding the true nature of the "tax money" being used for the performing arts money, to be sure, but another part was knee-jerk reaction on the part of the ultra-conservative Cuban community who considered just about anything supported by the *Herald* as diabolical. "It wasn't even debatable," Collins said of her efforts to discuss the possibility of the *Herald* site on conservative talk radio.

And though the trust had bowed to Collins's proposal that each county commissioner be able to appoint a representative to what had become an eighteen-member governing board, yet another voice clamored for further revision. At a January 29, 1991, meeting, newly elected Commissioner Arthur Teele rose to protest that Latins and blacks had too little guaranteed say in the performing arts center process and called for the addition of two more seats to the new board that would speak to those concerns. Asked what he thought about all this, Trust Chair Thomson gave a characteristically patient response: "We need their vote," he said of the project's dependence on the faith of the commissioners. "As bond issues come up, there'll be more and more votes."

The talk of moving the site, however, was of some concern to Thomson. Attorney Knox's proposal for Bicentennial Park not only lacked a firm commitment from the City of Miami to donate the land, but it would also mean the loss of $12 million in tax-increment funding that came with the Knight-Ridder site, he pointed out. Two other alternative sites had also been bandied about: the property north of Bayside Marketplace where American Airlines Arena now sits, and another in Overtown near the Miami Arena, but neither offered free property. "I have no question that the Knight-Ridder site is the best site the trust has been offered," Thomson said. As to the rash of new proposals, he opined, "This stuff is smoke. That's all it is."

In contrast to the continual indecision in Miami, work was already under way on the $53 million Kravis Center in West Palm Beach, which had a full-time managing director in place and a nonprofit governing board approved and was independent of city or county oversight. Said Assistant City Manager Pam Brangaccio, "We wanted the Kravis built, but we have too many other structures going up to govern it." Such governmental insouciance might have seemed surreal in Miami, though as Brangaccio pointed out, only $15 million of the total budget for the Palm Beach facility was coming from city and county funds.

In the weeks following, county leaders continued to issue stern warnings meant to show that they were indeed taking their responsibilities as watchdogs of the public trust seriously. Commissioner Gersten, for instance, expressed doubts to a *Herald* reporter about the practicality of raising the oft-mentioned $40 million in private donations that formed about 25 percent of the proposed performing arts center budget. The county should be building on the basis of "hard dollars in hand, not promises," Gersten said. He thought that the project should be downscaled to something in the $125 million range and went so far as to propose the substitution of "Honduran" marble for its Italian counterpart.

Cultural leaders may have owed a debt to Gersten for his ability to cobble together agreement among his fellow politicians, but it did not mean they were going to adopt him as the center's architect and designer. The trust would hire professional consultants in architecture, acoustics, and theater design and would also employ a cost estimator to come up with a workable plan and final budget. The first task was to ensure that the 3.45-acre Knight-Ridder tract was in fact of sufficient size to permit two major theaters to be constructed there.

"That site is marginally large enough for two buildings," Trust Chair Thomson told the *Herald* on March 4, 1991. But if studies were to say otherwise, Thomson allowed that the trust might have to ask for more space, and Knight-Ridder might say no. "Then we'll be looking for another site."

As for Gersten's notions about cutting the cost of the center, those might have made for good political rhetoric, but experience suggested that any change in figures would only head in the opposite direction. Broward's Kravis Center had been estimated at $30 million but ended up costing $56 million. While Miami's performing arts center advocates had been floating figures of $75 million for an opera hall and $65 million for a theater, and had proposed a contingency fund of nearly $30 million to cover overruns, those figures were now several years old. Also, still unresolved was the source of funding for the annual operating deficit, estimated at $1.2 million. While trust members theorized that an endowment would be created to cover that expense, there were no such funds yet on hand.

Arts group leaders explained that most such projects received little in private donations in the early stages. At the very least there would have to be conceptual drawings available to show prospective donors, the Miami Opera's Heuer said, simply because people always wanted to see where their money was going. One angel consistently referred to as a beacon for other philanthropists was Ted Arison, retired CEO of Carnival Cruise Lines and the founder of the successful New World Symphony. Indeed, Arison had committed $10 million to the center, associates said, but his money would be available only after a site was nailed down, a workable design for the two halls presented, and the other $30 million in private money raised.

Other matters, including the makeup of the performing arts center governing committee, also remained contentious. As a result of continuing political pressures, the board of fifteen originally proposed by the trust had now grown to twenty-two, with no guarantee that other politically appointed camels would not soon be nosing into the still un-erected tent. In addition, county commission staffers had recommended that the proposed contract with a head-hunting firm be scrapped and the search for a director be turned over to the county commissioners. Furthermore, that director would report to both the county manager and the trust, a proposal that many on the latter panel felt unworkable. "Please have the trust tell the commission that we want a contract that describes the trust's responsibility to design, finance, construct, and operate an arts center, and that it's solely the responsibility of an autonomous trust," Jacobson said to Thomson at a March 18, 1991, meeting. Jacobson's concern was that if those matters were left to the discretion of a historically fractious, ever-changing political body, there would never be agreement on anything having to do with the performing arts center.

Despite Jacobson's pleas, matters remained apparently at a standstill for nearly two months, until an announcement came that performing arts center supporters hoped might finally send the project "soaring like a rocket," as Commissioner Gersten had once wished might happen. On

June 19, 1991, *Herald* columnist Meadows wrote that Chicago retail giant Sears, Roebuck and Company was planning to donate its long-vacant downtown Miami property, at Northeast Thirteenth Street and Biscayne Boulevard, directly across the street from the Boulevard Shops site held by Knight-Ridder. The reported gift would settle the issue of whether or not there was sufficient room for two adjacent halls, for if Knight-Ridder was willing to go along and reallocate Boulevard frontage to the performing arts center, then the project would straddle Miami's signature street, with a symphony hall on the east, the opera house on the west, and the two major buildings to be connected, perhaps by a dramatic elevated walkway. Not only would the concept be viable in terms of space, it also seemed to address the perpetual bugaboo that some—including Knight-Ridder's Chapman—had always fretted over: visibility. Instead of being shoe-horned in between the *Herald* building and some unknown—perhaps colossal—future commercial development, Miami's performing arts center would have a rightful place of prominence.

The gift, as it turned out, was no sudden gesture of goodwill lobbed out of the blue down to Miami from the shores of Lake Michigan, but was part of a long-term strategy worked out over several months between Parker Thomson and Ross Associates Realtor Sheila Anderson. Back in July of 1989, when the trust put out a general call to owners of potential sites, Sears in fact made a proposal, but at the time was asking for $13.5 million for the property, which covered a city block of 3.5 acres, valued at $6.25 million. Because the store itself had been shuttered since 1983, and the company was saddled with an annual tax bill of nearly $230,000, it gave Thomson and Anderson the notion that a donation might be cadged in place of a purchase.

Early in 1990, Thomson suggested to Anderson that she might approach Sears headquarters to see if the company might be willing to donate the eye-catching tower portion of its property for use as a smaller, ancillary theater to be part of the performing arts center and thus ease concerns of those who thought the Knight-Ridder parcel inadequate. Anderson, a volunteer but not a trust member, readily accepted Thomson's charge and dashed off a letter to the chairman of the Sears board of directors. The chairman himself did not respond, but an assistant did call Anderson, wondering just what it was all about. The enterprising Anderson began a series of discussions with one Sears official after another, gradually working her way up the chain of power until, on August 15, she and Parker Thomson were on a plane bound for Chicago.

All the while, Thomson and Anderson kept the matter to themselves. Had Thomson shared the news with any other member of the trust, it would have been considered a meeting and therefore a violation of Sunshine Laws. In Chicago, the pair met with an attorney for Sears and four of the company's real estate officials. At that meeting, Thomson outlined the entire performing arts center proposal, but reiterated the fact that he was there to solicit a donation of the so-called Sears Tower, the first Art Deco structure in Miami and, though deteriorating, still considered a landmark.

Sears officials listened and then asked Thomson if he had a rendering of the proposed complex. Of course he did not, but Thomson assured the officials he would get them something. Upon his return, Thomson got in touch with William Cox, a Boca Raton architect who agreed to put together some drawings. By November 30, 1990, Cox's renderings, featuring a Tower façade with bright snappy awnings and "Miami Arts Center" decorating its front, were off to Sears.

"These look nice," was the initial word back to Anderson, but then the holidays came and went with no word from Sears. January passed and February of 1991 was nearly gone as well, when Anderson got a call from one of the real-estate executives with the company. That proposal about the Tower building was interesting, the Sears representative allowed, but what did Anderson think the response would be if Sears offered to donate the entire parcel for the project?

Anderson was pretty certain what the response would be, she assured the representative. The parcel sat squarely in a redevelopment district, was next door to the Dade County Schools building, was adjacent to several parking lots and promised to spur development in a long-depressed area further to the west. Though it is doubtful that she used the term, "Hallelujah!" is exactly what she might have said.

Surprisingly enough, no snags ensued with the company, no strings were attached, no unruly Sears director came out of the woodwork to complicate matters. By April of 1991, a formal letter of intent was miraculously sitting on Thomson's desk, along with proposals for the necessary title transfer and other paperwork attendant to the donation. At that point, Thomson, whose trust had no standing to accept or own property, had to approach the county, for obviously someone in authority would have to sign papers accepting the gift. Given his prior involvement, Joe Gersten, chair of the commission's finance committee, was the obvious choice. Gersten heard Anderson and Thomson's story, shook his head in amazement, and took a look at the papers. He called in county attorney Robert Ginsburg, who opined that Thomson could sign off on a letter of intent without making the matter public.

Thomson was only too happy to do so, and back to Chicago went a document stipulating that the trust would indeed accept the property, which some theorized was worth nearly $8 million by that point. While he waited for counter-signatures from the board of directors of Sears, Thomson went to Jim Batten, CEO of Knight-Ridder, to divulge what was in the works and float the idea for a project bridging Biscayne Boulevard. "I thought that the concept of straddling Biscayne Boulevard was an excellent one," Thomson recalls. "I thought the placement of the center there would help make it one of the great streets of the Americas, like the Malecón in Havana."

Batten was also well aware that in the end, the center would make any adjacent Knight-Ridder property more valuable, and the addition of the Sears parcel would take the onus off Knight-Ridder to make more property available if reports suggested such a need. Batten assured Thomson he would recommend the shift to the board of directors, and, once he had done so, agreement was swift. What Knight-Ridder had wanted all along was a spur to development in the area, Knight-Ridder's agent Blumberg told the *Herald*'s Meadows, "and now we have it."

Most civic leaders in Miami were more than pleased at the news, as were arts group representatives, who could at last relax their fears that the design of the project would have to be compromised because of the issues of space. However, those who have followed this saga thus far will not be surprised to hear there was a "but" that arose, nor would anyone doubt that the "but" was a big one. When she learned of the Sears plan, Commissioner Mary Collins was among the first to peer into the gift horse's mouth: "I still expect it to be controversial," she said. "I can't see the historic preservationists sitting still to let that building be torn down."

Bernard Zyscovich, chairman of the Miami Beach Design Preservation League, was quick to confirm Collins's fears. "It would be tragic to lose that building," he said. Added Robert Rickles, Miami Preservation Board member, "I think it's one of the most important buildings in downtown Miami." Opinions differed as to the architectural significance of the structure, but indeed the iconic tower had graced its corner since 1929, a veritable eternity in the city, which itself had not yet been in existence for a century.

Real estate agents who had been trying to peddle the property on behalf of Sears for the past decade were not so sure that the building could be saved for any purpose. "It is not structurally in condition," said Arlyne Cassut, who went on to theorize that perhaps a part of the façade might somehow be folded in as a design feature. Said Phillip Yaffa, a Chamber of Commerce member who had led an earlier effort to find a performing arts center site in the Omni area, "I hope preservation doesn't become an impediment. The tower is the only thing that's significant, and I don't think it's such a significant design."

At the blue-ribbon event arranged to announce the Sears gift, Parker Thomson did his best to reassure preservationists. His original proposal to Sears was for the use of a renovated Tower Building as a theater space and visual beacon for the performing arts center, he pointed out. He promised a thorough inspection to determine the soundness of the structure, to be followed by an announcement of more detailed plans. In response, Bernard Zyscovich told Thomson, "You have put to rest a lot of paranoia in the preservation community." Commissioner Gersten appeared before the assemblage of Miami's most prominent officials and arts leaders to formally accept the property on behalf of the county and to liken the occasion to the arrival of the first passenger train to the city in 1896 and the founding of Pan American's seaplane base in 1934. "Today will be added as the day Dade County was raised to the first ranks of great international cultural communities such as New York, London, and Sydney," he said.

As Thomson promised, the engineering report on the viability of the Sears Building was back by September 11, 1991. The county-sponsored study determined that it would cost about $750,000 to demolish the structure, and about $13.5 million to renovate it. The engineers cited the

presence of asbestos throughout the building construction, rusted rein-
forcing rods within the concrete walls, rotted floors, and trees growing
out of the roof. They also said that the electrical, plumbing, and mechani-
cal systems were beyond repair. The engineers said that preservation of
just the notable tower portion of the building, with its supporting walls
and façade, would cost $2.6 million. But preservationists argued against
that latter notion. "If a façade is totally overwhelmed with new construction, it becomes a meaningless fragment," said Thorn Grafton, historic
preservation architect retained by the county as a consultant on the evaluation. Informed of the report, the Preservation League's Zyscovich bris-
tled that there had been no intimation that the county would demolish
the building. Was Parker Thomson's promise not to count for anything?

There was added cogency to the report, because of the fact that the
county commission had delayed formal acceptance of the Sears Building until the engineering study was in hand. Now the county faced an
October 9 deadline to decide once and for all whether or not to accept
the gift. In the meantime, in a September 29, 1991, story, *Herald* writer
Meadows questioned the logic overriding not only the question of accepting the Sears gift but of proceeding with the performing arts center
project altogether. Accepting the Sears parcel was somewhat like receiving the gift of an elephant, suggested Warren Sumners, executive director
of Tampa's new performing arts center, which had opened in 1987. Even
if you got the elephant for free, Sumners pointed out, the costs of keeping it could be astronomical. "Our utility bill can be $35,000 to $40,000
a month," he said. Both Sumners and Nicki Grossman, Broward County
commissioner, warned of looming annual operating deficits that could
only be addressed by interest income from endowments dedicated to
such purposes. "To think you can run on earned income alone is delu-
sional," added Peal Beard, managing director of the West Palm Beach
Kravis Center. Beard said he kept watch on a dozen such centers around
the country, and none could keep the doors open without assistance.

Despite such fears and also concerns voiced by County Commissioner
Charles Dusseau—still lobbying for the relocation of the performing arts
center site to the Miami River property he championed—that an environmental cleanup of the Sears site might cost as much as $1 million, the
commission voted on October 1, 1991, to accept the gift. The question of

how much of the building to keep and how much to tear down would be resolved later—significantly later, as it turned out—but the property would be accepted. It was no Trojan horse, Joe Gersten advised his colleagues, reminding them that the parcel was valued by the tax assessor at $6.3 million.

Only a few days later Dusseau called a press conference of his own to announce that he had proposed a formal agreement between the three property owners of the Miami River site to pool and re-plat their holdings. The complex arrangement would result in the formation of three adjoining 4.75-acre strips, each fronting the north side of the Miami River, with the middle portion to be donated free of charge for the performing arts center. The remaining land would then be redistributed among the three owners, Dusseau explained. Though the notion came late, it nonetheless had some appeal to die-hard supporters of a "waterfront" site, albeit that the waterfront in this case was something of a technicality when compared to the bayfront settings of the previously mentioned Bicentennial and Bayfront Parks. The Miami River site, hemmed in by looming highway overpasses and fronting one of the more polluted estuaries in the nation, was tantamount to many South Florida house-hunters being led to "waterfront" property that turned out to have a view of a neighbor's back yard across a narrow, algae-choked drainage canal. Still, Dusseau's proposal seemed little more than a pipe dream, for as trust member and attorney Robert Sechen noted, no formal agreement had been signed by the parties.

In the meanwhile, longtime trust member Seth Gordon, bashed by many of his colleagues for suggesting the downscaling of the center to a single hall, announced that he was leaving the trust and would head up a new arts interest group to lobby on behalf of smaller-venue interests. Though Gordon claimed that his resignation was prompted by frustration that trust business had been brought to a virtual standstill by divisiveness and Sunshine Law regulations, others suggested that Gordon had become simply a gadfly convinced that the performing arts center was squeezing out the county's support for small arts organizations.

"Seth needs to start numbering his faxes so we can keep them all straight," Michael Spring told the *Herald* when the news broke. Spring, newly appointed executive director of the county's newly reorganized

Cultural Affairs Council (under the aegis of Commissioner Collins), was a longtime, trust-oriented employee of that agency (formerly the Cultural Affairs Department), who ascended in late 1990 when its former director, Ken Kahn, left for a similar position in Houston. The council had doled out more than $2 million to renovate neighborhood theaters in the previous three years, Spring said, and was currently accepting applications for a fourth round.

Alyce Robertson, current Downtown Development Authority director, remembers a conversation she had regarding Spring with the perpetually doubtful County Manager Avino. She had met Spring at a number of arts-related gatherings around town, and of all the people she had met in county government, she felt he had the best grasp of the value of the county's involvement with things cultural. "My bosses were way more interested in things like roads and solid waste management," she says, "so they'd always send me to what they called 'the garden parties.' When the interest in the PAC started to heat up, I told Joaquin that Michael would be the perfect point person from the county to keep tabs on it."

Parker Thomson, meanwhile, had directed much of his trust-related energies to the reformulation of the trust into a somewhat leaner body reconstituted to oversee what he hoped would be the imminent design, construction, and operation of the performing arts center. Target date for the county commission's action was November 19, 1991, and at that meeting, commissioners ratified the trust as a thirty-four-person entity and reappointed Thomson, along with six new members, including one Stuart Blumberg, who would become a key player in the mix.

Blumberg, a long-term Miami Beach resident and force within the Miami Beach Hotel Association, had approached Miami Beach Commissioner Sherman Winn, asking to be considered for appointment to, as he put it, "a group that I thought was going to leave an important legacy." Blumberg, who began as a bellhop at Bal Harbour's Americana Hotel (precursor to today's St. Regis) and became CEO of the Greater Miami and the Beaches Hotel Association for some twenty years, readily admits that his knowledge of matters cultural was not a strong point of his résumé: "I don't think I had ever attended a cultural event up unto that time," he says. "But I was a good businessman, and I thought I could help answer some practical financial questions that were bound to come up."

Commissioner Winn agreed, recommending Blumberg for a spot on the panel, and as Blumberg puts it, "I spent the next seventeen years asking people with great ideas very hard-nosed questions."

Complicating progress on the performing arts center—both in terms of government and private support—was the fact that the longtime behind-the-scenes power structure in Miami had—according to one's perspective—either shifted or vanished altogether. Through the 1980s, institutions such as Southeast Bank, CenTrust Bank, and Eastern Airlines, along with civic-minded corporate leaders such as Ted Arison, Frank Borman, Alvah Chapman, and others, formed a power core often referred to as the Non-Group, whose members could direct millions in corporate and personal support to civic projects they considered over lunch or during a cocktail cruise on Biscayne Bay. However, with a shifting population demographic, the collapse of the local banking industry, and the retirement of many of those aforementioned leaders, something of a power vacuum had developed. "Civic leadership today?" asked Parker Thomson during an interview with the *Herald*'s Meadows. "There isn't any."

The shift in banking from local entities to those held primarily by conglomerates based elsewhere made a profound impact, of course, but so had the influx of Cubans. Florida International University President Mitch Madique, who was born in Havana, told columnist Meadows that charity in his home country's culture was something taken care of within families, not by institutions such as the Red Cross or the United Way. Further complicating the issue was the hope of many older, still-influential Cubans of an overthrow of the Castro regime and a return to the homeland. If that possibility was ever laid to rest, Madique theorized, Cuban interest in Miami's civic affairs would grow rather than decrease. Very few prominent Cubans would go back, even given the chance, Madique contended. "When Cuba becomes a reality rather than an illusion, people will check that illusion and realize they're now American." But until that time came, the allegiance of the resident Cuban population in Miami would be shifting.

Such dour word on the dearth of philanthropic targets might have made for gloomy prospects, but as all involved in the effort to build a performing arts center understood, nature abhors a vacuum, and there was general consensus that a step-at-a-time approach would yield a grand conclusion, eventually. In early December, a commission subcommittee awarded a $200,000 contract to the New York firm of Jules Fisher to serve as principal consultants for the development of the performing arts center. The firm had provided similar services to the Broward Center and had also worked for a number of smaller venues in Miami Beach, Little Havana, and elsewhere. Shortly thereafter, Cultural Affairs Council Director Michael Spring and Assistant City Manager Dennis Carter were off to New York to attend an annual convention of performing arts center directors. They would not be interviewing candidates for such a position in Miami, the pair said, but they did intend to educate themselves and the potential pool of applicants on the matter.

At about the same time, on December 18, 1991, news came that the city's Historic Preservation Board had added the Sears Tower to its list of protected structures. While the designation meant only that any demolition plans could be stayed for up to six months, preservationists were heartened that it would mean a full public hearing be convened before any such actions were taken.

As the New Year turned, little of note took place concerning the performing arts center, though preservationists were distressed when work began on the dismantling of the red neon "Sears" signs that had graced the Sears Tower since the 1950s. Though it was a stipulation of the gift by the company—"They're not current. We don't use script any longer," said company spokesperson Gordon Jones—the news seemed a surprise to the Preservation League's Zyscovich. "My understanding was that the signs were part of the historic character of the building." The move was reminiscent of the loss of another iconic sign the previous year, when the famed dog-tugging-the-bikini-bottom of the "Coppertone Girl" sign, which had long graced the side of the Parkleigh House building, was removed to make way for Miami-Dade Community College expansion.

Matters remained essentially on hold through the first part of 1992 while the commission-approved consultants studied plans and county commissioners lobbied their counterparts on Miami Beach to formalize the plan to use convention development tax monies for performing arts center construction. That deal was at last finalized on April 22, when Miami Beach commissioners voted 5–2 to allow up to $92 million in future revenues to be diverted to the performing arts center. As part of the agreement, the county agreed to spend up to $2.75 million refurbishing smaller venues such as downtown's Gusman Theater and the Lincoln and Colony Theaters on Miami Beach. The work at Gusman included a makeover for a vestibule that had grown shabby over the years, including replacement of carpeting with tile, repairs to plaster and marble, and the installation of a more appropriately styled wooden concession stand.

By October of 1992, it seemed that matters were finally approaching a head. The trust had devoted three meetings during the year to detailed discussions with the consulting team, refining its criteria for design of the performing arts center and the selection of an appropriate site, which was still an open question despite the donation of the Sears parcel. "It was during this time that we decided that no matter where they stood, the buildings would be designed from the inside out," Chairman Thomson recalls. "I had heard too many horror stories about the experience of acousticians and theater designers having to make compromises because of the architectural design."

Despite the fact that the Knight-Ridder/Sears site had long seemed to have the inside track, the Miami River site championed by Commissioner Dusseau, though much smaller in size, remained in the running. According to a *Herald* piece by Beth Dunlop, architect Scott Wilson, one of the consultants, had examined drawings by both Hilario Candela for the Knight-Ridder site and Richard Heisenbottle for the Miami River site and determined that land offered at both was barely adequate for what the county and the trust wanted to be built. "The sites," said Wilson, "if they are adequate, they are marginal." Wilson had done drawings of his own for both sites, showing alternative configurations designed to maximize the drama of the finished complex.

Not only was the decision complicated in terms of present considerations, Wilson explained, but there was the future to consider as well. What, for instance, would the impact be of all the surrounding development to come, touted by backers of both sites? As Wilson pointed out, a mass of surrounding skyscrapers could render the performing arts center architecturally invisible. In any case, the matter was to be decided, once and for all, at a trust meeting set for October 26, 1992, where members would listen to a twenty-minute final presentation by backers of both sites, to be followed by the evaluations of the consultants. Then, the trust would vote.

"We have now formally been in this process since the end of 1988, almost four years," Trust Chair Thomson said. "Now is the time. We hope we will have two splendid alternatives to pick from." Added Cultural Affairs Council Director Michael Spring, "As much as we're picking a site, we're also picking a partner. We need to have a sense of where we're going in the short term and in the long term."

In fact, the trust did make its choice on that evening of October 26. After some lament that neither site was ideal in terms of proximity to downtown, waterfront visibility, size, or desirability of the surrounding neighborhood, members voted to make the Knight-Ridder/Sears site their choice. There was but one caveat: the land offered by Knight-Ridder was a bit too small and would require the concession of an additional half-acre or so to make everything work, but all concerned seemed optimistic that the matter was settled, once and for all. "It is going to be spectacular," said Knight-Ridder consultant Blumberg. "It will be one of the nicest places in downtown Miami."

Indeed, it seemed a milestone for a process that one might argue had been ongoing for nearly fifteen years, and the trust went immediately to work on refining a proposal that could be voted on by county commissioners by the first of the ensuing year. As that process went forward, however, there was one last wrench lobbed into the works: Commissioner Charles Dusseau announced that with the support of his colleagues Joe Gersten and Larry Hawkins, he would be introducing a proposal to authorize a study to see if the now county-owned Sears Building mightn't be suitable for a five-hundred-person homeless shelter. The proposal had nothing whatsoever to do with his support for a Miami River site for the performing arts center, Dusseau assured a *Herald* reporter on December 11, 1992. "They're not related," he insisted. "People can read into this whatever they want—and I am sure they will."

Despite Downtown Development Authority Director Matthew Schwartz's comment that "the consensus is that's absolutely the wrong site in downtown," and whether or not anyone took seriously Dusseau's suggestion that the homeless be housed in a building on the verge of ruin, Miami City Manager Cesar Odio said he would look into the matter of the structure's conforming with appropriate codes for such a purpose. When notified, the ever-diplomatic Parker Thomson said only, "It would certainly be nice if the commissioners waited until we had a chance to finish our plan." It was about as close to complaint as Thomson ever ventured, for as he recalls, when it came to advancing the prospects for a performing arts center in Miami, "we didn't need or want enemies."

As to why long-term performing arts center supporter Joe Gersten might have gotten involved with this apparent wrench flung into the works, there can be only speculation. "Joe Gersten wanted to be the county mayor," Thomson says today, "so supporting the concept of a homeless shelter would have been a political positive for him." Whether or not Gersten ever thought that using the Sears Building to house the homeless was a viable prospect will likely never be known, for the powerful commissioner's personal foibles would soon have him in an orbit far from Dade County's center of influence.

It would be the last newsworthy moment of 1992 for Thomson, save for a late-December notice in the *Herald*'s Home and Design section that he and his wife, Vann, had opened their Coral Gables home as one of four on that city's Garden Club annual holiday tour. While there is no mention in that story as to whether or not Charles Dusseau may have been among the eight hundred or so strolling through the home, Thomson says that if the commissioner had shown up at that event, "He would have been treated like anyone else."

10

· · · · · · · ·

In some ways, the events related to the saga of the performing arts center that closed out 1992 did constitute the "end of the beginning" for what was the most ambitious cultural undertaking in Miami's history. However, it would take another six months or so and considerable back and forth for the matter to finally be resolved.

In January of 1993, and though Charles Dusseau's suggestion that the county commission turn the Sears Building into a homeless shelter had come to nothing, arts groups were still haggling with the trust over the size of the proposed opera hall. The Miami City Ballet was reliant on an annual windfall from its holiday production of *The Nutcracker*, realizing about 50 percent of its income from that source. For that reason, the ballet wanted a 2,700-seat theater, but the Miami Opera manager countered that the budget for the performing arts center wouldn't allow for more than 2,400 seats. The ballet could continue to stage *The Nutcracker* at the Dade County Auditorium, with 2,500 seats, or the Gleason Theater, with 2,700, he suggested. Edward Villella, ballet artistic director, who had never deigned to appear before the trust, sent word through intermediaries that he was not pleased.

"I did meet with Edward Villella on more than one occasion," Parker Thomson recalls, "and we spoke—along with his business manager— several times on the phone, though it would be more accurate to say that I listened to them. Edward had strong opinions, but I had been impressed with him from the time he was being wooed to come to Miami and create the Miami City Ballet. What he accomplished was incredible."

Beyond Villella's dissatisfaction, supporters of neighborhood theaters and downtown's Gusman were also expressing concerns regarding the impending arrival of a $170 million leviathan on the arts scene, fearing that the new performing arts center would suck the cultural life out of their outlying venues. But the Cultural Affairs Council's Michael Spring countered that the trust was behind a plan to spend $8 million in council funds for upgrades to Gusman, the Dade County Auditorium, the Colony Theater on Miami Beach, and others.

Meanwhile, the trust was in negotiations with Knight-Ridder and the Florida Department of Transportation on the additional property needed to finalize the site and its financing plan, which they presented to the county commission on February 16, 1993. The commission, however, after hearing former staunch performing arts center supporter Joe Gersten proclaim, "What we have here, ladies and gentlemen, is a dollar-eating carnivore," were deadlocked 4–4 on whether or not to give final approval to the *Herald's* Omni-area site (the commission had been reduced to eight members because of the retirement of Harvey Ruvin to become county clerk). Among other concerns raised at the meeting was the exposure of the county to the oft-referenced annual operating deficits. In the end, the commission—distracted by changes in the County Charter that would eliminate the position of an elected mayor and establish district-based seats as opposed to those elected at-large—voted to have the entire proposal reconsidered by a joint meeting of its finance and cultural committees.

As to why Gersten had turned upon the performing arts center project, Parker Thomson can only theorize. "I think that when Joey [by then embroiled in a personal scandal that would lead to his political demise] realized that he could never be mayor, he turned on everyone and everything." As Thomson reasons, it was as if everything Gersten had ever supported was taken up with one goal in mind, and once it was clearly unattainable, he became venomous. "I remember him screaming at me about various issues from his commission seat at one point during that time, and all I did was nod and smile, which infuriated him even more," Thomson says. "But I didn't care. I had one thing on my mind, and that was the success of the performing arts center. By that point, what Joey thought about anything didn't carry much weight."

The prospect of a newly constituted county commission to deal with, including thirteen members each representing districts with special interests, was daunting to Trust Chair Thomson, however. "A great deal of education would need to be done with the new members," he said, urging that as much as possible regarding the performing arts center be determined by the present body. Emblematic of his fears was the comment of Bob Ruiz, candidate for the new commission seat representing Hialeah: "My area was not considered," Ruiz said, contending that the predominately Hispanic, working-class community north of the airport was a viable site for the performing arts center. "The commission might as well just wait until after the election." And Gersten continued his own bluster against the proposal. "I just don't understand the urgency," he told a *Herald* reporter shortly before a March 2, 1993, commission meeting where the question would be reconsidered. "Government shouldn't be signing blank checks."

At that March 2 meeting, Gersten again lambasted both the choice of the site and the financing plan for the performing arts center, alluding to ominous "powerful forces" within the community behind the proposal. By approving the performing arts center, he said, "We are doing a disservice to taxpayers." For their part, trust members said that without final approval of a site, it would be impossible to solicit private donations. In the end, commissioners voted 5–2 in favor of the Omni-area site, though they tabled the matter of the financing plan. Though they were among the four in opposition at the previous meeting, Commissioners Mary Collins and Larry Hawkins joined Charles Dusseau, Arthur Teele, and Sherman Winn in support of the site. Gersten and Alex Penelas remained opposed.

While trust member and Vice Chair Maria Elena Torano called the vote "a step forward," the matter of approval of the financing plan still loomed. While the matter simmered, Commissioner Gersten was forced to observe from a jail cell, where he had been remanded by Dade Circuit Judge Amy Dean on contempt charges, stemming from Gersten's refusal to answer questions from county prosecutors relating to the supposed theft of his car the previous spring. Though Gersten claimed his car had been stolen from his home, the three people apprehended while driving it said they took it from a crack house while Gersten was inside smoking crack cocaine and having sex with a prostitute.

Meanwhile, in the weeks previous to the commission vote on the financing plan, *Herald* publisher David Lawrence had spoken at some length with Edward Villella about the state of support for the arts in the greater Miami area. The temperamental Villella, then fifty-six, seemed uncertain as to whether the glass was half full or half empty. "The Miami

City Ballet has become a buzzword within the classical dance field," Villella said, "yet you wouldn't know it most of the time in Miami." But he despaired of the company's ability to reach the pinnacle of the national dance community without greater financial support. His budget was about $6 million annually (with a deficit approaching $1 million), while such companies as the Joffrey and the American Ballet Theatre operated on as much as $30 million. The community was short on the number of politicians who understood the value of culture, Villella added, saying that the proposed performing arts center was a "major statement that this city will or will not make. My sense of optimism depends on what day you talk with me."

In the end, Gersten's influence on the matter came to nothing, for the old commission was disbanded without taking a vote on the financing package, effectively passing the question along to those officials newly elected on April 20, and Gersten—with his reputation in tatters—was not among that group. Alex Penelas was back, however, and told *Herald* reporters that he was still opposed to the present location, despite Knight-Ridder's agreement to add property deemed necessary for the project. Hispanic radio commentators renewed their campaign against the performing arts center as well, characterizing the present proposal as a thinly veiled plot to enrich the much-despised *Herald*/Knight-Ridder cartel. Even longtime supporter Sherman Winn, reelected along with Penelas, told reporters he might reconsider a proposal to place the performing arts center on Miami Beach if it came up again.

By this point, the issue of the performing arts center had captured the attention of much of the county's electorate, and in May the new commissioners invited the public to share concerns and comments prior to the scheduled vote to finalize plans. According to the *Herald*, about three hundred people attended the May 25, 1993, meeting held at the Dade County Auditorium, many of them members of the Hispanic community exhorted to attend by Spanish-language radio commentators. A number of those present rose to protest the makeup of the Performing Arts Center Trust, which was about 70 percent white, non-Hispanic, an anomaly in a county that was made up of about 70 percent blacks and Hispanics. Others questioned the motives of Knight-Ridder in donating the land, a charge to which the company's Blumberg responded that while of course the company's surrounding holdings would increase in value, the gift would not have been given were it not for a civic purpose.

A number of critics railed against a center that they perceived was essentially of interest to the "elite," and Commissioner Penelas said that he would propose that $5 million of the performing arts center's budget be diverted to building a homeless shelter. Few seemed willing to concede the point that the tax monies to be used for the project would come from funds that could be used only for tourist development purposes.

For many of those opposed, the very fact that a performing arts center was being proposed in a county where there was no shortage of poverty was simply an affront. "I don't begrudge the rich people of this county a center, but there are very few people from Liberty City that are going to see the inside," said Garth Reeves, publisher of the *Miami Times*, the community's leading black newspaper. While no one among the members of the trust would have debated the needs of the homeless and other disadvantaged segments of the Miami-Dade populace, it was hard to discern just how much of the opposition was motivated by the opportunity for political posturing. Newly elected Commissioner Bruce Kaplan, for instance, vowed that he would seek assurances that neither "Knight-Ridder" nor "*Miami Herald*" would be included in the new center's name.

The recollection of Kaplan's move is something of a sore point for Parker Thomson. "Kaplan was a demagogue," he says, bluntly. "Knight-Ridder had never sought to have the facility named for the corporation or for the *Miami Herald* and understood that it would have required a gift of $25–35 million to make such a thing happen, so Kaplan's posturing was ridiculous, of no consequence." As to the comments of Reeves, Thomson is more diplomatic. "As it turns out, loads of African Americans have attended events at the PAC," he says, adding, "I have always said that support for the PAC was a mile wide and an inch deep, so there were commissioners and others who kept at arm's length on the project . . . just making sure that they weren't out in front of the mob until they were sure it was a parade waiting for you to be the drum major."

At their June 1, 1993, meeting set to decide the matter, Commissioner Javier Souto rose to protest that Bicentennial Park would be a better site for the performing arts center, and others complained that the "reverter" clause in the contract with Knight-Ridder could result in the center being taken over by the company sometime in the future. New Commissioner Maurice Ferre then succeeded in having a vote on the issue postponed until July, allowing for further study. As a *Herald* reporter covering the meeting noted, it was the fifth time the commission had put off a vote on the matter.

The *Herald* published an indignant editorial two days following the postponement, opining that if any other corporation but Knight-Ridder had offered $5 million worth of land, Metro Dade commissioners would have snapped it up in a heartbeat. The editorial also complained that the reverter clause simply required that the donated land be used solely for the purposes of a performing arts center. Such language was the stuff of many such agreements, even county agreements where public land was to be used by private developers for approved purposes.

Nonetheless, as behind-the-scenes negotiating continued prior to the commission's scheduled July 13 vote, Knight-Ridder agreed to drop all such language from the contract. In addition, the trust agreed to accelerate the schedule for the acquisition of private donations. The private, nonprofit South Florida Performing Arts Center Foundation, with prominent hotelier Sherwood "Woody" Weiser at its head, had been formed to secure those funds, and had pledged that $20 million of the projected $40 million total would be collected before construction began, with the remainder to be in the coffers by a hoped-for 1998 grand opening. Operating revenues would be guaranteed by setting aside $20 million of the donations into an endowment—income from that source, along with a portion drawn from the convention tax revenue stream, would cover the operating deficit and ensure that no property tax funds would be used to keep the doors open. Trust supporters also responded to the concerns that the performing arts center would consume all arts support from the county by asking the county commission for a $70,000 study to explore the viability of an arts and cultural center in South Dade.

Still, the question of whether commissioners would find such concessions sufficient was uncertain. In a *Herald* interview published on July 11, 1993, two days before the vote, Miami attorney Dan Paul, Parker Thomson's former partner said, "We are not as rich as we thought we were. We need to look at this more closely." It was something of a disappointment to have Paul weigh in thusly, recalls Thomson, but he believes that it might have been worse. "Our separation was not pleasant," Thomson says, "but Dan was a master of the one-liner, and if he had truly wanted to smear the project, he would have come up with something that would have been slashing. I suspect he was called for a comment because someone felt he'd be good for a slam. What he said was really pretty mild, in my opinion."

Indeed, reports from Tampa, West Palm Beach, and Ft. Lauderdale, where new performing arts centers had opened recently, were not encouraging. Tampa's center found its deficit projections $3.2 million short in its first two years of operation; Kravis Center supporters were scrambling to find $2 million to cover unexpected shortfalls for 1993; and the Broward Center ran $9 million over its construction budget, leaving county taxpayers stuck with a significant portion of the bill, along with $625,000 in unexpected operating costs. In response to concerns about such cost overruns, Cultural Affairs Council Director Michael Spring said that the county's planning was "the most comprehensive that has ever been done for a performing arts center" and pointed to the establishment of a $24.5 million line in the proposal budget set aside for construction escalations, some 20 percent of the projected $137.5 million cost. "We have established a budget, and we know it can be done for this," said a spokesperson for Jules Fisher Associates, consultants hired by the county. "It is not a lavish budget, but it's not too small, either."

Also on July 11, the *Herald* reported the results of a poll commissioned by the South Florida Performing Arts Center Foundation (SFPACF) showing that 75 percent of respondents were in support of a performing arts center similar to that proposed by the trust. That proportion held across all three major ethnic groups in the county, pollsters said. The poll also said that a "small majority" of respondents favored the site proposed in the Omni area.

Though some complained that the poll was limited to registered voters, and its questions were posed in such a way as to elicit a positive response, the results nonetheless rebutted assertions that taxpayers were resoundingly opposed to the "elitist" performing arts center, and on the morning of the commission's vote, the *Herald* editorialized once again in vigorous support of the proposal. "Greater Miami lacks what all world capitals have," the piece said, "a first-rate performing arts facility." Every pertinent aspect had been "studied, studied, and studied again," the writer said, and it all came down to one essential question. "Does the commission want to enrich Dade County's, and all of South Florida's, cultural life by building a showcase for the performing arts?" The piece concluded with a plea for a visionary commission to speak on behalf of a visionary community by saying, "Yes."

As for Thomson he was reasonably optimistic that the commission would comply with the urging of the *Herald*, though it is his assessment that the newspaper had positioned itself largely as "neutral" over the course of the process to that date. "I always believed that the editorial board of the paper was reluctant to appear to boost a project that would be perceived as a benefit to the stockholders of Knight-Ridder."

In any case, a reasonable observer might have predicted another set of endless diatribes to fill the commission chambers that day, and indeed the discussion did go on for hours. Commissioner Javier Souto again rose to plead his case for moving the performing arts center to Bicentennial Park. And Commissioner Natacha Millan argued that unshakable pledges from private donors should be in hand before the county anted up a penny. Commissioners also bowed to colleague Kaplan's insistence that $5 million of projected revenues from the Omni tax district funds sought for the performing arts center be redirected toward programs for the county's homeless, stipulated that funds would be set aside for investigating arts centers in both North and South Dade, and agreed to ensure the trust's thirty-four members would in fact consist of a more diverse body.

But most important, after securing the pledge of the trust that no further tax monies would ever be sought, instead of tabling the matter that they had considered on fourteen different occasions, and over the shouts of fellow commissioner Javier Souto—"You let me down, guys. You let me down"—on July 13, 1993, they voted 11–2 in favor of building a 2,480-seat opera house and a 1,900-seat symphony hall "of the highest acoustical and aesthetic quality" on the Omni area site, with even long-term foe Alex Penelas finally on board. According to the *Herald* reporter who covered the meeting, many in attendance rose to cheer.

"This is going to put Miami on the map as a cultural center," said Cultural Affairs Council Director Michael Spring. "It's going to be a great performing arts center."

A *Herald* editorial exulted in the decision, dubbing Commission Chairman Arthur Teele "a concertmaster" for maintaining order and focus during the meeting, and reserving special kudos for Trust Chair Thomson for the "untold hours" he and other trust members had devoted to "persuading Dade County's governors to make this historic leap of aspiration and faith."

When he was asked whether he thought the Performing Arts Center Foundation fund-raisers would be able to meet their $40 million goal, including $3 million to be in hand before an architect was hired and $17 million more before construction began, Thomson replied, "I expect them to exceed it."

In response to a reporter who wanted his reaction to the commission's historic vote, Thomson barely hesitated, "I'm relieved."

Smoke billows from buildings set ablaze during the Miami riots of 1980. Courtesy of State Archives of Florida.

Bird's-eye view of Philip Johnson's Miami-Dade Cultural Center, 1984. Courtesy of State Archives of Florida.

Joe Gersten faces the press after his release from jail in 1993 on contempt-of-court charges for refusal to answer questions regarding the alleged theft of his car in 1992. The incident marked the end of a once-promising political career. Courtesy of *Miami Herald*.

Cesar Pelli, *second from right*, and his design team (*from left*: Mariko Masuoka, Mitch Hirsch, partner Fred Clarke, and Roberto Espejo) study the original model for the selection competition in their Connecticut studios. Note that the Sears Tower is not yet a part of the layout. Courtesy of Pelli Clarke Pelli Architects and Robert Espejo. ©PCP Architects.

The Sears Building and Tower in 1957 during its heyday. Courtesy of David A. Kley-lien.

The proposed site of the performing arts center in 1996, looking south toward Miami from the Omni Hotel rooms where Pelli Clarke Pelli Architects displayed the model of their entry in the design competition charrette. The Sears Building and Tower sits at right center, with the *Herald* parcel (parking lot) directly eastward across Biscayne Boulevard. Courtesy of Pelli Clarke Pelli Architects. ©PCP Architects.

Above: Construction under way, with the concert hall superstructure in the foreground, the opera hall in the background, and the Sears Tower between. Courtesy of *Miami Herald*.

Left: The first section of the precast concrete roof of the concert hall is guided into place. Courtesy of Pelli Clarke Pelli Architects and Robert Espejo. ©PCP Architects.

Above: Traffic is rerouted on Biscayne Boulevard while the decorative walkway connecting the opera house and the concert hall is laid. Courtesy of Pelli Clarke Pelli Architects and Robert Espejo. ©PCP Architects.

Right: Late-night traffic is halted on Biscayne Boulevard as the girder supporting the Blumberg Bridge is hoisted into place. Courtesy of Pelli Clarke Pelli Architects and Robert Espejo. ©PCP Architects.

The first of the enormous reverberation doors is lifted into place at the concert hall. Courtesy of Pelli Clarke Pelli Architects and Robert Espejo. ©PCP Architects.

Work proceeds on the lobby of the opera house, highlighted by the inlaid terrazzo floor mural created by Jose Bedia as part of the Art in Public Places program. Courtesy of *Miami Herald*.

Lobby of the Ziff Ballet Opera House during an evening performance. Courtesy of Adrienne Arsht Center for the Performing Arts of Miami-Dade County.

Exterior view of the Carnival Tower as it appears today, housing the Café at Books and Books, with the opera house "lantern" in the background. Courtesy of Johnny Louis, jlnphotography.com. ©2017 Johnny Louis.

Evening event on the Parker and Vann Thomson Plaza for the Arts. Courtesy of Adrienne Arsht Center for the Performing Arts of Miami-Dade County.

The complete Arsht Center in formal dress, highlighting the nighttime Miami sky-line—Knight Concert Hall on the left, connected to the Ziff Ballet Opera House on the right by the Carnival Bridge, with the Carnival (formerly Sears) Tower in between. Courtesy of Patrick Farrell.

Parker and Vann Thomson, *left*, with Judy and Sherwood Weiser at the tuning event for the concert hall. Courtesy of Robin Hill. ©Robin Hill.

Adrienne Arsht, founding chair of the Adrienne Arsht Center Foundation, at the gala event celebrating the tenth anniversary of the center's opening. Courtesy of Adrienne Arsht Center for the Performing Arts of Miami-Dade County.

PART III

· · · · · · · · · · · · · ·

TASK AT HAND

Battles over Design and Budget, July 1993 to December 2000

11

. . . .

It had taken nearly five years for Parker Thomson to find the money and reach accord on a place for the performing arts center to be built. He was by the time of the fateful July 1993 vote a partner in the twelve-lawyer firm of Thomson, Muraro, Bohrer, and Razook and was of course heartened by the commissioners' vote, but if he sounded a bit reserved, it is only because he was a realist, even if he had an impossible dream, a realist who understood that there remained much to be done. "I was well aware of what had to come next," he recalls. "I was pretty sure that the guesstimate of cost was low and that it would be quite an undertaking to get the commission to approve a construction contract, for starters."

"When you are as conscious as I was—in a way nobody else, on or off the trust, could be—you can't get too excited over necessary successes along the way of a lengthy project," he added. "I couldn't feel confident of success until we—having picked an architect, and approved a design conforming to our prior inside-out approvals—got a construction contract signed, and shovels went into the ground."

In the immediate aftermath of the commissioners' vote, Thomson and the trust came up with a rough timeline for the major steps to come:

- By January 1, 1994, select an architect and raise $3 million in private funds.
- By January 1, 1996, begin construction, with $17 million more in private funds to be on hand.
- By July 1998, center to open, with $35 million in private funds to be in the bank.
- By 1999, a total of $40 million in private donations to be on hand.

To an ever-cautious individual such as Thomson, those dates may have seemed eminently reasonable. But as history has a way of proving, men might very well propose, but it is out of any individual's hands to dispose.

As he set to work on meeting those deadlines, Thomson took a moment to point out to reporters that the historic $172 million package approved by the county commission included $8 million for improvements in eleven existing venues within the county, including downtown's Gusman Theater, the Dade County Auditorium, and the 475-seat Colony Theater on Miami Beach's Lincoln Road. "I've always likened this project to sort of a wheel," Thomson told the *Herald*'s Laurie Horn. "The Performing Arts Center is the center of the wheel, but in a huge county, diverse ethnically and racially, you have to have venues out at the spokes."

Based on the premise that not every performance group in the county would be interested in or capable of mounting productions at a 2,480-seat opera/dance theater or a 1,900-seat symphony hall, the trust had formed an Existing Facilities Committee chaired by Stanley Levine. Committee members, along with the trust's consultants, visited various venues to solicit proposals from managers and performance groups for ways in which those facilities might be improved and coexist with the performing arts center. "We're going to have a community-wide integration of the arts [and] a project of cultural enrichment for the whole community," said Levine.

As a result of those discussions, included in the commissioners' approved package was $3.9 million to extend the stage, improve the lighting system, and modernize the dressing room at the Gusman Theater; nearly $1 million for Dade County Auditorium to upgrade the sound system, build a rehearsal hall/satellite theater space, and redo the lobby restrooms; and nearly $500,000 for various improvements to the Lyric Theater's sound, lighting, stage, and dressing rooms.

In addition, the performing arts center would institute a policy of half-off the regular rental rates to local groups, and, along with the major dance and symphonic halls, the center would also house a 250-seat, uncurtained "black box" theater that Cultural Affairs Council Director Michael Spring promised, "anybody can use."

It was all heady stuff, but at the forefront was the need to move forward on the design and building of the performing arts center itself. In order to hire an architect, the Trust Foundation, the nonprofit fundraising arm chaired by Southeast Bank CEO Douglas Ebert, was obligated to have $3 million of its $40 million in the coffers. It was a step that the trust hoped to take by the spring of 1994, said Michael Spring, who had taken charge of administrative details for the project. It was also Spring's hope, conveyed in an August 1993 interview with the *Herald's* Gail Meadows, that an executive director for the performing arts center would be on board by December. "We're moving now from planning to doing," Spring said. "It's time to assemble a staff."

As Meadows pointed out in her article, the latter was a step that the uninformed might question: why hire a director for a center that did not exist? But as experience in other communities had demonstrated, it was a prudent step intended to save headaches in the future. As department store titan Stanley Marcus told Meadows, the failure to put a director in charge early on during the construction of the performing arts center in Dallas was a serious mistake for that city. "We had an architect who had never designed a concert hall, a contractor who had never built one, a city that had never paid for one, and a committee that had never been involved with one." As a result, the Meyerson Symphony Center, completed in 1989, might have looked spectacular, but its cost had exploded from a planned $20 million to more than five times as much, and the design of the stage placed severe restrictions on the types of events that could be mounted there, denting the cash flow as a result.

Meantime, Trust Foundation Executive Director Ebert was making headway, having by September announced a $500,000 pledge from then-prominent member of the financial community Barnett Bank; another $500,000 from Equitable Life Insurance, owner of substantial property in the Omni area near the performing arts center site; and a $100,000 pledge from Florida Power and Light. And while the search for an architect was not formalized as quickly as had been hoped, Cultural Affairs Council Director Spring was besieged by inquiries from firms around the globe. By January 10, more than 350 requests from Australia, Japan, Belgium, Mexico, and elsewhere had come in, a phenomenon trumpeted in a *Herald* story. "It's massive and what we expected," Spring told writer Gail Meadows. "It's our next absolutely impossible task."

Ultimately, a deadline of February 28, 1994, was set for the receipt of preliminary applications from architects, with guidelines calling for designs that would somehow reflect "the diversity, excitement, and electricity" of Miami. To many, it indeed seemed an impossible task, given the divergent courses that architecture in Miami had taken in its one-hundred-year history. While the Mediterranean style had flourished in the

1920s—most notably in downtown's Freedom Tower and George Merrick's design of Coral Gables—Art Deco had thrived in the 1920s and 1930s as well, particularly on Miami Beach, and noted architects Andres Duany and Elizabeth Plater-Zyberk had also identified such strains as "Cracker" (think Southern Pioneer), and "frivolous Modernism," as typified in the hole-in-the-condo-tower montage opening of *Miami Vice*.

"I have no idea how a building can embody Dade County," Parker Thomson told the *Herald*'s architecture writer Peter Whoriskey in an interview published on the eve of the submission deadline, "But I am confident that the selection process will lead us to a solution."

At least two hearings were scheduled so that the public could share their feelings on the matter with a group of finalists to be selected from the architects submitting proposals. "We want the architects to get a feel for what Dade is, who the people are," Michael Spring told Whoriskey. Stylistic diversity would not be the only problem confronting the architects, Whoriskey pointed out. The guidelines also called for recognition of the Sears Building: "the ultimate design should consider the presence of this building on the site as part of a possible area master plan." And there was also the fact that busy four-lane Biscayne Boulevard would necessarily bisect the site.

Added to those considerations was the looming presence of the nearby I-395 overpass, as well as the shortcomings of two recent architectural features of the area, the fortress-like Metro-Dade Cultural Center and Miami Arena, the home of the Miami Heat. The latter, made virtually obsolete by cost-cutting measures imposed even before it was built, was about to be abandoned by its chief tenant, in search of a more spacious venue with expanded corporate suites.

All that was surely daunting enough, but there would be no shortage of those vying for the opportunity. By 4 p.m. on Monday, February 28, 1994, twenty-two qualifying firms from the United States, Canada, Mexico, and the Netherlands had submitted applications. The list included notable Miami firms Arquitectonica, which designed the famed Atlantis condominium, with its five-story "knockout" featured in the opening credits of *Miami Vice*; and Andres Duany and Elizabeth Plater-Zyberk, who designed the Florida Panhandle resort town of Seaside. Well-regarded out-of-town architects included Barton Myers, who had designed the Portland Center for the Performing Arts; Rem Koolhaas, who had designed the Netherlands Dance Theater in The Hague; and Cesar Pelli, designer of New York's World Financial Center and Carnegie Hall Tower, the Blumenthal Performing Arts Center in Charlotte, and the Aronoff Center in Cincinnati.

Roger Schluntz, dean of the University of Miami's School of Architecture, deemed it a "pretty good list," adding that there were easily ten firms included who were capable of doing a "world-class building." Cultural Affairs Council Director Spring proclaimed that the competition remained wide open, however, insisting that any of the lesser-known firms could seize the commission with the right design.

As to what that design would be, there was little in the initial stage to suggest it, for there was no call for drawings or discussion of specifics at that point. The list would be whittled down to twelve by a selection panel still to be appointed by County Manager Joaquin Avino, and those twelve would be invited to Miami for interviews, after which three finalists would be chosen. Those three would return to the city for a set of five-day sessions with performance groups, government and trust members, and the public. At that point, the three would be given a month to come up with drawings, a model, and a written explanation of the concept, at which time the selection panel—to be drawn from the thirty-four-member Performing Arts Center Trust, members of local government, and representatives of the architectural community—would rank the proposals and submit their findings to Avino. A revised timeline called for construction to begin in 1997.

Certainly the competing firms were drawn by the lure of a commission worth millions of dollars, but the heartening response also underscored the very reason for creating a performing arts center in Miami. "Miami is positioned to come of age in the next century, and architects find that fascinating," Architecture Dean Schluntz told the *Herald*'s Whoriskey. "It's a different culture. It's the gateway to three continents." Added Stanley Collyer, editor of *Competitions* magazine, "There are not too many bigger or more prestigious competitions in the country right now. Then there is also the Miami mystique. Everyone wants to go there."

Matters simmered until late July of 1994, when county commissioners finally agreed on a two-part selection panel process. It was announced in a *Herald* article of August 5 that a Professional Evaluation Committee would be formed initially, to include Jorge Hernandez, associate professor of architecture at the University of Miami; Vincent Scully, architectural writer and critic and visiting professor at the University of Miami; Karen D. Stein, senior managing editor of *Architectural Record*; Susanna Torre, chair of the Architecture and Environmental Design Department at Parsons School of Design; Jack Travis, Bronx-based architect and author of *African American Architects in Current Practice*; and Miami-based architect Carlos Zapata. That group would interview a number of the qualified architects who had applied for the commission and select a group of finalists.

Those finalists would present formal design concepts to a second panel, the Design Competition Selection Committee, which would have the charge of ranking the finalists for recommendation to the county manager, who would pass the findings along to the county commission for a final decision. The second committee was to include six representatives from the Performing Arts Center Trust—James Herron, Judy Weiser, Juan P. Loumiet, Florence Nichols, Amancio Suarez, and Maria Elena Torano—along with five senior managers chosen from Metro-Dade government.

On Wednesday, August 23, the Professional Evaluation Committee announced that just seven of the firms that had initially applied for the commission would be invited to Miami for face-to-face interviews, surprising some by eliminating one of the most notable of the applicants in their first cut: Michael Graves, lauded for his design of the fifteen-story Portland [Oregon] Municipal Services Building (1982) as well as the Swan and Dolphin Hotels at Disney World. Graves had become a postmodernist icon for his use of decorative flourishes and disavowal of the stark look characterizing many glass and steel skyscraping towers. Members of the committee, however, found fault with Graves's work for being *too* idiosyncratic, citing the guidelines that called for a center that would express "the diversity, excitement, and electricity of the community that is Dade County."

"Michael Graves's architecture always says, 'Graves,'" said panelist Carlos Zapata, a Miami Beach architect. "This building needs to find its own vocabulary. It needs to express the site."

The group also eliminated Richard Meier, designer of the High Museum of Art in Atlanta, a noted architect who would go on to design the Getty Center in Los Angeles. Janet Marie Smith, another evaluation panel member who had been involved with Baltimore's Camden Yards ballpark, said of Graves and Meier: "Their projects evolve into signature buildings. I don't think that is what the county is looking for."

The goal was seemingly clear: to select an architectural design that would express a place more than a designer, though even panel member Zapata acknowledged the difficulty of such a concept. "In this case, anyway, context is an illusion. It's based on a romantic idea. You have a big parking lot, you have a freeway overpass, and you have the blank walls of the Omni Mall."

For the *Herald*'s Whoriskey, who covered the meeting at which the panel's cuts were announced, there seemed a basic divide in the group. "If one side prevails," Whoriskey said, "the Performing Arts Center could look familiar—Art Deco or Mediterranean or Cracker. If the other prevails, expect the experimental."

At the time, Oriole Park at Camden Yards in Baltimore, then a three-year-old ballpark designed to look like one from the 1920s, was a darling of some. But others on the committee were calling for unusual designs that would express the community in a less expected manner. "When some of the most famous buildings were made, they were in fact very controversial," panelist Zapata said, pointing to the Eiffel Tower, the Guggenheim Museum, and the Chrysler Building as examples. "Why shouldn't architects today express themselves?"

University of Miami professor of architecture Jorge Hernandez pointed to the fact that Seville's Giralda Tower had influenced the Biltmore Hotel and Freedom Tower, suggesting that the design of Miami's performing arts center might in turn carry out that Mediterranean theme in its own way. The remark prompted fellow committee member Zapata to respond, "I have to say I do not feel an obligation to re-create an historical icon."

Zapata went on to suggest that an architect overly influenced by the existing context might end up designing a twin to the Sears Tower on the opposite side of Biscayne Boulevard. "I'm saying that on purpose to ridicule the process," Zapata said, "but it could get to that point."

It prompted venerable architectural historian Vincent Scully to respond, "It might not be the worst thing to do there—not at all. Why penalize one design for being reverent and respectful because the firm is not trying to stand on one finger?"

Such rarified joustings may remind some that there is seldom any final accounting for taste, especially where public money is involved. But reporter Whoriskey also noted another divide on the panel arising "from the demographics of Dade County," as he put it, with the group composed of "three non-Hispanic whites, three Hispanics, and one black member," three of them women, four of them men. The African American member, architect Jack Travis, spoke up to suggest giving the major pieces of the project less culturally charged designations. The symphony hall and opera/ballet house, Travis said, could be simply music and dance/theater, thus avoiding the saddling of the halls with traditional European baggage. "Miami, being of a non-Euro culture, has a unique opportunity to express that," Travis said.

Other panelists discouraged over-concern with political correctness. Said Jorge Hernandez, who seemed to express the sentiment closest to accord among the group, "I want it to be a Cuban building. I'm sure Jack wants it to be a black building, etc., etc. But in the end it should communicate to all of us."

By the evening's close, seven semifinalists were invited for a public interview by the evaluation panel on October 17, 1994, where the aim was to reduce the group to three, each of whom would be paid $50,000 to produce designs and models for public inspection and comment at a charrette to be scheduled in January. After one firm dropped out (New York's I. M. Pei, Cobb, Freed, and Partners), six remained to face the group of architects and critics charged with winnowing the list to a group of finalists, while the eleven-member Design Competition Selection Committee, chaired by Senior Assistant County Manager Dennis Carter, watched from the wings.

At that October 17 meeting, the professionals in the field got their final chance to influence the direction that the design of the Miami performing arts center would take. As evaluation panelist Janet Marie Smith put it, the job of her and her colleagues was "to rise above populist polemics" and come up with a list of finalists from which the selection committee, composed of county officials, business leaders, and arts groups representatives could not help but find a highly competent choice. To put it another way, the professionals were determined to make the list of finalists bullet-proof.

During the interviews, Connecticut's Cesar Pelli endeared himself to a number of panelists when he opined that the proposed performing arts center should be a public space that seemed to invite passers-by inside. "[It] should be the family room of Dade County," Pelli said, "not a building for the people who have the keys to the secret society." Another favorite was Dutchman Rem Koolhaas, who projected an insouciance that appealed to the more daring in the audience, including a number of architecture students who requested autographs following his presentation. When pressed about how he would fit his design into the context of structures surrounding the Omni site at Thirteenth Street and Biscayne Boulevard, Koolhaas responded, "I hope I don't sound like a smug European, but the beauty of this site is that there is nothing to weave together."

Evaluation Panel Chair Jorge Hernandez praised the uniqueness of Koolhaas's vision, saying that the former screenwriter (and designer of the Seattle Central Library) "opens our eyes to seeing things very differently." Also touted for boldness of vision was a firm well-known in Miami circles, Arquitectonica. That group was "synonymous with Miami for the larger world," proclaimed panelist Susanna Torre, chair of the architecture program at Parsons School of design. At the close of deliberations, the panel selected as its three finalists Cesar Pelli and Associates, Koolhaas's Office of Metropolitan Architecture, and Arquitectonica, to be joined on the design by former partners Andres Duany and Elizabeth Plater-Zyberk.

The three firms would return early in 1995 to participate in a public charrette where their models, drawings, and detailed design proposals would be presented to the public and, of course, to the Design Competition Selection Committee. Complicating the finalists' work was the vexing question of whether or not the raised overpass of Interstate 395, blighting the view southward from the performing arts center site, would remain. While some civic leaders proposed burying the roadway underground or simply dropping it into a below-ground channel, the cost of either alternative would add about $200 million to the already-planned roadway reconstruction. A below-ground I-395 would allow for unobstructed views from the performing arts center all the way to Biscayne Bay at that time, but that $200 million in added costs amounted to about twice what was budgeted for the center by itself.

If the roadway were to remain in place, performing arts center designers would have to take that fact into account, perhaps turning the entrances of the buildings to the north or, alternatively, erecting blank walls that would block the view of the highway from the center site. "We will instruct the competitors to assume one way or another," planning consultant Scott Wilson told the *Herald*'s Whoriskey, but as to which direction the decision would go, Wilson said, "We just don't know yet."

It was something of a riddle for competitors, but it would not automatically result in a deal-breaker for any of the final submissions. As the University of Miami Architecture Department Chairperson Schluntz pointed out, the purpose of the competition was to select a winning firm and not necessarily a final design. "The approach and the methods of the firms are just as important," Schluntz pointed out. The winning firm would have the opportunity to modify any aspect of the design before actual construction began.

While that matter simmered, a question of somewhat greater significance remained to be settled: the selection of a director for the performing arts center. As Lawrence Goldman, CEO of the $200 million New Jersey Performing Arts Center (still under construction at that time), told *Herald* columnist Gail Meadows, "Most of the projects that have gotten themselves into trouble financially or with schedule delays have reached that situation because they didn't have strong professional management on board." Without a management team in place, designers and contractors could plead a case for various changes directly to performing arts center board members lacking experience in design and construction management, and the result could be chaos, as in the case of the Dallas performing arts center, where costs had risen from a planned $20 million to $100 million by project's end.

"A normal office building would have about eighty pages of drawings," Goldman said by way of explanation. "[Our building] has fourteen hundred pages." Interviews with performing arts center managers around the state and the nation underscored the need for a firm hand at the controls of such an undertaking, for certain decisions could never be undone. One of the most striking such observations came from Judy Lisi, head of Tampa's Performing Arts Center, completed five years before she came on board. The theater, thought lovely in design by almost everyone, had one drawback, Lisi pointed out. "[It] faces the [Hillsborough] river, which means it looks beautiful from across the other side. But nobody approaches it that way. Unfortunately," Lisi said, "I can't turn the building around."

While Trust Chair Parker Thomson had long championed the hiring of a director for Miami's performing arts center, his efforts were hamstrung by the delay of County Manager Joaquin Avino in signing off on the job description for the position. Without the paperwork in place, no position could be advertised, no candidates interviewed or hired. And with the selection of an architect and final design looming, the need for a full-time director was nearing crisis stage. In addition, nine vacancies on the thirty-four-member Performing Arts Center Trust were coming up in December, and even Thomson's term as chair was set to expire on December 31, 1994. Reason seemed to dictate that a decision on the hiring of a director would have to be forthcoming soon. But, then again, reason has often proven to be a notoriously ineffective dictator.

12

· · · · · · · · ·

As the architectural firms busied themselves with their designs and the two far-flung firms moved to secure the services of local practitioners familiar with the Miami scene (former trust member and architect Raul Rodriguez was reported to have signed on with the Pelli firm, and Dutchman Koolhaas was negotiating a similar relationship with Hilario Candela, the local architect heavily involved with Knight-Ridder's Omni area planning), private fund-raising efforts were buoyed by the early December 1994 announcement of a $2.5 million gift from Ryder System Chairman Tony Burns. The money was available immediately, Burns said, without restriction. To Thomson and others, the gift was a welcome sign that influential benefactors in fact saw the need for the building of the center.

There was also a minor flap reported by the *Herald* near the end of the year between two of the competing firms when Rem Koolhaas requested a two-week extension of the deadline for supply of certain background information on the firm to county commissioners (certification that the firm did no business with Cuba, etc.), a deadline that Arquitectonica complained that it had spent its Thanksgiving holidays complying with. Also, by the end of the year, noted local architect Lester Pancoast had joined the design team of Arquitectonica, and Koolhaas enjoyed an exhibition of his daring work at the Museum of Modern Art in New York. But aside from assurances that the public charrette would indeed take place in early spring, the end of 1994 passed without further moment as it concerned the fate of Miami's performing arts center.

In mid-January of 1995, the *Herald's* Whoriskey traveled to New Haven to interview Cesar Pelli, coming away with a sense that this was one architect who subordinated his ego to the project at hand. "The city is more important than the building," Pelli told Whoriskey, "the building is more important than the architect." On the subject of breaking with tradition and reflecting the angst of modern living in design, Pelli was also reassuring. "There is a large current that says, 'We are living in a chaotic society. Therefore, our buildings should also be chaotic.' But that is like saying, 'We are living in a period where there is a lot of crime, so I'm going to take my kids to be mugged somewhere.'"

Pelli was expansive on the theme: "It is very common for an architect today to say, 'It is not my job as an artist to reassure the people.' That's absolute nonsense. One of the things that architects have to do is reassure people—that the building is comfortable, that it's not going to fall down on you, that it's going to be pleasant." Pelli's designs, which varied widely according to their surroundings, had their critics who faulted him for a certain conservative approach, especially in his work for corporations, and for a lack of individualistic flair, but the architect was resolute. "Architecture is not an art of isolated creation, like painting," Pelli insisted. "A painter gets up in the morning and decides, 'I'm going to paint a cathedral.' An architect can't do that. There is no blank canvas."

As to what he had in mind for Miami's performing arts center, Pelli was less forthcoming, saying only that he intended a center that would be appropriate for the place, details of which would be unveiled at the public charrette scheduled for February 2–6, 1995. "Miamians do not feel there is a Golden Age to re-create and protect," he said. "No. The attitude is, 'My God, let's carry on and get where we are going.'"

The question of the nature of the designs to be submitted might to that point have seemed completely open-ended, but scarcely two days after the interview with Pelli had seen print, a decision was made at a meeting of the trust that would demand a certain commonality, at least. After considerable debate at its January 17 meeting, members of the trust hammered out agreement on one guideline for the competing firms. All three were "encouraged to explore alternative approaches that incorporate significant structural and majority of exterior elements" of the long-shuttered and decrepit Sears building.

The codicil came into existence because of pressure from preservationist groups in Miami, including the Dade Heritage Trust, who argued that the Sears building predated even the much-touted Art Deco buildings of Miami Beach and had served as the center of downtown Miami retail since the 1920s. In response to one consultant's characterization of the building as like "a big ugly nose" on the face of the city's downtown, Heritage Trust Director Glenna Cook-McKitterick responded that the issue was preserving heritage, not beauty. "How many of your grandfathers have big, ugly noses?" she asked. Shot back architectural consultant Scott Wilson, "My grandfather had huge ears. But I would never wish them on my children."

Thus was inserted a feature of the project that in its own way would prove as controversial as any in the decades-long struggle to create a performing arts center in Miami. Certainly it seemed to put to rest Rem Koolhaas's contention that there was no context to be considered in a design for the site. The decision of the trust "may add another layer of complexity," opined architect Jorge Hernandez, a member of the evaluation panel that selected the three finalists. "But the Sears building gives the designer another string to weave into the quilt."

Shortly before February's planned charrette, the *Herald*'s Whoriskey ran the last in a series of interviews with the competing architectural firms, this with the local favorite Arquitectonica and four of its principals, Bernardo Fort-Brescia, Laurinda Spear, Andres Duany, and Elizabeth Plater-Zyberk. Though the two couples had split apart in 1980, Duany and Plater-Zyberk returned to the fold for the design of the Miami performing arts center, hoping to meld their own expertise in community design with their former partners' penchant for dramatic statement. Despite their international renown, the group acknowledged feeling somewhat at a disadvantage going up against their competitors, because of the very fact of their local connections. The "prophet without honor" factor was significant, all agreed, though as Duany offered, "I think one of the real advantages we have in this competition is that we've been thinking about Miami for a very long time."

Once again, little was divulged about what the firm would unveil at the upcoming charrette, but Duany promised one thing: "You'll notice in all of the towns we have planned, the civic buildings—anything like the Performing Arts Center—have very few restrictions. We want them to be spectacular. And we expect them to be spectacular."

When the firms finally presented their preliminary sketches at the charrette, all three had one somewhat anticlimactic feature in common: the proposals were subject to change, and the look of the buildings themselves was wholly undetermined. Plans floated by the Pelli group included one design with the opera house and the symphony hall both situated on the Sears parcel, with a park planned for the *Herald* parcel east of Biscayne Boulevard; a second plan submitted by Pelli located the opera house on the Sears parcel and the symphony hall across Biscayne, with the two connected by a Mediterranean-inspired colonnade.

The Koolhaas design also located both halls on the Sears site and called for a near-total demolition of the Sears building. Only the tower would be preserved, but it would be moved to another location on the performing arts center site. The Arquitectonica group located the opera house and symphony halls on opposite sides of Biscayne Boulevard, with the fronts of each building to be done in glass that would allow views of the lobbies and theater-goers from outside. "Think of these as a display window or a billboard for the culture of the city," said Arquitectonica's Bernardo Fort-Brescia. "It is not a place made of forms, but of people."

The plans submitted by Pelli were adjudged somewhat more classical in nature, but Fred Clarke, a member of that team, insisted that literally nothing was set in stone. All the groups would digest the responses to their preliminary presentations and use the rest of the month to complete final competition plans, including detailed drawings and models, due on February 28, 1995.

Trust member Stuart Blumberg remembers leaving his home on Miami Beach the morning of the charrette, informing his wife that he was just running out for bagels. "But then I thought, 'maybe I'll just drop by and see how those presentations are going.'" As he took a seat in the back of the room, Parker Thomson spotted him and took him aside. One of the members of the selection subcommittee had dropped out, and a substitute was needed. "In the end," Blumberg recalls, "I got home about nine o'clock that evening—a little late for breakfast and with another assignment to fulfill."

While Blumberg and the rest of the trust awaited the final submissions, Sherwood "Woody" Weiser, chairman of the board of the Performing Arts Center Foundation, the project's private fund-raising wing, was called upon to clarify reports that he had suggested elimination of the Sears Tower and Building in the ultimate design plans during a board meeting. While Weiser admitted in a February 15 letter to the *Herald* that he did not believe his group felt the retention of the tower or building was an "essential" feature of any design to be submitted, his comments caused concern among preservationist groups, leading the foundation to issue a resolution that the decision as to whether or not the buildings should be incorporated "should be determined by each architect on the basis of their view of what is necessary to create an outstanding architectural statement."

The announcement prompted the Miami Beach city commission to vote its own resolution, calling upon the Performing Arts Center Trust "to pay heed" to the Sears Building as "an important landmark." The Miami Beach commission was indeed aware that the Sears Building was situated in Miami, but, said Commissioner Nancy Liebman, former executive director of the Miami Design Preservation League, "We had the same resistance over here in the Art Deco capital of the world, and we showed how important landmarks are to a community. All we want is that [the Sears Building] be given a fair breathing chance."

Finally, on Tuesday, February 28, 1995, the three competing firms made public their intentions for Miami's performing arts center. Arquitectonica unveiled a design that it called "a billboard for the future," with glass-fronted halls situated across Biscayne Boulevard from each other and keeping the Sears Tower and base intact. The architects included small plazas in front of each building but kept the relationship between the two major halls intimate. "A problem of downtown Miami has always been too much open space," said the designers in their description. Keeping the buildings close would create a space that encouraged pedestrian activity. Their aim was to "demystify" the project, dispel the notion "that this facility was only for the elite," and create a space that would be "psychologically accessible to everyone."

The design by the Dutch firm headed by Rem Koolhaas also featured glass-fronted buildings facing south toward the city and the bay, but in this case combined both the opera house and the symphony hall into one structure to be built on the Sears parcel west of Biscayne Boulevard. The Knight-Ridder space across the street would be made into a park. One of the more novel features of the Koolhaas plan was the combined lobby that would serve both halls, eliminating various redundancies involved with lobbies in separate halls, and creating what Koolhaas called "a mixing chamber" that would mingle audiences for separate events. It would "turn the sum of visitors into a larger civic collective," the architect said. Though his plan would also preserve the Sears Tower, that structure would be relocated to a new location somewhere to be determined within the complex.

Though the design submitted by sixty-eight-year-old Cesar Pelli was considered in some respects to be the least adventurous of the three, his concept nonetheless was visually intriguing. His design featured matching buildings facing each other across Biscayne Boulevard, the opera hall oriented to the south and the symphony hall looking north, each fashioned, as Pelli put it, "like biblical mounts, to mark a place," connected across the boulevard by an oval public plaza marked by a colonnade. Pelli's design also preserved the Sears Tower, though he proposed to give the structure "new height and functional purpose by placing an observation room or café at its lower top," along with a "glowing construct similar to the old Sears design" to be added to call attention to the performing arts center's presence. *Herald* architecture critic Peter Whoriskey likened the concept to a set of irregular stucco layers rising from the site, "like mashing tectonic plates." For his part, Pelli hoped that observers would come away with the sense of two halves of an oval whole gesturing "with outstretched arms" toward the other. "The arts are joined in an embrace across Biscayne Boulevard," he poetically put it.

Though the proposals were made public on February 28, the eleven-member selection panel would not make its rankings known until the following Sunday, March 5. To assist the panel of arts leaders, businessmen, and county administrators—none of whom were architects—in making that final choice, a nonvoting panel of six professionals had been retained to advise the group. As time for the decision neared, the *Herald*'s Whoriskey approached the advisory panel, trying to get a sense of the favorite. Janet Marie Smith, the ballpark architect who had been a member of the professional evaluation panel, spoke highly of all three proposals but diplomatically declined to name a front-runner. Smith found Arquitectonica's proposal "very simpatico with Miami," and of Koolhaas she said, "I was impressed with the sheer beauty and sophistication of the building as a piece of art." She lauded Pelli's proposal for its approach to the open space around the buildings, a factor that had become more important to her as the process evolved. "I thought the oval plaza he created was a very convincing way to define an open space there," she said.

Carlos Zapata, an architect who had also served on the evaluation panel, leaned toward the Koolhaas design, and its concept of combining the two major halls. "I like the density that O.M.A. is proposing," he said. Karen Stein, senior editor at *Architectural Record*, also favored Koolhaas, calling him the "daring choice." Jack Travis, the African American architect who had served on the evaluation panel, spoke out on behalf of the community-centric approach taken by the Arquitectonica group, saying, "Andres Duany and Elizabeth Plater-Zyberk should be on whatever team wins."

In the end, however, it would be left to the eleven-member jury composed of five county administrators and six members of the Performing Arts Center Trust, including Stuart Blumberg, to make the final recommendation to the county commissioners. On Sunday, that group convened at the Crowne Plaza Hotel, a few blocks from where the center would one day be built, listening to a ninety-minute presentation from each of the competitors and considering public feedback from several hundred in attendance that touched on issues ranging from the sublime—"what will this building say about Miami?"—to the less so—"how are opera-goers supposed to get to the hall without being soaked when it's raining?"

Roberto Espejo, a Pelli team member, remembers the days-long process as both exhausting and surreal. "Each firm essentially maintained a daily open house at rooms in the hotel from 9 to 6. You might have a crowd of German tourists lathered in sunscreen dropping by on the way to the beach to gawk and offer suggestions, then the next hour you'd be entertaining a delegation from the ballet or the opera. I don't remember ever leaving the hotel during the whole time."

Following the proceedings that capped the final day of the grueling charrette, the eleven-member jury retired to chambers to debate its choice, finally emerging with a decision that would provide a much-needed focus for an undertaking that had been for so long a vital but only vaguely defined dream. Ultimately, seven of the eleven votes were cast on March 5, 1995, in favor of the jagged-mountains design of Argentinian-born architect Cesar Pelli.

Though the warmth and sincerity of Pelli and his vision were what swayed many—"His humanism seems to govern his architecture," said jury member James Herron—others leaned toward that choice for more practical reasons, including his design of arts centers in Cincinnati (the Aronoff Center, 1995) and North Carolina (Charlotte's Blumenthal Performing Arts Center, 1987) that had been completed on schedule and within their budgets. It was not only an aesthetically driven choice—the "tectonic plates" concept was a novel way of avoiding the "four blank walls" effect—but it was a pragmatic one as well, said jury member Laura de Ona, who added, "I'm not willing to gamble with the taxpayers' money." Indeed, Pelli's choice of a stucco exterior also seemed to promise budget friendliness, for the glass exteriors proposed by Koolhaas and Arquitectonica would have cost three to four times as much.

Even Pelli himself admitted that the decision might rankle some, particularly in the architectural community. But, he said, "This building should be able to be understood by everyone. If only architects understand this, then it is a failure. If architects also like it, then terrific. But it's not the most important thing." He also pointed to the importance of the plaza in his design. "In a Latin tradition, buildings with important public functions are placed around a plaza," he said, and he defended the notion that even one bisected by a busy thoroughfare such as Biscayne Boulevard could truly function as such. Comparing what he envisioned to the plaza in the center of the ill-fated arts complex designed more than a decade ago by Philip Johnson, Pelli said, "Oh, is it a dead plaza? [It] would benefit by a road going through it."

Roberto Espejo, the member of the Pelli team who would spend twelve years working on the project, the final half-dozen as on-site architect, says that from the outset Argentinian-born Pelli was galvanized by the possibility of designing a "statement" for what he considered to be "the gateway city to the Americas." Pelli was drawn not only by the prospect of collaborating with famed acoustic designer Russell Johnson, who had let it be known that the Miami performing arts center was his own "dream project," but by the prospect of designing what Pelli privately referred to as the "Sydney Opera House—East," Espejo says. "Cesar was excited. He wanted to prove to people that Miami was in fact a distinct cultural center."

"We were all very excited," says Mitch Hirsch, then design team leader and later principal in charge of the project for the firm (now PCP

Architects). "There were so many things: the chance to bring new 'land-forms' to the flat topography near the water; to provide what we were sure would be a catalyst for urban revitalization; to create these impressive buildings that would still not overpower pedestrians approaching on the streets; to play a part in showcasing Miami's diverse culture to the world. We all saw it as a chance to help create a cultural center for all the Americas."

For his part, selection panel member Blumberg recalls being swayed by Pelli's willingness to at least consider connecting the two halls with a pedestrian bridge. "I had this depressing vision of women in beautiful gowns and heels and men in tuxedos dashing across Biscayne Boulevard on a rainy night, dodging taxis and delivery vans, trying to make a curtain time," he says. "Common sense seemed to dictate the need for an elevated walkway."

County commissioners would in fact have the final say in the matter, but Maurice Ferre, a member of that body, opined that debate on the matter was at an end. "To substitute this process with a political decision would be wrong," Ferre said. "It would be a total travesty if we don't uphold the finding." Meantime, on the day following the choice of Pelli, the Performing Arts Center Foundation announced promising news of its own: five leading South Florida banks (Barnett, First Union, Sun Bank, Citibank Florida, and NationsBank) had joined to pledge a total of $2.05 million toward the project, bringing private donations to more than $4.5 million in total.

13

• • • • • • • •

A *Herald* editorial of March 7, 1995, applauded both the public spirit of the donations and the process by which architect Pelli had been chosen and urged the county commission to ratify the selection committee's work without delay. Since Pelli had promised to create one of the "great performing arts centers in the world," the editorial said, "Let's all not just let him, let's help him, get at it forthwith." It was a stirring endorsement of a dream that was more than two decades in the planning stages.

Still, it is possible that county commissioners did not understand the meaning of the term "forthwith," for it was not until June 20 that they got around to ratifying the choice of Pelli as architect for Miami's performing arts center. In the meantime, there was something of a scare for the project when State Representative Elaine Bloom of Miami Beach tacked on an amendment to a bill proposed by a colleague in the Florida legislature that would have affected the way in which bed tax revenues could be used in Dade County. In return for her support of HB 355, proposed by a New Smyrna Beach colleague who was trying to make changes in the way similar taxes were used in Volusia County, Bloom was able to include a rider on the bill giving priority for expenditure of Dade's monies to projects situated within one-half mile of the Miami Beach Convention Center. Bloom was looking for sources of funding for a proposed hotel parking garage in her district and insisted that she had no idea that her amendment would trump the language in the original convention tax agreement permitting use of the monies county-wide.

For his part, Parker Thomson, trust chairman, was flabbergasted. "When I last checked, the performing arts center is going to be a lot more than a half-mile away [from Miami Beach]. This could destroy funding for the performing arts center." Though the Florida House approved the measure by a vote of 103–9 on May 5, 1995, a flurry of phone calls to legislators by Michael Spring and Stuart Blumberg, explaining the consequences, persuaded the Florida Senate to decline its consideration of the bill.

If that near-disaster were not enough, there was a renewal of concern having to do with the Sears Building in June, when *Herald* columnist Meadows reported that the structure was causing problems for Dade officials charged with keeping the homeless from turning the abandoned structure into a de facto shelter. Every time that facilities management workers boarded up or placed blocks in doorways and windows, enterprising homeless people would find another way back inside. At the time of Meadows's writing, she said, draperies were once again bannering out of gutted window frames, practically advertising the tower as a place to flop. No other derelict building in the county's thirty-property inventory created such headaches, County Development and Facilities Management Director Diana Gonzalez told Meadows.

There was some good news for the project, however, when a long-rumored gift of $2.5 million from the Arthur F. and Alice E. Adams Foundation was announced by the Trust Foundation on April 21, bringing the total to about $7.5 million of the $48 million goal. "Opera was always my mother's primary goal," said son Henry C. Clark in making the announcement. "We could not think of a more fitting memorial than to have her name forever grace the opera hall entrance." But certain matters lingered between Dade County and architect Pelli. Though commissioners had approved the choice of Pelli as project designer in late March, the matter of negotiating a contract with the architect was no simple matter. It was October 12 before Michael Spring, director of the Cultural Affairs Council, told the *Herald*'s Peter Whoriskey that the process was nearing an end. "We are expecting to hear from them in writing tomorrow," Spring said.

It was reported at the time that the county and the firm had settled on a fee for Pelli of 13.5 percent of the total construction costs. While at the high end of public building commission fees, which might ordinarily top out at 11 or 12 percent, Pelli spokesperson Fred Clarke said that the county was getting a good deal, pointing out that the firm would also be providing oversight and planning for considerable surrounding development in the Omni neighborhood. "It's a very inclusive set of services," Clarke said. "They [the county] have cut themselves a very good deal, but it's one that we can live with." There were said to be a few minor points to be hammered out, but, said Clarke, "We have come to terms."

And while the county might have had trepidation, Roberto Espejo recalls that there was also some dissension within the firm as to the wisdom of proceeding with the project. According to Espejo, Clarke told Pelli in no uncertain terms, "This is the worst contract you've ever negotiated. We still have time to bail out."

But Pelli was adamant, says Espejo. "Cesar shook his head and very calmly told Fred, 'No, I have promised it to Parker [Thomson] and too many good people in Miami. We're going to do it.'"

While the details of the contract were being finalized, a pair of *Herald* articles appeared in the days before Christmas of 1995, wondering if indeed the arrival of a new performing arts center could reinvigorate a neighborhood that had been down on its luck for a good long time. Columnist Fred Tasker traced the history of the Omni neighborhood flanking Biscayne Boulevard back to its roots in 1912, when grand homes began to be built there, some sixteen years after the city's founding. In 1923 the Miramar Hotel was erected, and by 1927 Biscayne Boulevard, which had stopped at Thirteenth Street, was extended all the way to Thirty-Sixth Street. In the 1930s the Mayfair Theater went up, a movie theater with a garden lobby where maids served tea to guests waiting for the shows. But the gradual move to the suburbs, common to most American cities from mid-century forward, had brought great change to Miami's "uptown."

When race riots broke out in neighboring Overtown, just to the west, in 1980 and again in 1982, it was the death knell for an area that had come to be known as Edgewater. It had become 70 percent Hispanic and 20 percent African American, and the principal economic forces operating revolved around prostitution, burglary, and theft. Sears closed in 1983; Jefferson's Department Store was shuttered in 1985; and even the Omni Mall, at Fifteenth Street and Biscayne, much ballyhooed upon its 1977 opening, was in serious decline in 1995 (it closed just before the New Year of 2000).

Asked if he thought the arrival of a performing arts center could turn things around, Cephus McBride, a resident of Overtown, told the *Herald*'s Whoriskey, "To be honest with you, I don't think it will help anyone. It'll mean more crime. The BMWs, the Mercedes, Jaguars, that class of people will draw . . . well, the robbing class." Charlie Cavalaris, whose family had operated the nearby S&S Restaurant since 1942, told Whoriskey, "I don't think anyone walks here anymore, even during the day. They're too afraid."

Certainly, no one could be certain what a performing arts center could do in terms of reenergizing a neighborhood. "It's very difficult to tell what will work and what won't until afterward," ventured Marion Alberto, owner of a coin-operated laundry in the neighborhood. "And by then, of course, it's too late." There had been lofty hopes floated concerning the little-used Dade Cultural Center and the ill-fated Miami Arena, but as was the case with the struggling Gusman Theater, evening found the streets around those structures empty and forbidding.

As city planner and architect Joseph Kohl told Whoriskey, "If there was an easy solution to urban renewal, we would have discovered it already." But many remained undaunted. Said Michael Spring, pointing to the coming performing arts center, the planned relocation of the Florida Grand Opera nearby, the new Metromover stop, the presence of historic buildings, and of glittering Biscayne Bay, "When you add all these things together, you begin to wonder, 'Why couldn't this neighborhood take off?'" It was a theme not lost on architect Pelli, who said, "What we are trying to do as much as possible is bring the life inside the two main halls onto the street." Of the plaza that was central to his design, he added, "It must be a place where people feel safe and comfortable. People attract other people." Indeed, says Pelli associate Espejo, Pelli's vision was from the outset to "design from the inside out," always intending to extend the appeal of the performing spaces out to the community.

Meantime, negotiations with the Pelli firm had continued, until finally, on Valentine's Day of 1996, news came that the architect had put his signature on a contract with the Performing Arts Center Trust for $15.2 million. The document still awaited the approval of commissioners, but Steve Wolff, a member of the consulting firm retained by the county, called it a "a very competitive contract." It was expected that the design phase would take three years and construction another three years, with groundbreaking now projected for 1999. Officials noted that there was reason to hope that these were realistic dates, for the Cincinnati performing arts center that Pelli had designed (for $7.6 million) had been completed in October 1995, one month early and $135,000 under budget. In any case, the Performing Arts Center Foundation was now set to deliver $3.3 million in private donations to the county, which in turn hoped to have a construction manager for the project on board by July.

On March 21, 1996, commissioners in fact approved the contract with Pelli and also formalized an agreement with the city of Miami Beach for the use of convention tax monies so that $80 million in bonds might be issued in the coming summer to help pay for the performing arts center. At that same meeting the agreement with Knight-Ridder regarding the company's donation of 2.2 acres for the building site was formalized. In all, the project was now projected to cost $198 million, but the steps taken by the commission on that day, including the approval of a $10 million project liability insurance policy (at a premium of $811,318), constituted what Trust Chair Thomson termed, "The end of the beginning." Also at that meeting, Sherwood Weiser presented the $3.3 million check from the Trust Foundation to the Dade County Commission, "a remarkable sight," in the eyes of Cultural Affairs Council Director Michael Spring. In the audience were a number of trust members, Miami and Miami Beach officials, local architects Raul Rodriguez and Tony Quiroga, who had joined the Pelli team, attorney Robert Traurig for the Florida Grand Opera, and auto dealer Ron Esserman, chairman of the Miami City Ballet.

On April 2, 1996, the county authorized the placement of advertisements soliciting applications for the construction management of the project, and at a mid-May meeting of the Performing Arts Center Trust, the group appointed an eight-member committee to be headed by Stuart Blumberg to begin the search for an executive director. The trust proposed that a call for applications for the latter post be placed on June 1, with a deadline of August 2. The committee was to make its recommendation for a director to the county manager by September 1, with a start date targeted for October 1. "It's ambitious, I know," said Bill Johnson, the county's appointed manager for the project.

A bit too ambitious, as it turned out. On August 1, the day before the deadline and with forty-seven applications in hand, Johnson announced that, following consultations between County Manager Armando Vidal and Trust Chair Thomson, the search for an executive director would be put on hold. "There was a desire by all parties involved to spend money on construction instead," Johnson told the *Herald*'s Gail Meadows. "We'll resume [the search] in time to hire someone by late 1998," added committee chair Blumberg. In the meantime, for the next eighteen months or so, responsibility for keeping a handle on the vast project would remain in the hands of Cultural Affairs Council Director Michael Spring and two of his trusted staffers.

"For four years, I've screamed for an executive director," said Parker Thomson, but, as he explained, tough budgetary choices had resulted in the trimming of $4 million from the design and construction allocation. Where there was the choice between what he termed "soft" and "hard" costs, the choices were inevitable, he said.

The announcement raised concern among some who hoped to emulate West Palm Beach's example of hiring an executive director eight years ahead of that performing arts center's opening. The Broward Center had hired a director only two years before its opening and had been crippled by delays and cost overruns as a result.

"It was understandable why many people—particularly the performing arts groups—wanted an executive director who would serve as a cultural point person for the enterprise," says Stuart Blumberg today. "But to be honest, finding a capable executive director whose primary job for the foreseeable several years would be construction management would have been a difficult task. It would have been like looking for a bus driver before the bus had been built, and the likelihood that an effective construction manager would also be a programming and operations genius seemed slim."

Still, the news was not all downbeat, Bill Johnson insisted. After a series of meetings with theater consultants and acoustics experts, architect Pelli announced that he could accelerate his team's schedule and come up with detailed schematics by the end of 1996. It would allow for the center's opening in 2001 instead of 2002, according to Johnson.

All this took place against the backdrop of the race for the county's first "strong" mayor, wherein the position would be upgraded from a largely ceremonial status (as was the case during Stephen Clark's twenty-year tenure, 1974–1993) to a place where the newly elected chief had the power to veto the actions of commissioners. Those vying for the new spot found the matter of the performing arts center irresistible as campaign fodder. One candidate, former Miami Mayor Xavier Suarez, took the opportunity to criticize the choice of Pelli as architect for the performing arts center, asserting that local designers Bernardo Fort-Brescia and Laurinda Spear would have been better suited for the work. His principal opponent, Alex Penelas, countered that Suarez had been among the city commissioners who refused to hand over Bayfront property for the performing arts center site and lamented that the center would be virtually hidden behind the *Herald* building.

Meanwhile, with an interim deadline of October 8, 1996, for preliminary design presentations looming, tension heightened between Pelli's Connecticut-based design team and future arts users groups and others in Miami. At issue was the need to come up with a workable design to keep the project on pace while trying to balance requests for various features and equipment to be included that were not economically feasible. One of the so-called bid alternatives boosted by many was the inclusion of a $2 million concert-quality pipe organ that was presently unfunded. While the inclusion of such an accoutrement was iffy at best, Pelli agreed to save concert hall space for it in his renderings.

Another item high on the local wish list was the use of stone as an exterior finish in place of the far more economical stucco that Pelli had proposed, a substitution that would add about $8 million to the final tab. Fred Clarke, in charge of Pelli's team, pointed out that folding in numerous impractical items would only result in an unrealistic, unworkable design that would require eventual revision and create delays. But Stanley Arkin, the former Miami Beach commissioner and builder/developer now chairing the trust's construction oversight committee, faulted the architect for a failure to communicate with the trust as decisions were being debated. "In a one-hour meeting, we can't absorb all these details" tossed out by the design team, Arkin said.

As these matters were being sorted out, the county's Art in Public Places agencies had opened applications from artists across the United States, and a panel of experts was created to sift through the more than three hundred applications for the mandated $2.1 million in commissions to create art works for the center. Among them was one from Michele Oka Doner, who designed the striking bronze-inlay-embellished walkway at Miami International Airport's Concourse A. Ten finalists for the commissions were to be selected and brought to Miami for interviews that would include participation by Pelli's design team.

On October 9, 1996, the *Herald*'s Peter Whoriskey reported news that disconcerted preservationists: the cost of restoring the Sears Tower and folding it into Pelli's design was now pegged at $2.5 million, and there did not appear to be enough in the budget to include the structure in the final plans. Michael Spring insisted that while the intent had always been to save the structure, the matter had never been guaranteed. Still, Spring said, the matter was not yet decided. Determining precise figures on costs and completing engineering studies were the first steps. "We're actively pursuing its preservation," Spring said of the tower.

The news infuriated some in the historic preservation community. "I can't believe that they would consider doing anything else now," Becky Roper Matkov, executive director of the Dade Heritage Trust, told Whoriskey. "The citizens have been assured that the Sears Tower would be preserved as part of the overall plan." Supporters reiterated the status of the tower as the county's first and most distinctive example of Art Deco, generally conceded to be largely an American form, with relatively little tying it to traditional European architectural styles.

Complicating the matter, however, was the fact that the tower, the most notable aspect of the Sears Building design, was structurally supported by the far more pedestrian structure surrounding it, and that building, full of asbestos and beset with any number of flaws and failings, was necessarily going to be demolished. "We would love to have the Sears Tower," said Fred Clarke, spokesman for the Pelli team, but as he also pointed out, "there are a number of priorities, and not all of them are funded." On the wish list along with the tower, for instance, was the proposed pedestrian bridge over busy Biscayne Boulevard, and the question remained of just how elaborately designed and landscaped the pedestrian plaza spanning the two major buildings and the boulevard would be.

Finally, on November 12, the trust met and approved a priorities list of features compiled by attorney and trust member Al Cardenas, which narrowed some $60 million worth of add-ons to a short list of five essentials totaling more than $22 million additional: $5.3 million for purchase and installation of various necessary theater fixtures previously cut during the budget-cutting undertaken earlier in the year, when the decision was made to also defer the hiring of an executive director for the project; $5.3 million for parking facilities; $4 million to preserve the oft-threatened and maligned Sears Tower (Pelli had meantime reincorporated provision for the structure in his design); $4 million for the acquisition of land abutting the entrances and egresses on the adjacent MacArthur Causeway and I-395; and $3.5 million for what Parker Thomson and others had come to refer to privately as "Blumberg's Bridge," the elevated walkway to connect the two major theaters across Biscayne Boulevard.

Though the added features would raise the total budget for the project from $198 million to more than $220 million, Cardenas said that the trust would cover the additional costs from private donors and from government grants. The major components listed at the time, in addition to those added items were: $122.6 million for construction; the establishment of a $21 million operating endowment; the $15.2 million fee for Pelli; $6 million in emergency reserves; and $2 million for consultants' fees.

As to the matter of overseeing that $122 million or so of bricks-and-mortar construction activity, the process announced by the county's construction oversight manager Bill Johnson back in April to select a management firm was still under way. Eight firms competing for that $4 million contract made presentations to a joint trust and county management panel on October 30. At the end of the day, the panel ranked Parsons Brinckerhoff Construction Services of Tampa as the top choice, and County Manager Armando Vidal began negotiations with the firm. However, a glitch quickly arose when it was discovered that Parsons had neglected to include in its application letters of intent to hire the requisite numbers of African American, Hispanic, and female employees as part of its team. The second-ranked firm, CRSS Constructors of Coral Gables, wrote to Vidal arguing that, given their own compliance with the rules, they should be appointed in place of Parsons.

As the matter was being debated, the Art in Public Places committee met to consider the applications of three hundred artists vying for commissions to create art for the new performing arts center. Members viewed five slides for three seconds each from each applicant, then voted on whether or not an artist should survive for another round of consideration. At the end of those forty-five hundred seconds—or seventy minutes—of viewing (not accounting for breaks, brief discussions, and tallies that stretched the process over two days), thirteen artists were selected to be brought to Miami for further interviews. Artistic merit and achievement were high among the criteria for selection, of course, but other factors were given equal weight.

Among those not making the cut, for instance was Fernando Botero, the latter-day Rubens from Colombia, whose exuberant sculptures of rotund women had made him world-famous. Perhaps too famous, however, for panel member Barbara Young complained that Botero was becoming so familiar that his work would not contribute to a unique experience within Miami's performing arts center. For another thing, noted judge Daniel Perez, a Miami architect, "He's a great artist, but he's not a collaborator." Perez's comment spoke to the sense that placing art in public places requires a willingness to work with architects and designers as well as consider the public tastes in a given area. What might barely raise an eyebrow in San Francisco might seem scandalous in Des Moines, said Perez, who apparently thought the outrage bar in Miami pretty low.

The selection process continued into January of 1997, with individual artists interviewing with a panel that included trust members as well as Fred Clarke from the Pelli team, discussing how their various artistic visions might translate into decorative and evocative parts of the performing arts center experience. Artists began with a slide presentation of their recent works and were given the opportunity to explain—and in some cases defend—how the placement of their work might affect theater-goers. Following the presentation by Miami's Jose Bedia of a series of somewhat angry images relating to the conquest of Native Americans by Europeans, trust member Juan Loumiet ventured, "Your work is not only very strong, but it's . . . ah . . . not happy. This is a happy place we are designing here." The remark caused another panel member to remind Loumiet that much opera could scarcely be called "happy," while Bedia did his best to reassure the judges: "Humor is very important to me. . . . I think we can have a dialogue."

In another encounter described by the *Herald*'s Whoriskey, more than one of the panel of judges watched and listened to New Yorker Robert Appleton's call for a series of art-on-video-screen installations in the center, then suggested to the artist that if he weren't chosen to install art in the center, he might be willing to make up a few video directional signs to guide patrons around the place. Appleton seemed stunned by the suggestion, but when panelists were persistent, he finally sighed, "Yeah, yeah . . . if you'd like some signs that get you lost immediately, well, I'm your man."

As Whoriskey noted—and as the "Flying Bacon" episode in Miami's Art in Public Places past also attests—the two-day process was emblematic of the basic contradiction between the aims of government (the greatest good for the greatest number) and the mission of the individual artist to express a vision and inner conviction. As African American artist Gary Moore said, when asked if he could create works that would speak to all people, "Of course." However, he reminded the judges, "I am an artist of color. That's what I do. That's my vision. That's how I see the world."

As the judges pondered their final decisions on the art to be placed in the center, architect Pelli was back in Miami on January 13, 1997, with an update to the original design for the façades of the center's two major buildings. While he had not settled on the exact proportions of glass, stucco, and stone to be employed (pending final budget determinations), Pelli's new design was described by *Herald* architecture critic Whoriskey as containing façades of "soaring walls of glass that jut like ship prows." The result, Whoriskey said, was to lend the complex "sleeker, more modern lines and convert the lobbies into towering atrium spaces."

Pelli had also fleshed out his plan for the plaza that he intended to somehow pull the two buildings together despite their being bisected by the busy four-lane swath of Biscayne Boulevard. Pelli proposed the use of a great deal of landscaping and planters, a distinctive paving pattern stretching from door to door across the actual roadway and gutters of the boulevard, and finally a curved pedestrian bridge that would outline the plaza and span the street itself. Mitch Hirsch, one of the Pelli architectural team members, described the intended effect: "In a way, when you're driving down Biscayne Boulevard, you will be driving through the building." The fate of the Sears Tower, however, remained undetermined at the time of Pelli's update.

As all this was being digested, County Manager Armando Vidal put an end to the ongoing question of who would supervise the construction of the center by jettisoning both the first- and second-rated firms identified by the screening committee, choosing instead the third-ranked company, Church and Tower of Miami. Though the choice immediately raised howls of favoritism because of the firm's being controlled by well-known Cuban exile and activist Jorge Mas Canosa, Vidal pointed out that by law he was entitled to choose any of the top-three-rated firms on the committee's list. He had dropped the Parsons firm on the basis of the city attorney's refusal to certify the Tampa company's compliance with bid requirements. Vidal said that he passed over the number-two firm, CRSS, because of that company's spotty performance in supervising previous construction projects for the Dade County School Board. As reported by the *Miami Herald*, the school board had canceled a contract with CRSS in 1990 after administrators complained that CRSS was deficient in cost control and monitoring. In the end, the choice was a matter of little import to Trust Chair Thomson. "All I cared about [was] that all three were competent. Once that was decided, I shrugged."

Shortly thereafter, on March 10, 1997, the competition for the placement of art within the center came to a close when the selection panel announced its choice of seven of the thirteen who had been interviewed by the group in January. Five of the seven were from Miami, with four men and three women, four Hispanic, two non-Hispanic whites, and one African American, Gary Moore, who had steadfastly defended his vision as an artist of color during the interviews. Another notable selection was that of Cundo Bermudez, eighty-two, a Cuban exile who had risen to prominence in his home country and had seen his work hung at New York's Museum of Modern Art long before coming to Miami. Also selected was Jose Bedia, the artist whose work had seemed too "unhappy" for at least one member of the judging panel.

As for the center itself, there was something of a worrisome development in April of 1997, when county commissioners approved a deal brokered by newly elected "strong" Mayor Alex Penelas to in essence reimburse the Miami Heat for the construction of a new arena on Biscayne Bay by diverting $6.5 million yearly from the convention development tax revenues to the team. That money would be earmarked only after the apportionment of funds already approved for the performing arts center, but some worried that it would exhaust the bed tax revenues and mean the end of hopes for funding crucial add-ons to the center, including the salvaging of the Sears Tower and the construction of the pedestrian bridge. "If you are going to have a first-class facility, then you should have everything needed to make that a reality," said trust member Stuart Blumberg. Added trust vice president James Herron, "It seems like every time we are doing great, something comes not from left field, but from another planet."

At the meeting of the county commission on April 8, where the measure pertaining to the Heat was considered, Trust Chair Thomson assured commissioners that the issue was real: "This effective cap is a serious problem because it locks us in." But the vote to approve the deal with the Heat was approved, 9–2. In the end, a compromise was effected when commissioners agreed the following week that the performing arts center would be first in line for any surplus after the original performing arts center funds and the Heat monies were paid from revenues. It was not an ideal situation, said James Herron, but "It's the best we're going to do." The issue prompted considerable debate about the proper role of taxpayers' support for culture versus the subsidization of professional sports franchises, but in the end, of course, both entities walked away with considerable tax monies in hand.

"The episode really underscores Parker Thomson's political expertise," recalls Bill Johnson. "Instead of trying to stonewall the inevitable, Parker worked out a compromise, and ultimately the center project won."

14

. . . .

Something of a more pluralistic phase in fund-raising appeared in July of 1997, when the trust foundation put out the call to the general public, as it were, advising that a donation of $100,000 would guarantee a patron a plum seat in one of the major halls in perpetuity, along with a bronze plaque affixed to the back of the seat. Box seats were likewise available, for a donation of $250,000. And membership in the founders' society, with access to the patrons' lounge, could be had for $500,000. These were not inconsequential offers, of course, and reflected the trust's hopes that the undertaking would rouse significant response among affluent residents.

However, just as this drive gathered momentum, Judy Weiser, long-time South Florida arts patron and wife of Sherwood "Woody" Weiser, chair of the trust's foundation wing, rose before a September 16 meeting of the trust to lament that—shortly before its scheduled unveiling on October 12—Cesar Pelli's design for the center was lacking in both character and heart. "It's not modern, contemporary, or Mediterranean," she said. "I don't feel this is the building we had hoped it would be." Pelli's project manager, Phil Bernstein, responded that the basic design of the building had been out in the open for several years now, and that the stucco façade, an element that Ms. Weiser found particularly distasteful, was dictated by budget. Stanley Arkin, the trust's construction committee chairperson, expressed hopes that additional monies would be found to upgrade the exterior finish, but Ms. Weiser was dubious that stone was going to make that much difference in the end.

Pelli associate Roberto Espejo well remembers sitting in on the pivotal discussion. "Ms. Weiser asked Cesar point blank, 'Is this really what you'd call world-class architecture, Mr. Pelli?' and Cesar looked back at her and said, 'Maybe not the exterior, but certainly the inside and the acoustical design is.'"

At that point, Ms. Weiser asked, "Well, what would it take to make it world-class?" Pelli responded mildly, says Espejo. "Restore the original dimensions of the forms [some of the angularities had been minimized as cost-cutting measures]. Create the façades with glass and bring back the lanterns [meaning the glass side walls]. Use stone for the exterior finish instead of stucco."

"But the Sydney Opera House uses stucco," one trust member responded.

"No," Pelli said, patiently. "That is a very specialized stone composite. Not inexpensive. But it looks good, and it will last forever." Then he added, "There really is no such thing as a world-class stucco building."

According to Espejo, it was a watershed moment in the process. "There was never really any question after that meeting," he says. "I knew that the building would eventually have a stone and glass façade."

In an October 12 *Herald* article, architecture critic Peter Whoriskey attempted to clarify what the substance was behind Weiser's remarks. The design of the performing arts center had come to represent something far beyond the utilitarian nature of the buildings themselves. For Miamians who had long sought the establishment of a performing arts center in the city, the enterprise was as much an overarching statement of the value of culture to a place as it was the construction of two theaters where musical and theatrical productions might be effectively mounted.

For such individuals, the old saw "good enough for government work" was anathema. However, for politicians with one eye always on an upcoming election, the trick was to balance the pressures coming from a relatively small, if influential, group of culturally committed individuals against the criticisms of opponents with quite different interests—everything from the welfare of the homeless to the coddling of professional sports franchises. Then of course there was the vast majority of an electorate generally sympathetic to the notion of culture but also easily swayed by those warning of higher taxes to come, not to mention "the wasteful expenditure of public funds on monuments to the interests of the privileged classes."

Whoriskey pointed to a number of "missed chances" that Miami had experienced when attempting to create an overarching architectural statement that would somehow express the nature and ambition of a singular place, pointing to Philip Johnson's foreboding, fortress-like library and museum complex, the run-of-the-mill nature of Bayside Marketplace, and the white elephant of Miami Arena, where cost-cutting measures imposed on the building during the construction phase rendered it virtually obsolete before a spectator ever ventured inside.

That spectacular failure, which had led to the call for a new arena for the Miami Heat, was something that galvanized performing arts center supporters when the subject of capping bed tax revenues for the center was recently proposed. "What's at stake is trying to produce a building that is truly, truly distinctive," Parker Thomson told Whoriskey. "The decisions that will be made now will be with us for years to come." And, he might well have added, "Anything that is worth doing is worth doing right."

Without doubt, much about the center was being done "right." From the outset, the trust had insisted that acoustics and other aspects of interior function were primary over all else, for after all, the shows would be mounted on the inside of the buildings. However, given that far more people would pass by the performing arts center on a daily basis than would ever venture inside its doors, the nature of the façades would indeed constitute a "function" for thousands of residents and visitors each day. Anyone who has gawked at the Eiffel Tower, the Guggenheim Museum, or the Sydney Opera House can attest that one not need ascend, enter, or judge interior acoustics in order to be amazed. (In fact, while the latter is one of the iconic visual images of world architecture, the interior acoustics and sightlines of that building are generally agreed to be substandard.) At any rate, the likelihood of the exterior of Pelli's complex "amazing" anyone seemed much in doubt at the time Whoriskey was writing. As Judy Weiser told Whoriskey, "As it stands now, I don't think anyone would consider it a wonderful building. But we're still hoping."

Because of that hope and also forecasts that predicted an unexpectedly bountiful rise in hotel tax revenues, the trust and county commissioners pushed back the final unveiling of Pelli's design until November of 1997, in hopes that a number of the more spectacular elements of the original proposal might be restored. The extra time would also give Pelli the opportunity to nail down the costs of the upgrades, including the replacement of a stucco exterior with stone, the cost of which was ball-parked at $14 million. "I don't think anyone wants to see a building open up that they're not proud of," Stuart Blumberg, chair of the trust's management committee, said, "but we need to know how much the package is going to cost."

For their part, the Pelli design team was insistent that despite all concerns, their customers would be more than satisfied. "It will definitely be a landmark building—there is no question about that," said Pelli spokesperson Fred Clarke.

At its November 11 meeting, the trust voted to formally request the restoration of items that would add as much as $54.5 million to the $198 million project, including the use of hand-set stone and granite for the façade, the restoration of nearly 20 percent of the buildings' height, the increase in the size of windows and glass entrances, the reinstatement of ground-level awnings, and a plaza fountain, among other things. The decision was made after an announcement from the county's finance director (after prodding from hotel tax expert Blumberg) that indeed some $71.6 million more in convention development tax revenues would be available during the necessary term than was previously thought.

As for prospects for the commission's approval, Parker Thomson was optimistic. "So far they have been very responsive to our needs," he said, "but we've got to sell it." (Convention development tax revenues totaled just over $22 million in 1997 and were projected by the Peat Marwick study to rise to about $47.5 million in 2014. Actual revenues for 2014, according to Blumberg, were $70 million, with projections for future years pegged to rise by more than 10 percent per annum.)

Part of Thomson's sales pitch would include the announcement that as of Monday, November 17, the foundation trust—with $2.7 million in new pledges—had passed the halfway point in securing its target goal. The news did not come without a bit of controversy, however, for the giver of the largest single donation of $1 million delivered some pithy remarks along with his contribution. Annenberg publishing heir Gilbert Kahn lamented the fact that the building site was not on Biscayne Bay. "When you see a picture of the Sydney Opera House, you never have to ask what it is," he said. And he also had some words of advice concerning the cost of saving the Sears Tower. "It's the ugliest building in Miami, and I've been here 36 years," he told the *Herald*'s Gail Meadows. "Incorporating it into the design is even more ridiculous."

Despite Kahn's remarks, county commissioners seemed pleased at the news that the private sector was indeed ponying up in accordance with what had been promised. At their November 18, 1997, meeting, they heard architect Pelli defend the proposed $54 million increase in the budget in blunt terms: "You can have a good, workable center, or, if you pass this amendment, you can have a noble, durable, magnificent center, a center that will put Miami on the map," Pelli said.

One commissioner, Natacha Millan, was not swayed, given her concern that other social needs in the county were going unmet. "As long as I have to look at the dark side of this community, I cannot vote on $54 million for a signature building, because we need signature people here."

Her words prompted a response from colleague Miguel Diaz de la Porta, reminding those present that Millan had recently voted to approve spending $240 million on a new arena for the Miami Heat. Millan grumbled back that the Heat had already proven it had an audience, while doubt remained about the need for a cultural arts center. "I'm not interested in building a monument to the wealthy in this community," she said.

Millan's sentiments were not shared by most commissioners, however. "I would hate for the people to call this building *el cheapo*," Javier Souto said in response to Pelli's urgings. "This could very well be the resurgence of all this area downtown." Added Commissioner Jimmy Morales, "I view this as not only creating a building that will hopefully outlive us, but also as a promotion of arts and culture."

Certainly one of the most compelling items considered was the report from accountants KPMG Peat Marwick that, based on projected increases in bed tax revenues, it seemed there would in fact be money in the coffers available to pay for the restoration of various features. With little debate, the measure to increase the construction budget by $54 million was approved by a vote of 11–1. The magnitude of the vote was not lost on Trust Chair Parker Thomson, who told reporters, "This gives us a chance to produce really top-flight buildings."

The decision by commissioners allowed the trust to close out its 1997 activities on a high note, but just as quickly new trouble surfaced, when a minority firm subcontracted by Church and Tower, newly appointed construction management supervisors for the project, complained to the county that a signature of one of the firm's partners on bid documents had been forged. Alberto Ribas, a partner in the firm of Brizuela and Ribas, said that another firm member, John Duret, had (without Ribas's knowledge or approval) signed a document agreeing to reduce the share of Brizuela and Ribas in the work from 10 percent to 5 percent, shifting that lost 5 percent to another company, CAP Engineering. Given that the original winner of the bid application process, Parsons Brinckerhoff, had been disqualified for irregularities pertaining to minority participation in the contract, it seemed highly possible that the contract with Church and Tower would likewise be canceled.

The news was distressing for the trust, for as Parker Thomson told the *Herald*, "We are now in construction drawings, and we need to know at all times that we are on budget," he said. "The construction manager is crucial to ensuring that the project is on time and on budget." Whatever the outcome with Church and Tower might be, without continuing professional oversight, keeping the project under control would be nearly impossible.

Though there was heartening news in February of 1998, when the Knight Foundation made a $2.4 million pledge to the project, bringing total private gift-giving to $29.2 million, the situation with Church and Tower remained in flux. On March 5, 1998, Mayor Alex Penelas called for the resignation of County Manager Armando Vidal, saying that Vidal had proven himself incapable of running "a competent, ethical government," and that Vidal had reduced the county's image to that of a "hall of shame." Beyond the issue that concerned performing arts center oversight, another of the allegations against Vidal was that he was negligent in allowing overpayments regarding a county paving contract let to Church and Tower.

The question on Church and Tower's appointment to oversight of the center's construction lingered on into April, even as architect Pelli returned to Miami on the fourteenth of that month to unveil the details of wood-burnished, acoustically high-tech designs for the interiors of the opera/ballet and symphony halls. "You'll feel like you're inside a violin," said Florida Grand Opera's Robert Heuer of what was proposed for the maple-redolent concert hall, adding that he also approved of the "cozy and elegant" look of the opera house. For his part, Pelli promised, "This is a place that will transport you to another world."

Following the architect's presentation to the trust, Foundation Chair Sherwood Weiser asked the main body to once again consider the need to hire an executive director for the center. The project was scheduled to break ground in 1999, he reminded them, and was only four years away from its projected opening. "There are groups that want to book this venue already," Weiser said. Though recently deposed County Manager Armando Vidal had asked that a $6 million reserve fund be in place before the position was authorized, Weiser pointed out that those monies were now in place, and there was no reason not to move forward. At that same meeting, trust members were assured that a decision on the continued involvement of Church and Tower in the project would be made by April 24.

That date came and went without a decision, but soon after, on April 28, the entire South Florida community was rocked by an announcement from P. Anthony Ridder that the Knight-Ridder Corporation, owner of the *Herald*, would be moving its headquarters from Miami to Northern California's Silicon Valley, where modern news-gathering technology was centered and where the company held interests in a number of other newspapers. The loss of one of the region's few Fortune 500 companies was indeed a blow, but Ridder made assurances that the company had no intention of selling the *Herald*. While many were stunned at the prospect of losing the leadership and philanthropic support that the company had long provided, Ridder insisted that the company's commitment to civic involvement in Miami, including support of the performing arts center, remained firm. The headquarters of the John S. and James L. Knight Foundation, an independent philanthropic entity, Ridder also announced, would remain in Miami.

Arts leaders did their best to keep a stiff upper lip in the wake of the news. "It's akin to losing a diamond tie clip from your tie," said Alejandro Aguirre, the chairman of the advisory group to the county's Cultural Affairs Council. "You've lost the diamond, but you still have your tie." Still, the loss promised a difficult road ahead for fund-raisers trying to replace an almost-certain diminishing flow of contributions from a giant the size of Knight-Ridder.

While the community struggled to absorb news of the impending loss, the thread suspending the Damoclean sword above Church and

Tower's fortunes was finally severed on June 1, 1998, when Bill Johnson, the county's construction oversight official, wrote a memo affirming that the signature of a subcontractor involved in the bidding process had been forged and that, at the very least, the company "should have confirmed the accuracy of all information in its proposal." Though Johnson claimed that dropping Church and Tower would not delay the project, set to break ground in 1999, Trust Chair Parker Thomson was hardly enthused by the news. As he told a *Herald* reporter, "I am not worried about delay. I am worried about getting the job done."

As the massive task of actually constructing the center loomed, considerable attention was also devoted to the question of just how the center would operate following its opening, now targeted for 2002. Though no full-time director had been authorized, Steve Wolff, a budget consultant retained by the trust, was busy creating projections for use of the center, trying to balance the needs of the five major Miami arts user groups (Florida Grand Opera, Florida Philharmonic, New World Symphony, Concert Association of Florida, and Miami City Ballet) against date allocations for the mounting of major Broadway touring shows, any of which were likely to bring in far more cash to the coffers. Wolff estimated that expenses for the center's first year would total approximately $8.7 million, while revenues were pegged at $6.6 million. While Wolff maintained that his estimate of about 75 percent of the center's costs being covered by revenues was accurate, a *Herald* news story of June 14 claimed the national average was only 55 percent.

Even using Wolff's figures, the trust was still facing a significant budget deficit of nearly $2 million, a shortfall that would have to be made up by corporate sponsorships of events, proceeds from the foundation endowment, and other fund-raising activities. Complicating the matter was the need to bring a staff on board in the planned four-year interim between commencement of construction and the opening, and those personnel costs were estimated by Wolff at around $3.3 million.

In September of 1998, nine months shy of the projected groundbreaking set for May 1, 1999, a three-dimensional model of Cesar Pelli's amended design was unveiled by the trust at a meeting intended to kick off the trust foundation's final fund-raising phase. To that date, more than $31 million in pledges had come in, leaving $10–12 million to be raised in advance of groundbreaking. The hope was that the model would aid donors in visualizing just how their dollars would be used. "Last year we raised $8.5 million," said Foundation Chairman Sherwood Weiser, who expressed confidence that the final donations would arrive on time for commencement of construction. At the same time, County Commission Chairwoman Margolis told the *Herald*'s Gail Meadows that the county had been successful in selling $201 million of the $223 million in bonds authorized to finance the project and said further that commissioners expected that once the center opened, the county's economy would realize a "ripple effect" of $10 million a year or more.

In October columnist Meadows reported that private fund-raising had reached $32 million, with eleven of the fifteen boxes in the concert hall snapped up at $250,000 apiece, and eleven of the seventeen boxes in the opera hall taken. Though Ryder System's $2.5 million gift had secured naming rights to the concert hall lobby, and a similar gift from the Arthur E. and Alice E. Adams Foundation secured the designation for the opera theater lobby, a number of other opportunities, including the naming of the center itself, remained available. During its October meeting, trust member Stanley Arkin shared plans for the creation of a seventy-five-seat café in the ground floor of the Sears Tower. "And we are not talking about Starbucks," Arkin added.

With the turn of the New Year to 1999, plans were still on for that May 1 groundbreaking. A huge banner was draped across the façade of the dilapidated Sears Building, announcing the site as that of a performing arts center that would open in 2002. That January was also the occasion for disheartening news, however, when word began to circulate that the Concert Association of Florida, headed for some thirty years by legendary impresario Judy Drucker, was in serious financial trouble. Paid subscriptions for the concert association's offerings at the 2,400-seat Dade County Auditorium had fallen to about 1,000, and it was becoming harder to raise money to offset operating losses, Drucker said, because donors were funneling contributions to the performing arts center project. The concert association had lost $450,000 in the final quarter of 1998, reported the *Herald*'s Meadows, and long-term debt had reached nearly $900,000. Furthermore, Drucker had precious little capital to fall back on, given that the total endowment of the association stood at $600,000.

The members of the Performing Arts Center Trust were well aware of the issues confronting the concert association, said Cultural Affairs Council Director Michael Spring. In fact, county commissioners had authorized the disbursement of as much as $900,000 in operating funds grants to struggling companies during the coming year, Spring said, suggesting that Drucker's organization might be in line for substantial help.

Meanwhile, the trust finally opened interviews with candidates for the long-delayed position of executive director. A search committee headed by the trust's Juan Loumiet and County Manager Merrett Stierheim interviewed eight candidates in late January of 1999 and identified a set of four finalists for the $125–150,000 post. That group was asked to return for second interviews before the selection would be made. Former County Manager Ray Goode, a member of the interview committee, pointed out the difficulty of identifying a quality candidate when he described the size of the available talent pool to the *Herald*. "There are only 20, 40, or 50 significant arts centers in the nation," Goode said. "It's a relatively small universe."

At about the same time, news came to the trust that the local engineering firm picked by architect Pelli to provide the construction drawings for the opera house might not in fact be able to meet the March 1 deadline. David Wolfberg, one of the principals in the South Miami firm of Wolfberg Alvarez, had no comment for reporters, but Bill Johnson, the county official who had been overseeing construction matters, had plenty to say. "I don't want to sound nasty or arrogant, but they've had three years," Johnson said. "If the deadline is missed, it will impact the overall completion schedule [fall of 2002]."

Still, planning for a May 2, 1999, groundbreaking continued, with a gala celebration planned under tents to be set up near the site on the previous day, including appearances by Broadway stars, acclaimed concert musicians, and a special performance of the New World Symphony, with the Florida Philharmonic's James Judd joining his New World Symphony counterpart Michael Tilson Thomas in conducting. And on April 15, 1999, the project took another major step forward when the trust finally announced the hiring of an executive director. Selected from the group of eight first interviewed in January, Tom Tomlinson had been managing director of the Michigan Opera Theatre and Detroit Opera

House since 1997. At his new post, it was said, Tomlinson would be paid $175,000, along with various benefits, making his the third-highest salary behind County Manager Stierheim ($260,000) and County Attorney Robert Ginsburg ($195,000). Tomlinson told the *Herald*'s Gail Meadows that his goals went further than preparing for an opening night in 2002. His concern was far more with the center's making the Miami of twenty years hence a different place, "about a center becoming an integral part of the community." Tomlinson was to attend the groundbreaking festivities and begin his duties as chief on May 15, 1999. With a full-time director at last in place, a new era seemed poised to begin.

15

. . . .

By late April of 1999, a week or so before that planned groundbreaking, Foundation Executive Director Nancy Herstand gave columnist Meadows the heartening news that fund-raising from the private sector had reached $35 million, and that she expected another $3–5 million would be in the coffers by the end of June. If that happened, the group would have completed the bulk of its goal nearly three years ahead of deadline (the center's opening), thereby offering proof that influential Miami residents saw the importance of the performing arts center.

Still very much up for grabs, Herstand continued, were naming rights to each of the two main halls, at $10 million each, and for the entire complex, which carried a $20 million tag. Almost immediately Sunglass Hut founder Sanford Ziff offered the trust $12 million in exchange for naming rights to the opera hall, but the gift that he proposed was in the form of a life insurance policy. Once he and his wife, Dolores, died, Ziff explained (he was then seventy-three, his wife seventy-four), the $12 million benefit would go to the foundation trust. Though it was a welcome gesture, Foundation Executive Director Sherwood Weiser said that the foundation's response was essentially, "Thanks, Mr. Ziff, but no thanks."

From the first discussion of its formation, Stuart Blumberg had argued that gifts accepted by the foundation trust would have to be in cash. "If we go to the county and say we have $20 million, but only $1 million is in cash, they'll throw us out," he said, and eventually Weiser agreed. The agreement between the trust and the county was that the entire amount of private funding (now calculated at $43.2 million) had to be cash on hand as of the completion of the project (an $18 million interim payment would be due from the trust to the county on the day of groundbreaking).

While Ziff was proposing to pay the $300–400,000 annual premiums on such a policy, fund-raising professionals pointed out that until the policy was paid in full, there could be no guarantee of a final payout. (Blumberg likes to point out that his hard-nosed policy did not deter donors:

"To the best of my knowledge," he says today, "every pledge made to the project was honored.")

At the same time, columnist Meadows reported news that Ted Arison, Carnival Cruise Lines founder, had confirmed his commitment to a $10 million gift to the foundation in exchange for naming rights to the center's concert hall. That gift would not be forthcoming until construction was completed, however.

By this point, it had also become clear that the groundbreaking celebration scheduled for May 1 would be only symbolic in nature. Though a number of Broadway and symphonic luminaries did in fact appear at the event, staged by top-shelf Miami party planner Barton G. (tickets were $250 to $1,000), the event, drawing about six hundred people, had become what Foundation Trust Executive Director Herstand described as a way "to honor the donors of $100,000 and over." It had become apparent over recent months that the pieces would not be in place to begin construction until the fall, at the earliest. The absence of a full-time executive director was a major hindrance, as had been the inability to find and keep a construction management firm in place.

However, an executive director for the center was now in place, with Tomlinson replacing de facto director Michael Spring, and county commissioners had moved to shore up their oversight of the actual building of the project by hiring Gail Thompson to join the staff of County Manager Stierheim. Thompson had served as vice president in charge of construction of the New Jersey Performing Arts Center in Newark and was successful in bringing that $180 million project to completion on time and essentially within its budget. In Miami, Thompson would be charged with similar responsibilities, taking over the duties in-house that had originally been proposed for the two now-discharged independent construction management firms. A major difference between the posts, however, was that in Newark, Thompson reported directly to the CEO of the center. In Miami, Thompson would be a county employee, answering to the county manager and, in effect, to the county commissioners. Though no one was saying as much, the hiring of Thompson amounted to another cost-saving measure, for instead of a $4 million-plus contract, the county had simply added another middle-management position for less than $200,000 per year.

Hopes were still high for a fall 2002 opening, but, on the other hand, no one believed that the center could be constructed in less than three years, which meant that ground would indeed have to be broken before the end of 1999. The first step in making that happen was to invite bids from construction companies capable of doing the complex work and choose from the applicants before July was out, something of a tall order. As Michael Spring opined to columnist Meadows on the eve of the May gala, "These theaters are enormously complex. There's nothing that comes close except hospitals and nuclear power plants."

Still, a call for bids was announced on June 25 for a project described by Spring thusly: "It's going to be so complex, your head will spin." In fact, there were only three firms in the running, all of which had submitted extensive prequalification documentation packages to the county several months previously: Clark Construction, a national firm that in 1995 had taken over George Hyman Construction, builders of the Broward Center for the Performing Arts; Odebrecht, a leading Brazilian company involved in the construction of the new American Airlines Arena in downtown Miami; and Morse Diesel Construction of Chicago, which was partnering with Odebrecht in building the arena.

County Project Director Gail Thompson announced that those three firms would have six weeks to study construction drawings (still in flux themselves) and submit final bids on a project estimated at $168 million. It was her intention to make a recommendation to commissioners by September 21, 1999, with groundbreaking to take place before the end of the same year. As to that figure of $168 million, the trust's construction committee chairperson, Stanley Arkin, whose family were longtime Miami builders, told the *Herald* that project consultants had assured the trust that what was being asked for in the plans was equal to what the budget should be.

Furthermore, he said, meticulous review had shaved about $20 million worth of features from the project. "We've pared it down to what's needed," Arkin said, "both from an aesthetic standpoint and a resident-company standpoint." If the bids came in a bit over the mark, Arkin suggested there might be room for negotiation, but a significant difference would require line-by-line negotiation. Arkin was a bit skeptical that all of it could be wrapped up within six weeks, but Thompson remained optimistic. "The opportunity to build this project ought to be attractive enough to keep those pencils sharp," she said.

For his part, Trust Chair Parker Thomson echoed his longtime patient overview. "I think we've done everything we can," he told columnist Meadows. "I expect the construction firms will come in reasonably close to our estimate." As for what would happen in the coming weeks, Thomson explained that any of the firms could ask for more detail on any of the drawings, and if such requests were made, the responses would be shared with all bidders. One observation of his was telling, however: Pelli's unique design was a challenging one for all construction trades— "there are no right angles anywhere," Thomson pointed out.

While the companies pored over documents, Sherwood Weiser carried on with fund-raising efforts for the trust foundation, announcing a number of gifts just short of the June 30 deadline referred to back in May by executive director Herstand. Gifts from Publix Supermarkets and Bank of America (known as Nations Bank in South Florida at the time) pushed the total to more than $37 million of the $43.2 million target.

On September 9, 1999, just one day short of the deadline for submission of bids, Odebrecht threw something of a wrench into the works when spokesperson David Kessler announced that the company was withdrawing from the competition. The project simply promised too many headaches over the next three years, Kessler said, adding that the lack of a construction management firm to serve as a buffer between the customer and the contractor was a major concern for his company. Gail Thompson was quick to respond. While she lamented the withdrawal of Odebrecht from the bidding process, she defended the county's decision to dispense with a middleman to oversee the project's construction. "I've never seen a project run better than when it's run by the owners," she said. "It's a far more efficient way."

Meanwhile, staff at Morse Diesel and Clark Construction labored away in order to meet the September 10 deadline, and while the packages found their way to Thompson's desk on time, the results were not quite what she or the trust had hoped for. Morse Diesel, it turned out, was offering to build the performing arts center for $233.5 million, some $65.5 million more than was projected. Clark Construction was the lower bidder at just under $214 million, $46 million over estimates.

In any such bidding process, error in calculation or confusion about the nature of plans can affect the final estimates, of course, but the fact that both contractors had come in with figures so much higher than anticipated—one at 27 percent above target, the other at nearly 40 percent—was a considerable blow. While she would go over the figures line by line with both bidders, Thompson declared, such a review would be a lengthy one. It was the end of any hopes for a groundbreaking in 1999 and an opening in 2002. The opening of the Miami performing arts center was officially moved back for a year, to fall 2003. Representatives for both companies welcomed the consultations, though Morse Diesel spokesperson Steve Arnold cautioned that perhaps the county and the trust had formed unreasonable expectations, given the nature of the Pelli design. "There is no normalcy to this project," Arnold told the *Herald*. "It's the most complicated thing I've ever been involved in, in more than 30 years in the business."

It was not the only blow to the process, for scarcely had Thompson announced the delay than the two local firms engaged by architect Pelli to create the working construction drawings announced their intention to quit the project. Wolfberg Alvarez, which had already had its issues with Pelli regarding deadlines for drawings for the opera house, and Rodriguez and Quiroga, the Coral Gables firm that had drawn up the plans for the concert hall, issued word that they intended to sever ties with Pelli immediately. There was some speculation that the decisions were connected to the issue of Thompson's oversight, given architect Raul Rodriguez's comment, "What it means is that we decline to be involved in construction administration." Whether it was the lack of a construction management entity to mediate between contractors and the production architects, a persistent lack of communication between Pelli and the local firms, or the chronic difficulties in prying payment out of a cumbersome system, as some maintained, is difficult to ascertain with certainty, but one thing is sure: the contract with the county stipulated Pelli as the architect of record, and the Pelli firm was ultimately responsible for providing working building plans to contractors.

Roberto Espejo vividly recalls the moment when word reached Pelli's offices that the Miami architects were bowing out. "What are we going to do now?" he remembers asking Pelli.

"We're going to accept their resignations," was Pelli's response.

"But it means we'll be responsible for drawings we didn't do," Espejo protested. In fact, the Connecticut-based firm would be responsible for the multitude of code compliance details that are normally called out by firms familiar with local building requirements.

"Yes," Pelli told him. "But still we're going to get this job done."

Gail Thompson maintained that there was no connection with this latest setback to the earlier decision by Odebrecht to pull out because of the lack of a construction management firm. Nor, she told *Herald* columnist Meadows, did the resignations have anything to do with the unexpectedly high bids that had recently come in, and it had nothing to do with builders' disinterest in the project overall. "It's a scary project with a high level of details and finishes and a rigorous schedule," she said. "We're in a market where there are easier things to do." Such factors not only encouraged the design subcontractors to extricate themselves once their contracted work was essentially completed, but it also explained the size of the bids that were submitted. With competition limited to two firms, the result might have been expected, she said: "[It] means you get high bids."

The announcement of the size of the bids and the resulting delay as those figures were pondered was disheartening for supporters, of course, but there was also a bit of countervailing news from the foundation. Ever since sunglasses magnate Sanford Ziff had made his offer of a $12 million gift, there were those within the foundation wing who were determined to find a way to broker some kind of compromise there. Foundation Treasurer Ron Esserman, himself a highly successful businessman and founder of an extensive South Florida string of auto dealerships, sought out Ziff for a meeting shortly after his initial offer was turned down. Though the two had never met, Esserman approached Ziff on familiar terms. "Sandy," he said, "I feel like a kid in a pile of manure. There must be a pony in there somewhere."

When Ziff reiterated his original offer, Esserman, who did not come by his salesman's reputation by accident, commiserated with Ziff, but reminded him that the foundation's hands were tied. The county's demand was that the funds be in cash in the bank at the time of completion of the center. He too would like to see the Ziffs' name gracing the theater, but there was no way around the requirement that cash be placed on the barrelhead. Finally, Ziff relented. He would give the foundation $2.6 million in cash and assigned immediate ownership of a life insurance policy of sufficient value to bring his gift to a total of $10 million. As Esserman pointed out when the gift was announced at a gathering that included Florida Secretary of State Katherine Harris and Miami-Dade Mayor Alex Penelas on September 23, 1999, Ziff's gift was the first to include collateral for the pledge. "All we had from everyone else," Esserman pointed out, "was a promise."

With that gift, which equaled the sum of the pledge of Carnival Cruise Line founder Ted Arison (which was not yet officially announced), the foundation surpassed its goal of $43.2 million and very nearly covered attendant fund-raising costs of $5 million as well. Ziff explained the reasons for his change of heart to the assembled crowd by saying, "I want this to inspire others to give. I want this center to rank up there with Lincoln Center, the Kennedy Center, and the opera house in Sydney." As for Ted Arison, he would not live to see his pledge made good, for shortly more than a week after Ziff made his announcement, the cruise line founder, Miami Heat owner, and chief patron of the New World Symphony died of heart failure at his home in Tel Aviv on October 1 at the age of seventy-five.

While Arison's passing was widely mourned within the South Florida community, County Project Manager Gail Thompson remained hard at work on the question of bringing the costs of the center's construction into line with previous estimates. In an October 5 interview with *Herald* architecture writer Peter Whoriskey, she attributed the difference between the county's figures and the bids to a combination of factors: there was the fact that the county's cost consultants had not seen the final construction plans; an ongoing construction boom was driving up prices across all sectors; and indeed there had been "a few" errors on the plans themselves.

After preliminary meetings with Clark Construction and Morse Diesel, Thompson said that she had already identified ways to save "millions," including such measures as reducing the thickness of the roof slabs atop the halls from twelve inches to ten and negotiating better prices on various features with the builders. "There are many things we can do to save money without impacting the architecture or the acoustics," she said, noting that she had been successful in reducing the construction budget at the New Jersey Performing Arts Center from 20 percent higher than expected to 8 percent higher. Were she to be similarly successful in Miami, it would amount to an $18 million savings from the low bid, or somewhere just below the $200 million mark.

While matters with the contractors simmered, Thompson made an attempt to move forward on one front at least—namely, the demolition of the Sears Building on the west side of Biscayne Boulevard, where the opera house would eventually be located. She had already received interest from half a dozen demolition contractors for a job that she had estimated to cost about $800,000, and in early December of 1999, she announced plans to award a contract within weeks. If all went well, she told reporters, work on that initial phase of the project could begin by late January 2000.

Though project supporters might have expected worse as 2000 was ushered in, the new millennium brought more problems. Foremost among them was the need to salvage the Sears Tower from the decay that sprawled about it, but it was indeed constructed as a part of the ancient complex and had never been designed to stand on its own. Demolishing the surrounding structures would require significant care not to damage the seven-story octagonal tower and also would necessitate the erection of temporary bracing until the new surrounding walls of the opera house were put into place. Only two of the demolition companies who surveyed the prospects were interested in doing such complicated work. And while consultants had budgeted such costs at approximately $2 million, in addition to the demolition itself, the contractors, as one might suppose, saw it differently. One company put the total cost at $6 million, the other at $4.6 million.

That price tag, said Trust Chair Parker Thomson "will only increase the flak about [the Tower's] preservation. It's an issue that has been in dispute for a long time." Still, some trust members hoped that the latest higher-than-expected bid incident would not derail the project. In the larger scheme of things, the low bid was "only" $2.6 million over the projected cost, and as the foundation's Sherwood Weiser put it, "We don't need another issue to debate. There are other items in the budget they are looking at, and, hopefully, we will find significant savings in there. I wouldn't pick on this one item yet."

As for the larger matter of the overall budget, County Project Manager Thompson was successful in convincing the county commissioners to reject the bids of Clark Construction and Morse Diesel and to reopen applications from firms that would agree to bid on and build the center on a "Construction Manager at Risk" basis, meaning that firms would have to guarantee the final price of the work. Four firms had indicated an interest in submitting such bids by a June deadline, Trust Chair Parker Thomson announced at the group's meeting of April 4, 2000, with a decision to be made in July and an official groundbreaking proposed for September. "We've spent ten years plus in design and financing," Thomson said. "Now we're finally ready to start the physical work."

In fact, it might be reckoned that the physical work actually began on that same day in the spring of 2000, for it was that very morning that at long last demolition began on the crumbling Sears building. At the controls of the oversized machine snatching the first clawful of debris was Miami-Dade Mayor Alex Penelas. "In 1990, when I was first elected to the County Commission, the performing arts center was the first item I was asked for a vote on," Penelas told the *Herald*'s Gail Meadows. Penelas was quickly replaced at the wheel of the machine by a more seasoned operator, Tim Grady, who estimated that it would take somewhere between four to six weeks to clear the lot, with the exception of the fabled tower, which had yet again survived attempts to toss it out of the mix.

Anyone who took the beginning of demolition of the Sears building as a harbinger of the onset of actual construction, however, would have been sadly disappointed, for the attempt to settle on terms with a contractor was quickly becoming a nightmare. On June 9, the deadline for submission of bids, only one firm, Turner Construction, complied with the county's requirements. County Manager Stierheim said that while one other firm, PAC Builders—a conglomerate formed between Odebrecht, Haskell, and EllisDon companies—had also applied to bid on the project, assistant county attorney John McInnis disqualified that entity because all required paperwork had not been filed.

Stierheim said that the county would begin negotiations on a price with Turner, a national firm with South Florida roots going back to the 1920s, including such projects as Miami's Ingraham Building and the legendary Breakers Hotel in Palm Beach. More significantly, Turner had been the lead contractor for the New Jersey Center for the Performing Arts, a fact that promised a comfortable relationship with County Project Manager Gail Thompson. If Turner's interest seemed promising, however, by the following Tuesday, all had changed.

County attorney Robert Cuevas announced on that day that he had authorized an extension for submission of materials to PAC Builders, and that he would review that entity's application after all. The decision was a blow not only to Turner but to those who hoped for agreement on contract terms and approval by county commissioners on July 25, 2000, their final meeting before the summer recess. The decision particularly rankled officials at Turner, for that company was one of those disqualified from the competition for the ill-fated construction management position back in 1997.

The matter began to take on proportions of a comedy of errors when PAC Builders filed the necessary paperwork about an hour later than the Tuesday noon deadline set by Cuevas. Instead of a second disqualification, however, Cuevas announced that he would simply wait until the following day, Wednesday, to review the materials and make his decision. The matter actually came to a head on Thursday, June 15, when Cuevas declared that after all the scrambling, PAC Builders still had not satisfied the county's requirements (primarily involving a rundown of subcontractors and their scheduled participation in the project).

While Turner officials proclaimed themselves "ecstatic" at the news, and PAC Builders said that they would fight the matter no more, it was scarcely the end of the story. When Turner followed up the announcement of their selection with an actual dollar figure to do the work, on June 20, a new chorus of wails arose. Gail Thompson and county construction consultants had been at work on a review of cost estimates for the work ever since the original bids had been thrown out the previous year, and they had come up with what they considered a far more realistic estimate than the $168 million bricks-and-mortar figure that had been floating around since 1999 and earlier. Given present-day realities,

Thompson and the consultants figured, it would actually take about $198 million to build the center, a figure that County Manager Stierheim had already passed along to county commissioners.

However, when Turner presented its preliminary figures, the collective gulp from county officials and trust members might have roused Wagner and Bach from their eternal slumbers. The company was proposing to build the center at a cost of $253 million, $20 million over the previous year's high bid of $233 million, and about $40 million more than the previous low bid. When Project Manager Thompson told company officials that she would not even take that figure to commissioners, Turner officials agreed to a compromise: the company would find a way to fashion a bid of $210 million, though they would have to negotiate various methods of cost-cutting with the county before a contract could be finalized.

"When I heard that $253 million figure," says Pelli's Roberto Espejo, "that was the time I began to wonder if this project was ever going to happen." But work between Thompson and the company continued at a frenzied pace over the following weeks, until it was announced on July 11 that an agreement had been hammered out for Turner to build the center for a total of $208 million. The savings were achieved by meticulous review of the drawings, which allowed for the elimination of duplicate and unnecessary items, Thompson said, and by changing of specifications for various aspects of construction materials, including the substitution of poured concrete for a number of steel beams, and the like. Given that $201 million in bonds had been sold, earning $17 million in the interim, and that nearly $50 million in private donations had been secured, it seemed that all was finally in place. The contract would be finalized and filed with the county clerk on the following Friday, in time for consideration by commissioners on July 25.

Of course, those who have followed the saga to this point will not be surprised at what happened next. In fact, Project Manager Thompson was forced to announce, Turner officials may have claimed a bid of $208 million, but, when push came to shove, the firm had balked at signing off on the "At Risk" provisions of the contract that guaranteed that price—such a cap was simply unrealistic in the company's eyes. Another of the items complicating the matter, as it turned out, was a clause that Thompson had agreed to and hoped to find approval for from her superiors: she and Turner had agreed to exempt from the contract $22 million in costs for the heating and air-conditioning systems for the complex. According to the deal that Thompson had brokered with the company, that equipment would be purchased via lease and paid for by earnings on bond monies during the three years of construction. When County Manager Stierheim saw that clause, however, he slammed the brakes on the deal. In his eyes, it was nothing less than a bait-and-switch maneuver. The price tag faced by the county was in actuality at $230 million, and Turner would not even guarantee to complete the work at that price.

With all hopes of an imminent agreement evaporated, Thompson instead came to the commission on July 25, 2000, seeking permission to resolicit bids from all four companies that had expressed interest in the job, including Turner, PAC Builders, Morse Diesel, and Clark Construction, the entity that had once seemed so outlandish with its "low" bid of $214 million. Companies would have until August 25 to prepare bids, and Thompson hoped to be back before commissioners on September 7 with a contract and a recommendation. At that same meeting, given the apparent certainty that the increased cost of the center would require a proportional increase in the funds to come from the private sector, Trust Chair Parker Thomson told commissioners that the trust's foundation arm would immediately raise its fund-raising goal by $20 million.

The developments and the attendant delay were of great concern to many, of course, with some beginning to doubt once again that the project would ever get off the ground. *Herald* music critic James Roos, in a rundown during the renewed bidding process, pleaded with those who suggested scaling back the project to instead keep their eyes on the prize: the goal of building a world-class facility that would spur tourism and development in the center of the gateway city to Latin America. And *Herald* columnist Gail Meadows reminded readers of the realities of the county's financial position on the matter. County Manager Stierheim was in the process of revising the 2001–2002 fiscal year budget to reflect such items as the $201 million in bonds sold in 1997, significant millions in interest earned on those bonds, $3.7 million in state grants, and $6.7 million in additional projected revenues from the convention development tax.

There seemed enough in the coffers to absorb higher costs, but Meadows repeated a jab that critics had first hurled at the prospects of a Miami performing arts center almost a decade before: "In my lifetime?"

Ultimately, the county and the bidders were unable to hammer out details of any final bids in time for that September meeting, ending hopes of a groundbreaking for yet another year. In addition, two original bidders—Clark Construction and Morse Diesel—dropped out of the process, and it was November 3, 2000, before the new proposals of Turner Construction and PAC Builders were opened. And when that opening finally took place, sticker shock was once more the order of the day. Turner Construction, which had bowled over Gail Thompson with its suggestion that the county pay $253 million for the center back in June, was this time offering to do the job for $332 million. PAC Builders presented a bid of $280 million (it had been learned that the company had submitted an unopened bid of $249.5 million in June).

County Manager Stierheim seemed beaten by the most recent numbers. "I don't know whether we can put this thing together or not," he said in a *Herald* interview. "I'm extremely disappointed. Some people seem to think they've got us over a barrel." Turner representatives contested that view, however, saying that the county's insistence on guaranteed pricing for more than five hundred items in the budget was to account for the size of the company's bid. Turner President Michael Smith claimed that the firm had never guaranteed a single line item in all the years of its existence, and that the amount of the final estimate was the simple result of the company's need to protect its position. PAC Builders spokesman Jorge Luis Lopez seemed more philosophical about the county's demands, however, saying, "Line-item guarantees have become an important way of assuring no risks on behalf of the client." To center backers, though, it seemed a "damned if you do, damned if you don't" position. They could either insist on a fixed price for the work and get an inflated bid or gamble that costs would stay relatively steady over a three-year period of complex construction. Either way, it was becoming clear that the undertaking was going to cost far, far more than was anticipated.

Only Trust Chair Parker Thomson seemed unfazed by the latest figures. "Regardless of what the numbers are, we're doing it," he said. In his "it is what it is" way, he remained confident that the trust would be able to put together a financing package that would cover the ever-escalating costs.

Shortly after that set of bids had been released (some could still remember the good old days when $168 million seemed a sizable figure), Miami-Dade Mayor Alex Penelas made headlines with a suggestion that the center should be reduced to a single hall. "We could build one hall now and look at how to build the second hall later," Penelas told the *Herald*. That familiar canard elicited little support from cultural leaders, however. Such a step would simply be short-sighted, the trust foundation's Nancy Herstand said. "You would get the same situation you have now at the performing arts centers in Broward and Palm Beach. They can't accommodate the performance load." In fact, Tom Tomlinson, the performing arts center's executive director, had projected that each of the halls would be occupied for as many as three hundred days per year with the remainder set aside for maintenance. And Parker Thomson was quick to counter as well. "We'll get this done [as proposed]," he said. "We'll find a way to get this done."

However, the prospect of getting it done seemed to be getting more complicated by the day. Part of Mayor Penelas's reluctance to commit further public monies to the performing arts center was because of his vision for the building of a new baseball stadium for the Miami Marlins, new museums of science and art downtown, and the completion of a regional performing arts center in South Dade. While some contended that an ever-growing flow of bed tax monies could pay for all those things and still cover cost escalations for the performing arts center, others were not so sure. County Budget Director David Morris allowed that bed tax revenues had in fact exceeded projections, but as County Manager Stierheim reminded readers during a *Herald* interview, "if tourism falls off, you still have to meet your obligations." Budget Director Morris also clarified the status of the bond monies available for the performing arts center. When the county upped its budget for the center's construction to $205 million from $168 million, the difference was made up by the interest earned on those bonds sold in 1997 (and guaranteed by bed tax revenues). There in fact was no "extra pot" of $46.3 million or even $17 million, Morris said.

Meanwhile, Parker Thomson weighed in that the bids recently submitted, including that of PAC Builders, were "ridiculous." The trust was irrevocably committed to constructing two halls, he said, pointing out that redesigning the center as a single hall would itself trigger untold millions in architects' costs and delays. By the time a new hall was ready to begin construction, it would be another three years and what might construction costs have risen to by then? There would be two halls built as designed, Thomson vowed, and he was equally adamant about another thing: "that price is coming down."

What followed was an intense month of negotiations with PAC Builders aimed at accomplishing that very mission until finally, on December 13, 2000, County Manager Stierheim announced that he had an agreement in hand. He intended to go before the county commission on the following Tuesday and ask approval of a contract for $255 million with PAC Builders, a consortium formed between Odebrecht, the Haskell Company of Jacksonville, and EllisDon Construction, a Canadian firm that built the Athletes' Village for the 1996 Olympic Games in Atlanta. The consortium, formed expressly for the purpose of bidding on the Miami performing arts center, agreed on $255 million as a "target" price, with the understanding that the company and the county would begin a six-month period of negotiations with labor unions with the goal of making that figure a reality. The intended date for groundbreaking was the summer of 2001, with completion three years following.

Stierheim explained that the county was covering the additional $50 million in budget from the additional $20 million in private funding pledged by the trust and another $30 million in additional interest from the 1997 bond proceeds, along with additional proceeds from the ever-burgeoning convention development proceeds. In addition, Stierheim was proposing the establishment of a $24 million contingency fund to cover unavoidable cost increases, though he insisted, "I have no intention of spending that money."

One of the chief negotiating points was the contractors' reluctance to be held responsible for errors or omissions in the building plans, Stierheim said, but the county had agreed to assume that risk and would look into doubling the $10 million insurance policy already in force. However, PAC Builders would assume any increases in construction materials and the like.

A *Herald* editorial of December 16, 2000, lauded the news, calling for commission approval and declaring it "time to put away the discount-store mentality that has kept Miami-Dade in a cultural vacuum." No property or sales taxes would be involved, the piece reminded readers, and pointed to the centers in neighboring Broward and Palm Beach Counties as successful cultural beacons that delivered benefits far beyond those measured in dollars.

Finally, on Tuesday, December 20, 2000, with several hundred in attendance in its chambers, the county commission took up Stierheim's proposal. Though Commissioners Natacha Seijas and Miriam Alonso expressed some concerns about the price tag, Commissioner Dennis Moss countered, "Great communities have great things. I believe we have an opportunity today to move forward with constructing a great venue in the community." In the end, the group voted 11–0 to approve the contract, and the chambers erupted in joy.

Performing Arts Center Executive Director Tom Tomlinson applauded the commissioners' decision by telling reporters, "I believe that the arts have the power to bring a community together in a way that no other enterprise can, particularly a place like Miami with such enormous diversity." As for long-suffering, endlessly patient Trust Chair Parker Thomson, he recollects feeling nothing less than pure relief, for he had not known with certainty what the final vote was going to be. "With the authorization of the contract," he says, "I knew that one way or another, this project would get done. We'd been having a *conversation* for a number of years. Now, talk had turned to reality."

PART IV

· · · · · · · · · · · · · ·

IF YOU BUILD IT

Cost Escalations, Finger Pointing, Grand Opening,
Almost Closing, December 2000 to the Present

16

. . . .

If the beginning of the new millennium had begun with trepidation re-garding the future of the performing arts center, the events at the end of that year seemed to mark a new beginning. The *Miami Herald* called the commission's actions on December 20, 2000, "a resounding climax to a 21-year-long dream," and lauded the work of that body, Mayor Alex Pene-las, County Manager Merrett Stierheim, Sherwood "Woody" Weiser, Ryder Systems' Tony Burns, and, of course, Parker Thomson. The action might be viewed, in fact, as the pivotal moment in the rebirth of down-town Miami, the editorial concluded.

For this writer, who first laid eyes on that "downtown" in 1967, during a side trip on a spring break foray from Ohio to Ft. Lauderdale, the con-cept of the city's having died and moved to the point of rebirth within that brief period of thirty-three years seemed an odd one. Of course, things were not nearly so grand in downtown Miami as they were out on Miami Beach in 1967, but there was still some life to be found in the city's center, even then. There remained stand-alone movie theaters to be found—including the Lyric, with its balcony still open, showing *Cool Hand Luke*. And the nighttime streets still contained traffic and enough of a pulse to entrance a pack of college-aged Buckeyes.

By the time of this Buckeye's return in 1981, things had changed, how-ever, with even the action on Miami Beach largely confined to the Hotel District far north of that city's center, and "culture" still more or less de-fined by ever-dimming memories of what the likes of Jackie Gleason and the Rat Pack had once wrought.

That by the year 2000, a city with more than its share of societal and infrastructural issues to contend with could manage agreement on such an investment as the performing arts center required seemed little short of astonishing. After all, scarcely six months before the commis-sion endorsed the beginning of construction on the center, the entire South Florida community was consumed with—and essentially evenly divided over—the issue of whether a seven-year-old child named Elian Gonzalez should be returned to his father in Cuba or stay in Miami with relatives his mother was trying to reach by raft when she drowned with her son in her arms. The Elian saga was only the most recent thread of a decidedly singular, complexly woven, socially fraught backdrop against which Thomson and the other dedicated volunteers of the trust had managed to keep their focus steady over the years, a remarkable feat in itself.

However, despite the success of late December of 2000, much effort lay ahead. Says Thomson, "There was a *world* of work to be done—we all knew that—though none of us realized just how big the job would be. We thought we'd be building a building, but we ended up virtually rebuilding a city."

Adrienne Arsht, a longtime resident of Washington, D.C., who still divides her time between the nation's capital and Miami, agrees with Thomson's characterization. "The Lincoln Center and the Kennedy Center have been extremely important to New York and to the country," she says. "But so has the center been in Miami. And compared to a place like Philadelphia's Kimmel Center [completed in 2001], there's no comparison in terms of the degree of impact. I mean, the Kimmel is a fine venue, but a city like Philadelphia has so many other things. Adding something like the performing arts center to Miami was obviously going to be transformational."

The first order of business in the actual building process was finalizing the contract, the hope being that negotiations between PAC Builders and construction trades would result in keeping that budget firm at $255 million, a tall order in a white-hot construction market. However, if those talks resulted in an escalation of that figure, the whole matter would have to go before the county commission again. "*That*," said the PAC Builders project manager to the *Herald*'s Gail Meadows in early January of 2001, "is the *last* thing I want to do." Still, the prospect placed quite the burden on the company and performing arts center supporters. Were the issue to go before commissioners anew, one available option for that body would be to simply refuse to endorse *any* funding for building the performing arts center.

Matters were complicated shortly after the first of the year 2001, when Tom Tomlinson, who had been on the job only a year and a half, announced his resignation as executive director of the center. Though Tomlinson told Meadows on February 7, "I had absolutely no personal problems with any of the project's participants," he did express frustration that eighteen months had passed since his hiring and a date for groundbreaking was still hazy. Cultural Affairs Council Director Michael Spring, who had served as the de facto executive director for the county for a number of years before Tomlinson's hiring, was to take over the position once again, while a search for a permanent successor proceeded.

Several weeks later, in a March 25, 2001, *Herald* story, columnist Meadows reported that Tomlinson's departure, lamented by some arts activists in Miami, was prompted by Tomlinson's insistence on hiring his life partner, Geoff Corbin, for the $99,000 position of director of external affairs (i.e., booking director) for the performing arts center. Though Trust Chair Parker Thomson would say at the time only that Tomlinson resigned "for personal reasons," at least one member of the trust said that Thomson and Tomlinson had not gotten along from the beginning. They might not have quarreled in public, Meadows's source said, "but they would have sat beside each other forever with knots in their stomachs." Whatever his reasons, it was not the first time Tomlinson had left such a position abruptly, Meadows noted, for in 1996, he had quit the post as chief operating officer of the Orange County Performing Arts Center in Costa Mesa without notice and with vague justification.

"I don't know about 'knots in my stomach,'" Thomson recollects today. "I had decided early on that I personally would live with any important decision we made. If you don't make decisions, you don't get anywhere. You don't always make the best decisions, of course, but I certainly didn't have acrimonious feelings toward Mr. Tomlinson—it was just time for him to go."

Meantime, the prospect of Miami's performing arts center actually taking physical shape had intrigued observers far away from Dade County. The ambitious undertaking, with separate halls for theater and concerts, had earned comparisons to the Lincoln Center and the Kennedy Center from observers far removed from the fray. "I saw the model in Cesar Pelli's office, and it's breathtaking," said Mark Light, president of the Dayton, Ohio, Arts Center Foundation. Light told one *Herald* reporter in a March 2001 interview, "A performing arts center project like you have in Miami exists mainly to feed the soul, and change the city."

Adds Michael Spring today, "You have to understand that at first, we were just trying to compete culturally with cities like Atlanta and Philadelphia and Boston. But as the project became more and more of a reality, we decided we were on track to outdo them."

As for the task of trimming some $24 million from the preliminary construction budget by an August 22 deadline, PAC Builders' Jesus Vazquez was resolute. "There has been too much effort and money put into this project already for anybody to come and say it's not going to happen."

Preliminary work at the site actually began in mid-June, when crews began drilling operations to test for possible soil contamination and to determine the depth of the underlying water table so that the exact nature of the buildings' foundations could be determined. But still doubts persisted about whether or not a budget would ultimately be approved by county commissioners.

At a July 13 summit, County Project Manager Gail Thompson brought together representatives of PAC Builders, a number of major subcontractors with whom the company was negotiating, trust members, fund-raisers, county officials, and representatives of architect Pelli to try to determine where matters stood on the budget. At that meeting, PAC Builders' Vazquez announced that the company had been able to shave about $15 million off the total bill, $11 million of which was realized by negotiations with subcontractors. The company identified another $4 million in savings by "value engineering"—that is, finding alternative materials and procedures that would have no effect on the quality of the finished project, such as the substitution of thinner doors and cheaper hardware in areas of the buildings the public would never visit.

However, some of Vazquez's suggestions for ways to cut the remaining $8 to $9 million overage created a fresh firestorm of criticism. When he suggested that substituting precast concrete panels for the stone exteriors called for in the plans would save $4.6 million, Vazquez was inviting a storm of protest from those who wanted the building to look world-class as well as *be* world-class. And—controversial a notion as it was—simply demolishing the Sears Tower would trim another $2.3 million, he reminded everyone. Doing away with special reverberation doors and curtains would save another $1 million, as would the elimination of the small "black-box" theater envisioned for the use of local theater groups presenting experimental works. Axing the bridge that would span Biscayne Boulevard and connect the two main halls would save $700,000, and doing away with the café in the tower or anywhere else it might be put on the property would realize another half-million or so.

The suggestions, all dutifully reported by the media, brought howls of protest from various quarters, along with suggestions that PAC Builders consider reducing their projected $18 million in profits from the job before contemplating cutting anything else. The mere mention of demolishing the Sears Tower brought a stinging response from Dade Heritage Trust Executive Director Becky Roper Matkov, who called it "a totally unacceptable option." Such a step would constitute what she termed "a total reneging of the assurances we have received."

Parker Thomson issued a typical call for reason in the wake of the meeting, pointing out that Vazquez had simply done what was asked of the company: "present as complete a list as they could of ways that you could reduce the overall price with no evaluation of whether they were practical or impractical." As for certain of those proposals, Thomson told *Herald* writer Stephen Smith, "There ain't a prayer in heaven" that the stone exteriors of the buildings would turn back to concrete and stucco, and furthermore, Thomson said, "there ain't a prayer in hell" that the Sears Tower would be torn down. Ways would be found to reconcile the budget figures by August 22, Thomson promised, and he was confident that nothing of material significance would have to be changed.

On the subject of the tower, Thomson was particularly adamant. "There are a lot of people who don't like the Sears Tower, and that's tough," he told Smith in a July 31 interview. But the point of incorporating the structure into the performing arts center's design went beyond matters of aesthetics. Since 1929 it had stood as a kind of sentinel at the gateway to the city, and to destroy it would be a blow to the very impulse that center backers had called for from the original mandate to designers to come up with a design bespeaking the place. The fact that the structure might seem ungainly or inelegant to some was irrelevant, Thomson insisted. "It's a vertical symbol of Miami."

The matter came to a head on Wednesday, August 22, 2001, nine months after the selection of PAC Builders, when the company appeared before County Manager Steve Shiver (Merrett Stierheim had resigned according to his prearranged schedule earlier in the year). In Shiver's offices that day, the company gave assurances that it would in fact guarantee the building of the complex for $255 million. They had realized the savings by a combination of value engineering, aggressive negotiations with subcontractors, and by shaving $3 million or so off their projected profit of $18.3 million and another $2.4 million from projected overhead costs.

De facto executive director Michael Spring, back on the job since Tomlinson's departure, was quick to assure reporters that nothing of substance had been cut from the design. Though there were modifications to elevator design, food-service equipment, exterior awnings, sound hardware, and interior finishing touches to the Sears Tower, the tower itself would remain; stone would indeed grace the buildings' exteriors; and the acoustical design would stay intact. "It has taken sweat and blood to get here," Parker Thomson said after the announcement, though he was his typically cautious self. "I'm pleased, sure. But, I'll be more pleased when it's built."

County Project Manager Gail Thompson also expressed relief, telling the *Herald*'s Smith, "There were certain points [over the past six months] when we weren't confident that we would get to this point, because the numbers just weren't coming together. And that's when you dig deeper, on all sides."

As to how deep the digging was, reporter Smith reminded readers that the $255 million figure represented solely the costs of bricks and mortar. All told, including architect's fees, insurance, permits, and various administrative costs, the price tag for the center now stood at $334 million, a far cry from the $156 million or so that consultants had floated back in 1986. Backers were quick to remind everyone that private donations would rise in accordance with formula requirements, however, and that the cost to county taxpayers remained at zero. As pointed out by trust member Stuart Blumberg, the significant increase in bed tax revenues, far beyond what had been projected, would prove sufficient to cover the increases and more. All that remained now was for county commissioners to give their stamp of approval to the final budget at their first meeting in September.

That meeting was scheduled for September 11, 2001, a day on which events of far greater moment took place. Any discussion of the tragedy of that day goes far beyond the purview of this book, but the very mention of 9/11 is a reminder of how long had been the struggle of supporters to create a center of culture in Miami and of how complex the backdrop of that struggle had been. Its supporters would argue that the very concept of vitalizing the culture of a city and a nation is to be understood as one of the bedrock countervailing forces that operate against currents of negativity, cynicism, and destruction. Likewise, they would contend that the support of culture reflects the most noble aspirations of the species, and that the making of art represents the very antithesis of evil and negativity—or as one catchphrase goes, "There are no living nihilists." The drive to create a performing arts center, then, is to those who support such views as valuable an undertaking to a nation and a place and to the prospect of world peace as is diplomacy and spending on defense.

In any event, it was September 25 before county commissioners met to consider the budget presented by PAC Builders, and to his credit, County Manager Shiver stood to point out that the September 11 attacks had resulted in an immediate precipitous drop in tourism everywhere, and it was difficult to know what the long-term effects on the county's bed tax revenues might be. "Sorry to dampen the moment," Shiver told commissioners, "but it is absolutely important to be clear."

It was a rather remarkable testament to the resolve of commissioners, then, that they brushed aside such concerns and in the end voted unanimously to approve the budget for the undertaking.

"Elated, ecstatic, that's how I feel," County Project Manager Gail Thompson said, despite all, following the meeting. "This is the moment we've been waiting for."

Still, performing arts center supporters were charged with raising some $30 million in additional private donations to support the project, and the economic climate—with tourism projected to be down by 20 percent or more—was not promising. Even before the September 11 attacks, the nation's economy was softening, and fund-raisers for all five major arts organizations slated as major users of the performing arts center were having issues with finances. Only the New World Symphony, with an endowment of nearly $70 million, much of it provided by gifts from Ted Arison, was on solid financial ground. The Florida Grand Opera, Miami City Ballet, Florida Philharmonic, and the Concert Association of Florida were all operating with endowments far below what could cover protracted operating deficits. "There were hard times before," said Concert Association President Judy Drucker in a *Herald* interview of November 18. "September 11 was just the kiss of death."

There was some good news in December, when soil samples taken from the site suggested that far less contaminated soil than was feared would have to be taken from the performing arts center site, and a newly formed trust committee began interviewing candidates for an executive director to replace the departed Tomlinson. Despite the problems, hope remained that construction would soon begin and that indeed 2004 would see the long-anticipated opening of Miami's performing arts center.

17

. . . .

By February of 2002, foundations were indeed being poured at the performing arts center site, and competition for the position of executive director was narrowed to three: Michael Hardy, president of Louisville's Kentucky Center for the Arts; Colin Jackson, president of the EPCOR Centre for the Performing Arts in Calgary, Alberta; and Lawrence Simpson, Cuyahoga Community College playhouse director.

The matter was resolved in April, when Hardy, fifty-six, landed the job, effective June 1, 2002, at a salary of $185,000, with a $15,000 signing bonus and a contract including various performance bonuses. Hardy, with a Ph.D. from the University of Michigan, an M.A. from the University of North Carolina, and a bachelor's degree from Duke, had held his Kentucky post since 1998, where he managed an eighty-seven-person staff and an annual budget of $8 million. For six years prior he had served as executive director of the International Society for the Performing Arts, an association of performing arts executives from more than fifty countries. It seemed he was the right person for the job.

Meantime, construction work was well under way. The *Herald*'s Gail Meadows toured the site in early April and described the view from an adjacent rooftop as "a series of ancient tombs full of vertical mummies." She was referring to foundation pilings that studded the site, some plunging as deep as eighty feet into the somewhat soggy ground. Eventually, there would be a thousand such piles supporting the foundation of the concert hall and seven hundred more for the opera house.

As architect Roberto Espejo, appointed as Pelli supervisor at the site, put it, "We keep being reminded that, during *The Nutcracker* at the Met in New York, a sixty-foot Christmas tree comes up from below. We're going to be able to do that here too." The work, however, was complicated by encounters with pockets of groundwater that had to be pumped away by engines the size of pickup trucks, at a rate of twenty-five hundred gallons per minute. "The place was one big Slurpee," as Espejo described it. Perhaps the most interesting development was the fact that a practical use had been found for the much-maligned Sears Tower. In addition to the café planned for its main floor, the tower's second floor would house air-conditioning machinery servicing the opera house.

While this work was going on, Miami Mayor Manny Diaz reopened the call for a long-sought modification to the I-395 overpass, the elevated section of freeway connecting I-95 to the west with Miami Beach across Biscayne Bay via the MacArthur Bridge. That freeway would not only be an eyesore to behold from the new performing arts center, just to the north, but it had already been long criticized by social activists for decimating the nearby Omni and Overtown neighborhoods. Diaz pointed out that the footprint of the roadway was occupying several hundred acres of land that would be worth a fortune to developers if the overpass were turned underground. Such a project would involve digging a twenty- to thirty-foot-deep, one-hundred-foot-wide tunnel about five blocks long from North Miami Avenue and Bayshore Drive, and according to preliminary design estimates, would cost about $275 million.

As intriguing as the plan sounded, however, few saw it as practical. Not only was the price tag steep, but Florida Department of Transportation officials thought the idea dangerous. To avoid creating a roller-coaster effect for drivers dropping into the tunnel, then climbing onto the MacArthur Bridge within moments, the entrance to any such tunnel would have to be moved further west, exponentially raising costs.

In an interview with reporters two weeks before he began his new job, performing arts center Executive Director Hardy identified one of the major challenges facing him: bringing the divergent forces behind the project together into a unified whole. "You have a Performing Arts Center Trust, a Performing Arts Center Foundation, a Performing Arts Center management company, [and] Performing Arts Center Builders," Hardy said. "Different organizations doing different parts of this job rather than one organization that includes all of them happening together." Indeed, Hardy's task of aligning the common goals of those entities—not to mention those of county government and elected officials—would be a daunting one. Still, Hardy spoke eagerly of learning to speak Spanish and familiarizing himself with Miami's diverse cultural landscape. "The performing arts center of the future is going to embrace the community in its entirety," he said. "You make your market 100 percent of the population instead of 5 percent of the population."

As construction moved forward, attention inevitably turned to the prospect of what would eventuate from all that labor, particularly regarding the sound within the new halls. Negative reviews of the sound qualities of the newly opened music hall at the Kimmel Center in Philadelphia—Verizon Hall, where Russell Johnson, acoustician in charge of sound design for Miami's center, had done the work—raised concerns in some. If Johnson and his company, Artec, had created in Philadelphia what the *Washington Post* termed "an acoustical Sahara," what did that portend for Miami? The *Herald*'s music critic James Roos chimed in, calling the Verizon "a nightmare" and lamenting that the orchestra sounded lost in the 2,550-seat hall.

Michael Spring and others associated with the project downplayed such fears, pointing out that fine-tuning the sound at Verizon would go on for months after opening night, as Johnson and his team tinkered with various components affecting the sonic experience in contemporary theaters. As a *Herald* piece of July 21, 2002, noted, the two main halls planned for the Miami performing arts center would in effect be acoustical chambers completely isolated from the physical structures surrounding them, like nested boxes, with exterior sounds such as thunderstorms and the interior hum of elevators and air-conditioning systems cut off physically from patrons in their seats.

The two inner halls would be joined to the outer shells by six-inch flexible rubberized members that would dampen any sound transmission between the two structures, and indeed, visitors to "back of the house" areas today can see the joints marking the line where inner and outer structures meet. Similarly, two separate roofs were built: one to absorb the clatter of rain or hail, the other an inner dome reflecting the sounds of performances back down to audiences. Even the air-conditioning system was designed to allow cold air to descend upon patrons according to the silent laws of physics (warm air rises, cold air sinks) rather than be forced by churning fans. The ducts themselves would be connected to rails and supporting members by rubberized connectors in the same fashion as the inner walls were joined to the outer.

"We're building a building inside a building," said Pelli's Roberto Espejo. "You will be able to knock on one side of the wall, put a stethoscope on the other side, and not hear anything." In fact, there are actually three walls that insulate performers and audiences from the outside world. There is the inner shell of performance space, with its walls buffered and connected by a thick rubber seal to the surrounding space that houses offices, lobbies, storage, and the like. That outer shell is also covered with its own sprayed rubberized membrane that the stone façade itself does not actually touch. Instead, the stone slabs are attached to that second wall by a complex series of hooks that create another three-inch sound barrier.

"You could drop a delivery truck from a crane onto the walkway there," says Espejo, during a present-day tour, pointing to a spot on the exterior concourse, "and no one inside the opera house would hear a thing." In fact, the architects had been required to design the buildings around acoustician Johnson's specifications, not the other way around, as had sometimes been the case with other venues earlier in the century. Indeed, acoustics at New York's Lincoln Center Philharmonic Hall (now Avery Fisher Hall) had long been the subject of lament—and of considerable costly redesign—since its opening in 1962, forty years before. Such an arrangement led to various disagreements, misunderstandings, and, inevitably, an escalation in costs at Miami's performing arts center, but it followed the resolute mantra of Thomson and the trust: build from the inside out.

In addition to the basic design, a number of high-tech features were included in the plans to allow Johnson to fine-tune the sound that was produced by performers inside the chambers-within-chambers. An inverted acoustic dome studded with a number of smaller mini-domes would be set into the ceiling of the opera hall to help disperse sound, and a series of motorized fabric curtains and banners would be placed on the walls. The latter would be retracted for opera, which requires a crisp, drier sound for unamplified speech and singing, then unfurled during productions using amplified music sources to dampen unwanted reverberation.

Johnson designed the 2,200-seat concert hall after Boston's legendary Symphony Hall, constructed in a time-honored rectangular shape proven to convey orchestral sound more clearly and evenly than any other. There would be no sound-swallowing proscenium framing the stage, which would instead extend naked out into the audience. In fact, a balcony would wrap all the way around the back of the stage to enhance the intimacy of performances for audiences. To tailor acoustics according to the size of the performing group—from string quartets to symphony orchestras—the concert hall would feature a wood-encased, nautilus-like acoustic canopy thirty-five feet in diameter that could be lowered in varying segments over the platform when smaller groups performed and raised during full orchestra concerts. In addition, a series of one hundred huge motorized reverberation doors, controlled by computers, would be placed in the walls. The doors could be closed flush to diminish the size of the hall's acoustical envelope for chamber music and pivoted open for the likes of Tchaikovsky or Kiss.

Such design features portended that the quality of acoustics would be no issue at Miami's performing arts center, and indeed Johnson maintained that the smaller size of the hall alone portended a better experience—"every seat you remove from the 2,500-seat level ensures better sound." But as the University of Miami's Professor of Music Engineering Kenneth Pohlmann said, "All you can do is put your hall in the hands of a good steward and cross your fingers." The final answer would come on opening night.

More significant concerns surfaced in September of 2002, when news came of a delay in the delivery of steel needed for the project, and Executive Director Hardy announced that, as a result, the 2004 opening was in doubt. County Project Manager Gail Thompson explained that the steel, purchased from ADF International of Terrebonne, Quebec, would not arrive until mid-October at the earliest, because of difficulties in the complex design process. Drawings had to be completed before the steel members could be fabricated, and those drawings also had to be reviewed by architect Pelli's on-site construction team. When it was announced that the steel, originally scheduled to be delivered on September 16, would not arrive until November 25, Thompson said that crews would nevertheless press forward, moving other facets of the project ahead of schedule in the meantime, then work nights and weekends once the steel arrived, in order to allow for a late 2004 opening. Even in that best-case scenario, Hardy said, the 2004–2005 season would have to be a partial one.

Project Manager Thompson was also still dourly contemplating a $16 million list of items that had been trimmed from the budget during the previous year's negotiations, all of which various segments of the major users groups wanted to see somehow returned. Some still lobbied for a formidable pipe organ in the concert hall; others pointed to the need for a special scenery lift in the opera house; and yet others called for a soundproof drop door for the opera stage, through which backdrops and scenery could be raised and lowered. While the $255 million construction budget contained no wiggle room, Thompson was hopeful that government grants and private sources might be found to cover some of the costs.

Trust construction committee chairman Stanley Arkin gave the go-ahead to the opera house lift, the door, and also the inclusion of a marble wall where the names of donors might be chiseled, saying that the $2.5 million needed could come from the existing pot, then be somehow reimbursed down the line, all maneuvers that pointed up the difficulties of maintaining a balance between "good enough" and "world class." Also in October, Foundation Director Sherwood Weiser announced that his group had raised their goal to $80 million, up from $63.2 million, in order to cover administrative overhead and preopening staffing costs (Executive Director Hardy was seeking to hire an operations manager and a communications manager at $100,000 each annually) and guarantee that the doors would stay open for the center's first ten to twelve years.

By March of 2003, Hardy had put together his core group of executives and had included a programming chief, Australian native Justin Macdonnell, as well, but plans for an opening in 2004 had faded. Instead, Hardy was contemplating a "soft opening" that might begin the following spring and last for several months, leading up to a full season beginning in fall of 2005.

By this time, the long-awaited steel had begun to arrive from the Canadian manufacturer, and construction teams had already placed beams at the 130-foot apex of the concert hall, and similar work was well under way at the 150-foot-high opera house on the west side of Biscayne Boulevard. However, the delays in material delivery had contributed to a deficit in the construction budget, projected at $25 million at the time, according to a story by the *Herald*'s Meadows. The county had appointed a dispute resolution board to try to iron out the differences, said Project Manager Gail Thompson, but meantime, the demanding work, where no two steel beams were identical, proceeded on, buoyed by reports from a stress-analysis lab that the building would indeed meet South Florida's enhanced building code and be able to withstand 140-mile-per-hour winds as well as hurricane-driven downpours.

Late in April of 2003, word came that one of the intended principal tenants for the performing arts center, the Florida Philharmonic, would be unable to meet its May 23 payroll of $350,000 and might be forced into bankruptcy. The orchestra, founded in 1984 and performing an average of forty-three weeks a year, had been plagued by financial problems for years, its permanent endowment about a quarter of the $40 million or so recommended by arts group consultants. In 2001, orchestra members were forced into a pay cut (average salaries were between $37,000 and $50,000), and later in 2001 longtime music director James Judd resigned.

The news regarding the Philharmonic, which had been running annual deficits of $1 million or more since 1999, was less than a happy harbinger for performing arts center supporters. A *Herald* story of May 5 wondered if, in light of the Philharmonic's difficulties, the South Florida community could support an opera house expected to be in use 220 nights a year and a concert hall operating for 150 nights. The last projected operating budget had been prepared in 1998, the story pointed out, and even if the Florida Philharmonic was to survive, all five major user groups together would provide only about 10 percent of the center's annual operating revenues. With an operating budget projected at approximately $15 million, it meant that about $1.5 million might be derived from rentals from the big five. Revenues from the convention development tax were projected at $1.4 million. Another $1 million would come from interest on the Performing Arts Center Foundation Trust and grants from Miami-Dade County's Cultural Affairs Council. The Performing Arts Center Foundation hoped to chip in $5 million from annual giving appeals, something of a tall order in challenging times. But even with generous giving, that left a gaping $6 million hole for outside programming revenues to make up.

Executive Director Hardy was forthright: "Right now our proposed operating budget shows a $2 million gap. We're working toward closing it before we open." Longtime Miami philanthropist and Philharmonic supporter Taffy Gould was not optimistic, especially concerning the prospect of a continued giving appeal by the Performing Arts Center Foundation. Such efforts would be in direct competition for the same source of dollars as those of the five major cultural organizations, she pointed out. "The fund-raising for that Performing Arts Center really did in these five groups."

Florida Grand Opera's Robert Heuer was more hopeful. "I think there's a huge amount of money that has gone untapped in this community," he said. And Randy Cohen, executive with Washington, D.C.-based Americans for the Arts, added, "It's a really tight fund-raising environment right now in every city. But the economy will turn around, and so will the fund-raising environment."

As for Trust Chair Parker Thomson, he provided his customary steadying words. "Everybody said we couldn't get the center built. We've met every challenge so far. We sure as hell expect to meet this one."

A little more than a week later, on May 12, 2003, a *Herald* story appeared, with details on the previously publicized $25 million construction cost overrun, and stating that most of the cost was attributed by PAC Builders to nine months of delays related to laggardly steel delivery, which in turn was attributable to flaws in the original design of the girders. The county, on the other hand, was claiming that PAC Builders was at fault for failure to communicate promptly or correctly with the steel subcontractor. While mediators were at work trying to resolve this finger-pointing scenario, County Manager Steve Shiver announced that whatever the outcome, $25 million might be an underestimate of cost overruns, and that the project was, in fact, "a train ready to wreck." Of this latest news, Trust Chair Parker Thomson said, "We're not construction people, and we can't say whose fault it is. But delay is a cost, and somebody is going to have to eat some of it."

As for news on the fate of the Philharmonic, it was not long in coming. On May 14, that organization announced it would file for bankruptcy, and while there were hopes expressed that a buyer might be found who would attempt to reorganize the company, the possibilities were dim. It was unfortunate news on many fronts, but an ancillary factor not to be overlooked, said Performing Arts Center Director Hardy, was the blow to Philharmonic subscribers who might feel ill-treated and lose interest in supporting other cultural institutions.

As for the issue with PAC Builders, the dispute over cost overruns would only grow more acrimonious. On August 12, the trust's construction committee, chaired by Stanley Arkin, filed a report citing that construction—only 30 percent completed after nearly two-thirds of the allotted time had elapsed—would be further delayed by the need to correct serious faults in sound-baffling equipment and other errors.

Pelli's on-site architect Roberto Espejo provides some insight into the delay referred to by Arkin. The set of eighty-four massive concrete reverberation "doors" that Johnson had designed into the concert hall were being fabricated by a firm in Sarasota. The company had agreed to pour two of the doors and then bring Espejo up for an inspection before proceeding with the rest. However, according to Espejo, the company, under pressure to meet deadlines for delivery, had decided on its own to expedite the process and thus fabricated all eighty-four doors at once, pouring the concrete into forms laid out in an area exposed to the elements.

When he arrived in Sarasota, Espejo found that the panels were marred by rainwater that had puddled on the concrete during curing. "We were talking about maybe $750,000 worth of panels," Espejo said, "and I rejected every one of them on the spot." The panels were a key element in Johnson's design, Espejo points out, and while the acoustics expert had called for essentially the same devices in the design of the Philadelphia performing arts center, "they value-engineered out the concrete there and filled the panel shells with sand, claiming the function would be identical. When Philadelphia opened, the acoustics were panned, and Johnson was livid." In Espejo's eyes, the doors were a crucial part of the design for Miami's performing arts center, scarcely to be treated like roadway dividers or parking garage flooring.

The Sarasota firm of course protested Espejo's decision, proposing to plaster over the imperfections in roughly half of the panels that would be visible to the public, but Espejo was doubtful about the fix. "What if the

Cleveland Symphony cranks up the volume and chunks of concrete start raining down on the audience from those vibrating twelve-ton doors?" he asked.

The impasse led to a visit to Espejo's trailer on the performing arts center construction site by the county's Bill Johnson. "He was furious with me," Espejo recalls, "because I was holding up the job, but I pointed out that it was *my* job to make sure the center was built the way it was designed."

"Well, at least accept the half that nobody will ever see," Johnson demanded. "If something cracks there, we'll deal with it then."

Finally, Espejo gave in. Johnson was the customer's representative. If he was willing to accept refurbished doors, Espejo would go along.

With that, the two left Espejo's trailer, with the architect escorting Johnson to his car. "It was close to quitting time," Espejo recalls, "and there were a lot of crew and supervisors heading for the gates. All of a sudden, it was like a switch went off—a delayed reaction or something—and out of nowhere, Bill turned on me and started reading me the riot act. Basically he said that he had never dealt with anyone like me in his life. I was the most unreasonable, fault-finding, miserable nit-picking jerk he had ever encountered, and I was single-handedly responsible for driving this project into the ground for no good reason . . . and then he really got going.

"By that time, everyone had stopped to watch. I was astonished, but it was clear there wasn't anything I could say. When Bill finally ran out of gas, I just said, 'Are we finished now? Can I go back to my trailer?' And Bill turned and stomped away."

It was the lowest moment of his experience on the job, Espejo recalls. "I'm like standing there humiliated, thinking 'this job really sucks,' when one of the construction guys comes up to me and says, 'Wow, that was great, the way you handled that!' and a bunch of other guys came over and started clapping me on the back, and before you know it, we—myself and a bunch of guys I had been giving a hard time to for all these months, guys that would punch the side of my trailer in anger on the way out the gates—we were on our way to a bar for drinks. After that day, I'd go up to someone to point out a mistake, and it was like, 'Whatever you say, Mr. Espejo.'"

By way of epilogue, Espejo points out that in the end it took more than nine months for the set of repaired and remanufactured doors to be delivered to the site, and by that time, all the steel had been erected in the concert hall's roof, leaving no way for the huge panels to be lowered into place by crane as originally intended. "In the end, we had to put in a whole system of temporary support columns beneath the stage, bring the panels in through the stage doors and lift them up into place, but that's the way it goes sometimes." He shrugs. "They work like a charm, though. And nothing's fallen off yet," he adds.

Espejo's efforts aside, the county's Gail Thompson had by this time lost all faith in the project's principal contractors. On August 29, 2003, she wrote to the new county manager, George Burgess, pointing out, "with two years of construction behind us and as much time left to go, we do not believe that PAC Builders is capable of significant improvement in this regard." On September 9, citing fears that the budget might well soar as much as $50 million over what was authorized, the Performing Arts Center Trust voted unanimously to have the contract with PAC Builders voided.

For its part, PAC Builders responded by saying that the trust had acted rashly and that any errors that the company might have made could be corrected. County Manager Burgess attempted to reach a compromise on the matter, suggesting that the costs of correcting errors be shared by drawing equally upon the contingency funds of both the contractors and the county, with a final responsibility to be determined by mediators while construction proceeded apace.

It was a worrisome scenario, but worse yet, the contractors had not even begun work on the most ticklish part of the whole enterprise: the interiors of the halls themselves, where the stages and woodwork and stonework and associated mechanics and electronics demanded perfection from craftsmen, and the slightest changes would set in motion a cascade of related modifications. "What we're building is an instrument," Jim Gray, a spokesperson for PAC Builders, told the *Herald* on November 3. And because of the fact that the design of that instrument was meant to be unique, almost nothing in the process was standard. As was mentioned, Sydney's famed opera house, so often held up as an ideal by Miami's performing arts center supporters, was originally proposed to cost $7 million and take four years to build. In the end, the iconic Australian structure required fourteen years and $102 million to complete.

In any case, said Trust Chair Parker Thomson, Miami's performing arts center would be built as it was designed. "We won't sacrifice quality to keep on schedule," he said, while floating a new opening date of February 2006. "Timing is utterly outside our control."

By December 2003, the *Herald* was reporting that overruns had reached almost $60 million, about $22 million of it attributable solely to maintaining payroll and other expenses while construction was delayed, and another $12 million attributed to design error and delivery problems with the steel. At its December 16 meeting, the county commission heard colleague Katy Sorenson declare, "We have gone through everything from therapy to litigation. This psychodrama has to end." In response the body approved $750,000 to hire a consultant with arts project oversight experience to filter all future change requests from contractors. Meantime, however, there was still no resolution to the issue that had already developed, with the contractors adamant that incorrect construction drawings were provided to them by the county and that the corrections that had to be made were no fault of the builders. As PAC Builders spokesperson Steve Halverson put it, "Changes have been made for which compensation is due."

18

. . . .

With matters between the county and the builders at an apparent impasse as the New Year turned, the Performing Arts Center Trust and the Performing Arts Center Foundation met in mid-January of 2004 to form a joint venture that would allow the trust to conduct its own fund-raising efforts aimed at covering operating expenses once the center opened, while preventing any duplication of efforts and double-dunning of potential donors already tapped by Weiser and the foundation. While the foundation had as one of its goals the raising of a $21 million operating endowment, its primary focus had always been to come up with the private sector's share of construction expenses, tabbed at $42.2 million before the current specter of cost overruns threatened to push the figures higher. "If we didn't do this, the trust would have to hire its own fund-raising staff, and they might end up approaching the same donors," Performing Arts Center Executive Director Michael Hardy explained.

At a March 12 meeting of the county's Recreational and Cultural Affairs Committee, County Project Manager Thompson shared the news that the projected completion date of the center had been pushed back once again, this time to summer of 2006. Furthermore, Thompson said, change orders continued to flow in from the builders at the rate of about $1 million per week, with some estimates of total overruns now at $100 million. "I find it appalling, unacceptable," a frustrated Commissioner Dennis Moss told reporters. Assistant County Manager Bill Johnson, still helping to ride herd on the project, said that he proposed to the builders that the most recent delay be the last, and that PAC Builders should agree in writing to pay penalties if the center were not completed in June of 2006. Not surprisingly, the contractors did not warmly receive Johnson's proposal.

A bit of good news came the following week when Sherwood Weiser announced a $1 million gift to the foundation from former Cuban refugee Paul Cejas, founder of Care Florida Health Systems and former U.S. Ambassador to Belgium under Bill Clinton. The gift brought the foundation's total to $54.4 million of the $80.2 million it was charged with raising. Another ray of sunshine came before the month was out when construction workers celebrated the positioning of the final piece of steel in the framework of the Ziff Opera House on March 26. And further good news came from Tallahassee in April, when, following a visit by Michael Spring and Stuart Blumberg to confer with legislators, state legislators voted $500,000 toward the construction of the elevated pedestrian bridge that would connect the two main buildings of the complex.

In May, the county's oversight team took something of a blow when Bill Johnson, forty-nine, and on the job with county government since 1980, announced his plans to take a job with Miami developer Jorge Perez and his Related Group. Though he did not give an exact timetable for his departure nor say exactly how much he would be making with Perez, it was understood he'd get a sizable raise over the $220,000 the county was paying him at the time. Johnson, a native Ohioan, had come to Miami with a history degree and an M.A. in public administration to serve an internship under then–County Manager Merrett Stierheim. Over the years leading up to the county's involvement in the building of the performing arts center, Johnson had risen through the ranks to become assistant county manager and had overseen the land acquisition and construction of a number of county building projects, including several police department headquarters and training facilities.

At the time of the public charrette arranged to select the performing arts center architect, Johnson was assigned responsibility for the county's oversight on its construction. "It wasn't a task I sought out," Johnson recalls, "but then again, Joaquin Avino [county manager at the time] made it clear it wasn't exactly a request." While Johnson's experience with construction oversight was not insignificant, those previous undertakings paled in comparison with the performing arts center. "This was one of the most complex building projects ever undertaken in South Florida," he says. "It wasn't unlike building a nuclear power plant. Still, I didn't think it was going to be impossible. I just understood that it wasn't going to be simple."

By 2004, Johnson's characterization of the matter had been more than amply borne out. "There was a lot of talk about budget overruns at the time," he says, "but I am not sure that 'overrun' is the proper concept." In

Johnson's view, the project had never been comprehensively and realistically budgeted in the first place. With separate contracts in place for the theater designers, the acoustician, and the architect and a three-headed construction firm at the head of a group of more than seventy subcontractors, containing costs had become a near impossibility. "There were literally thousands of unanswered RFIs [contractors' requests for further information] pending at the time, and everyone on both sides, design and construction, was clamoring to be paid for additional work." Indeed, even Pelli's firm announced that it too was seeking more money for its efforts, though it was not clear just how much they wanted beyond the $25.35 million already agreed upon.

While PAC Builders had originally agreed to complete the job by October 15, 2004, their target date was now May 31, 2006. The company claimed that vague drawings from the architect had resulted in most of the delays, but the county's Gail Thompson countered that PAC Builders had been given six months to study those drawings before agreeing to the $255 million price tag. Thompson said that the builder submitted only about four hundred requests for clarification during the time it was preparing its bid, but had sent in more than five thousand since. The builders had also filed 991 change orders required by plans clarifications and were asking for $47 million to cover those changes. Furthermore, her office was now estimating that further delays would cost another $14 million. It was bad news that traveled from commission chambers to the pages of the newspaper in what seemed a never-ending flow.

Amidst threats from commissioners and some trust members that both the contractors and the architects should be fired, then–County Manager George Burgess was working diligently to find a compromise. If the dispute ended up in court, he said, "You might not resolve it for fifteen years." Though Trust Chair Parker Thomson was well aware that jettisoning the contractor and the architect at this stage could be calamitous, "The only thing worse would be to continue the way we are."

Matters were further complicated when performing arts center Executive Director Hardy delivered another reality pill to County Manager Burgess. In addition to the cost overruns, Hardy suggested that the center would need an additional $30 million infusion to cover a number of essential items lopped off the budget during the value-engineering process that reduced the original budget from $279 million to $255 million back in 2001. In a document entitled "A Status Report to the Community," Hardy outlined a staggering array of both essential and optional items, including $7.3 million to restore such necessary items as security systems, paint, rugs, lighting fixtures, pianos, and sewing machines for costumes; $10 million for maintenance trucks and the long-debated pipe organ; $10 million in preopening operating expenses for salary, rent, and other costs occasioned by the twenty-month delay in opening; $6–7 million to offset operating deficits the performing arts center expected between opening day in October 2006 and 2010, the earliest possible time to break even; and $5–6 million yearly, to cover the operating deficits of the center's resident companies.

County Manager Burgess professed astonishment at some of the items on Hardy's list, but Hardy (echoing the theme put forward by Bill Johnson) was adamant that original projections had simply been short-sighted and overly optimistic. His figures reflected reality—and if the project were to be completed, the money would have to come from somewhere.

Meantime, in mid-June of 2004, Burgess announced plans to do at long last what had been called for at the outset of the project: hire an independent construction management firm to oversee the work. Burgess proposed that Value Management Services, an Ohio-based firm headed by engineering consultant Ron Austin, take over oversight of the remainder of the work, replacing Gail Thompson, the county's project manager on the project since 2000. Burgess was also proposing to hire another architect, GBBN of Cincinnati, to help the Pelli firm respond more quickly to on-the-ground clarifications and modifications sought by builders. Thompson would stay on as an administrator associated with other details of the project, Burgess and Assistant County Manager Bill Johnson proposed.

While Burgess's plans awaited commissioners' approval, Thompson let it be known what she thought of the idea by summarily tendering her resignation. In response to the county's offer of another position, she wrote to Burgess, "I find that it is not consistent with my career goals." In the wake of her departure, performing arts center officials declined to blame Thompson for construction problems on the project. In a

Herald story of June 29, Sherwood Weiser said, "I don't think anyone in the situation she was placed in could have or would have done better." Added Trust Chair Parker Thomson, "If you want to assess blame, there's enough to go around for a lot of people." He explained, "It's a distressed project and way behind. And it was time to do anything to get this project on track."

In hindsight, most agree that Thompson had been put in something of an untenable position from the beginning. In Newark, she worked under an established executive director responsible for interfacing with government officials, freeing her to focus solely on getting a building completed. In Miami, she had found herself caught between a three-headed construction firm and a diverse group of politically motivated commissioners, including some who would wish the project away in a heartbeat.

Bill Johnson remembers the fraught period as the only time he began to wonder if the performing arts center would indeed be built. At least one of his former bosses suggested to him, "Bill, this is the end," and there were others in county government who thought that the size of the various claims from designers and contractors would simply sink the ship. "Better that we cut our losses and simply walk away," Johnson heard from more than one insider.

With nearly a quarter of a century of experience in the complex workings of county government, Johnson might have yielded to the pressure and taken the easy way out to that plum position offered up by the private sector. "There were a lot of sleepless nights," he recalls. But in the end, motivated by his belief in the inherent value of the undertaking, he announced a ninety-day deferment of his new partnership with developer Perez and returned to the performing arts center fray. In what he recalls as his most significant action, he convened a lunch meeting that included nearly one hundred representatives of designers and contractors, where he called for "a new day" moving forward.

"It was simply a matter of opening up the lines of communication and reminding everyone that we would have to cooperate from there on out if this job was going to get done," Johnson says. "And I reminded everyone how much would be lost by everyone if it didn't get done. We were involved in a partnership, and we had to start acting like it.

"I also assured everyone in the room that I would personally consider every claim outstanding and that everyone was going to be fairly treated," Johnson adds. "And I instituted a policy that if an RFI came in from a contractor, it would be answered within seventy-two hours, or I would hear about it. Enough was enough."

It is hard to know what might have happened had Johnson exited on the heels of Gail Thompson's 2004 departure and left the teetering project in the politicians' hands, but Parker Thomson for one is grateful that it did not turn out that way. "Bill is one of those rare, engaging human beings who can get people to come around by the sheer force of his personality," Thomson says.

Johnson was also astute enough to know that he would need the help of an experienced independent construction manager and outside claims analyst, and thus he urged County Manager Burgess to carry the fight for such a hire back to the county commissioners. In the end, and after considerable lament, commissioners voted on July 28 to back plans to bring in outside help and settle outstanding claims with both PAC Builders and Pelli for about fifty cents on the dollar.

"I feel like an abused wife who isn't leaving a relationship even though she still may be abused in the future," groused Commission Chair Barbara Carey-Schuler. But in a vote of 8–4, she and others also approved the establishment of a $15 million fund to cover future contingencies. Still, following the vote, Commissioner Dorrin Rolle warned, "There are land mines here, and we're going to step on them in the future. You're going to be back for more money," he grumbled to Burgess. The additional $67.7 million authorized by the vote brought the revised cost of the performing arts center to just under $412 million. To a community kept meticulously abreast of center affairs by the media for at least fifteen years, the escalation might have seemed incomprehensible, but perhaps just as amazing was the lack of any focused community protest. Citizens were either numb by now or they had fallen in with Parker Thomson's view: one way or another the performing arts center would get done.

Ron Austin, the engineer who took over as construction oversight manager and facilitator—his fees to be paid in part by the county, in part by the trust—had been involved with architect Pelli in a similar post during construction of both the Aronoff Center in Cincinnati and another smaller performing arts venue in Dayton, Ohio. While the outside architects, GBBN, would be working with Pelli on ironing out on-the-ground production design issues, Austin would spend most of his time working with PAC Builders and the various subcontractors. He had in fact been engaged by Odebrecht as a consultant back in the days when the Brazilian contractor was contemplating making a solo bid on the project.

"I listened to them back then as they outlined their expertise in building dams and hospitals and skyscrapers in various places around the world, and then I advised them to forget about getting involved with a PAC," Austin says. "They were a little surprised, but I pointed out to them that building a performance hall was unlike any other type of construction. People who had welded steel beams and panels together might think they could build a submarine, but that is not necessarily the case."

Austin was in general agreement with Bill Johnson that any mistakes that had been made at the outset on the design and budgeting of the project meant little. "The important thing was to get the project back on track and have people communicating," he says, though he admits that when he approached individual contractors, he would have to listen to literally hours of complaint about past grievances.

"It was a major issue not to have production architects in place, because there is a big difference between what a design architect does and what a production architect does." As an example, Austin describes his review of the original Pelli plans, which called out the external dimensions of the walls, as one might expect. "But when I examined the details of each individual section, angle by angle, marching around the perimeter and getting back to the starting point, I found a gap of eight inches. You can't just turn the builders loose, section by section, telling yourself, 'Oh well, we'll just build a little extra eight-inch wall if it doesn't work out.' You have to adjust the plans to make sure everything joins up like it's supposed to. All those beams have to be fabricated exactly, to the inch and on the right angles. When you're building a submarine, you don't take the attitude that you'll just use a bigger hammer and pound things into place somehow."

When Austin arrived in Miami in mid-2004, he found a project paralyzed by the fear held by virtually every party involved that if something went wrong, then the individual firm was going to be held accountable.

No one wanted to assume a risk that could sink an entire company, so the round of finger-pointing and requests for further information had escalated to the point where nothing was getting done. "At one point, I sat down for lunch and sketched out a flowchart of the way things *ought* to be working and handed it to Bill Johnson," Austin says. "'Someone has to break the logjam,' I told him. 'I don't know who that is, but if it doesn't happen, this project is going down the tubes.'"

Austin had barely returned to his Ohio home for the weekend following that conversation, when the phone rang, with County Manager George Burgess on the other end. "I'm about to fire the contractors," Austin recalls Burgess saying, "but Parker Thomson says I should talk to you first."

In short order, Austin was on his way back to Miami to detail a previously unthinkable solution to the impasse: the "at risk" provisions of the contract would have to be rescinded, and the county would have to make a major leap of faith that contractors would deal with them in good faith. "The county attorneys started tearing their hair," Austin says, but Burgess bought into the concept.

"This is how we're going to do it," Burgess told the county attorneys. "Draw it up." And then Burgess turned to Austin, who had yet to agree to take on the full-time job of construction oversight. "As for *you*," Austin recalls Burgess saying, "I'm holding you responsible for making it work. And don't think that Ohio is far enough for you to run if you don't pull it off. I'll find you wherever you go." At six feet, four inches, and about 240 pounds, and a construction site veteran, Austin had rarely been physically intimidated. "But I was that day," he recalls, as Burgess backed him up against a wall of a conference room. "George got my full attention."

It was no easy process, Austin says, "but little by little we were able to regain people's trust. The contractors gradually came to understand that they would be treated fairly, and in turn they gave it their all."

"All projects eventually get done," says Jesus Vazquez, who was project executive for PAC Builders. "But some take longer than others. In this case, it was a first-of-its-kind undertaking for everybody, and we were all being educated as we went. Risk management had become the big issue holding up the project, and every question we might have about the plans had to be signed off on by the sound designer, the theater designer, and the architect, not to mention the county. No contractor was willing to accept responsibility for issues beyond company control, and in a project of this size and complexity, unexpected problems were popping up all the time."

As Vazquez points out, most building projects have repetitive elements that, once engineered, can be chunked out easily, or "produced," in assembly-line fashion. But there were no repetitive elements in the complex nature of Pelli's design. "A lot of times, we just couldn't get walls to close," Vazquez says, echoing the description of problems Ron Austin had spotted in the plans. "BIM [Building Information Management] technology was really just in its infancy back then. Today, computer programming could cope with these problems in advance, but back then it was a lot of tedious, seat-of-the-pants work." With a laugh, Vazquez adds, "The fact is that no contractor who has ever won a performing arts center contract has ever bid on a second one."

In Vazquez's view, County Manager George Burgess had gone out on a very important limb to revitalize a troubled project. "When George Burgess was able to convince the commissioners to listen to reason," he says, "it was a real turning point. Once the 'at-risk' stipulations were removed, everyone started to work together, and problems eventually got resolved."

Of course, there were times that Austin also had to convince Bill Johnson to give on certain matters, a process that did not always go smoothly. Johnson, for one, recalls a day early in 2006 when Austin came into his office high up in the county building to suggest that PAC Builders simply weren't going to be able to meet the August target date for obtaining the temporary certificate of occupancy. Johnson thought about it briefly before he responded, "So what if I said I was going to throw you out that window, then?"

Johnson wasn't smiling. Austin gazed out at the landscape of Miami stretching away for miles below. "I'd say that we were going to meet that deadline," Austin answered.

In any event, the move by commissioners to increase the budget and bring in independent construction oversight and architectural firms would put an end to center-related controversy, for a time, at least. By the end of September, a still-on-the-job Bill Johnson termed construction on the project two-thirds complete, and, in a September 29, 2004, interview with the *Herald*'s Fred Tasker, he expressed confidence that the center would indeed open in August of 2006. During a tour of the construction site, observers were given a look at progress on the much-discussed main reverberation doors, the set of forty-foot-high, twelve-thousand-pound concrete slabs that would open and close in accordance with acoustical needs.

By January of 2005, the *Herald* was reporting the project 70 percent complete and on track for an October opening the following year. The glass fronts for both the Ziff Opera House and the Carnival Symphony Hall, each 120 feet wide and 100 feet high, were in place, and the Blumberg Bridge linking the two buildings now created what architect Espejo termed "the handshake" spanning Biscayne Boulevard. Blumberg, on vacation in Los Angeles when Saturday-night traffic on Biscayne Boulevard was stopped and the bridge support beams were hoisted into place, recalls Parker Thomson sending him a cellphone photograph of the moment. "A wonderful feeling," Blumberg recalls.

More than 180,000 square feet of quarried granite from Brazil and Sardinia was being affixed to the buildings' exteriors, and work would soon turn to finishing of the interiors and the fine-tuning of acoustics. "This physical thing on Biscayne Boulevard has exceeded my wildest creative imagination," proclaimed Espejo, who had been at work on the project for a decade. Pelli himself added, "These will be two splendid, incredible structures that will be the pride of Miami for generations to come."

Pelli's optimistic vision had not taken shape without significant strife, of course. As any homeowner who has ever wondered of an architect if there mightn't be a cheaper way to achieve some desired effect in a new home or a remodel can attest, desires and practicality are often in conflict. Espejo is fond of recollecting the time when he was called out of his trailer by Bill Johnson and Ron Austin, along with PAC Builders project manager Jesus Vazquez, to take a look at a sample of a material Austin wanted to use for paving the exterior entryways to the halls. The sample was of a granite composite that Gail Thompson had conceived of before her departure, an amalgam that she felt would be "just as good as" solid stone and cheaper besides.

"That's a concrete product," Espejo pointed out. "It's got granite in there, but it's not the same as solid stone. Concrete is going to absorb moisture and mildew. You'll be cleaning it all the time."

"So we'll clean it," Austin said. "Big deal."

"On top of that, it's the wrong color," Espejo said. "Look at it. There's a lot of pink in there. We need something more natural, to match the granite on the façade."

By this point, Austin had lost his temper. "You architects get something in your heads, and you never want to compromise. You can't even tell me the name of the color you want, but you sure as hell can tell me you don't want to save a couple of dollars when it's possible . . ."

It was at about that point, as he was trying to muster some response, Espejo recalls, when a shadow swept over their group gathered outside the buildings. Espejo hadn't even had time to glance up when a huge, plate-sized mass of bird dung splatted onto the shoulder of Austin's shirt. Everyone in the group stood transfixed, with Austin's expression suggesting that Espejo had somehow arranged it all.

Espejo seized the moment, framing the dripping mess on Austin's shoulder with his thumbs and outstretched index fingers like a cameraman. "Actually, *that* is the color we've been looking for," he told Austin, as Johnson and Vazquez dissolved in laughter.

Espejo also likes to describe another instance where the cost-cutting impulse might have resulted in a truly unfortunate outcome. "We had gone to Italy to pick out some of the stone for the façade when the quarry master asked me if we had any smaller installations we might need marble for. There was the matter of what to use to create the bottom of the plaza fountain, I said, but even I had decided that we would cast some kind of composite material. Marble would be just too expensive. But the quarry master pressed me on the design, and after I described it—a representation of a sand-rippled sea bottom—he shook his head. 'So you're going to cast three hundred different pieces, not one of them with the same dimensions? You'll have to build three hundred different molds. That's going to cost you a fortune.'"

"He took me to a spot in the quarry where there was this beautiful Travertine marble just the color of what we were wanting to replicate,"

Espejo recalls. "He explained that with new computer-driven saws they were now using to extract the marble, they could cut the pieces exactly to size and for way less than what all that molding and casting would have cost. In the end, we got a far more beautiful fountain that will last forever, and we saved enough money to use marble for the paving stones on the plaza too," Espejo says. "It's the same marble they used to line the Trevi Fountain in Rome, by the way."

These and similar stories are diverting, of course, but they are also emblematic of the new can-do spirit that had come to prevail on the project, uniting even those with differing attitudes and methods. Also in January of 2005 came the welcome news that the Florida Department of Transportation was in negotiations to purchase three parcels of land adjacent to the performing arts center that had been slated for development by private owners. The possibility that condos or office towers might end up looming over the performing arts center like the skyscrapers dwarfing the wizard's cottage in the classic film *Metropolis* had worried center supporters for years, but the cost for the trust to purchase the properties was out of the question. However, if the state purchased the parcels to allow for a widening of I-395, at least one issue would cancel out another. Whatever was decided about that freeway—whether it was to become a tunnel, a giant ditch, or a soaring overpass—it seemed now that the performing arts center would never live in the shadows of colossi.

"Thank God," Trust Chair Thomson announced. "The PAC buildings are going to change Miami. They need to be seen." The issue persists to the present, however, for at the time of this writing, one high-rise condominium project was under way just across the street north of the opera hall, with a second soon to begin groundbreaking just to the east, opposite the concert hall. In addition, yet another round of proposals for the endlessly proposed redesign of I-395 was called for in mid-2015, bringing revitalization to the phrase "in my lifetime."

Soon after word of the Department of Transportation's intention came, in March of 2005, the Performing Arts Center Foundation began a new type of donations drive intended to engage a far broader cross-section of Miami's citizenry than those with the spare six-, seven-, or eight-figure gifts to hand over. For as little as $50, it was announced, a donor would get on an e-mail list to carry news of late-breaking additions to the performance schedule, and $250 would ensure that one's name was etched into one of 12,012 terra-cotta paving stones covering the grand entrances to the main halls. A gift of $1,000 would allow entrance to one of the patrons' lounges during intermissions. "The time has come to let the public feel that this center is not just about rich people," Albert Milan, the foundation's executive director, told reporters.

More good news came in May of 2005, when Executive Director Hardy announced that the prestigious Cleveland Orchestra would enter into a ten-year agreement for a series of three-week residencies at the center beginning in January of 2007. The agreement was particularly meaningful, given the recent demise of the Florida Philharmonic, which had been slated as the center's resident symphony. Hardy termed the addition of the Cleveland Orchestra "a major jewel in our crown" and credited Dan Lewis, a former board member of the Florida Philharmonic and also a trustee of the Cleveland Orchestra, with helping make the connection.

Fears that the Cleveland Orchestra might arrive and find nowhere to play were stoked when an August issue of the *Herald* carried news of a shortage of laborers on the project. According to Assistant County Manager Bill Johnson, there were about 550 construction workers on the job, but, he said, "we need 250 more." Part of the problem was that competing projects in the downtown area were offering laborers up to thirty dollars an hour, while performing arts center jobs were paying twenty-two dollars. The shortage had the greatest impact on the exterior stone work, but Johnson said that would not affect plans for the center's opening. "We're still on schedule for completion [of construction] on August 4, 2006," he said.

However, by September 14, 2005, County Manager Burgess was back before county commissioners to announce that more money would in fact be needed for the 84-percent-completed project. He was asking for another $34.4 million, Burgess said, some $13 million of which would go for higher wages that would lure additional workers needed to complete the work on time. Another $11 million or so was needed to cover additional cost overruns caused by plans problems and associated change orders. Burgess also requested roughly $6 million to establish a contingency fund as well as another $3.4 million to hire specialty craftsmen for certain parts of the interior finish work, to correct various previous errors in construction, and to hire additional maintenance staff and security to correct a growing graffiti problem at the unfinished project. (Parker Thomson recalls a conversation of the period with Ron Austin as they viewed an example of a colorful bit of graffiti painted on one of the highest concrete slabs in the structure. "What are you going to do if you catch the guy?" Thomson wondered. Austin pointed at the spot, which was difficult for even experienced riggers to reach. "I'll hire him," Austin replied. "We need guys who will do anything to get the job done.")

For his part, Burgess proposed that most of the money to cover the additional costs would come not from the trusty convention development tax revenue stream, but from the City of Miami's Omni Area Redevelopment Area property tax revenues, which had been augmented in recent years by rising property values attributable to the performing arts center. Trust Chair Thomson vowed the group would do its part, pledging to raise an additional $1.5 million per year over the following twenty years. Whatever was necessary would be done, Thomson said. "It's crucial to get the PAC open on time. We have a lot of commitments coming up with the opening—Broadway Series contracts, bringing employees on line, and the like."

At that stage of the game in 2005, there was in fact little to be done but to keep calm and carry on. Critics grumbled, of course (County Commission Chairman Joe Martinez told one civic group the project had been a "fiasco from the get-go" financially), but as others pointed out, delays and cost overruns seemed the order of the day for such complicated projects. The recently opened Disney Hall in downtown Los Angeles was finished ten years behind schedule and at $164 million over its budget. And, by comparison, Miami's dual-hall performing arts center was a far more complex undertaking.

"There was a lot of talk about unnecessary cost overruns and contractors taking advantage," Ron Austin says, "but the truth of the matter is that Odebrecht was often floating millions of dollars in costs for months, waiting to be paid by the county for ordinary expenditures. They were bending over backward because the company wanted to establish a positive presence in the United States. When I came on board, the project had been essentially stalled for six months. Work was six hundred days behind schedule, and there were about $100 million in unpaid claims, most of them well-founded. The contractors ended up settling for about half of that, which I considered a bargain for the county. If there are any unsung heroes in this process, I would say it was Odebrecht."

In an October 30, 2005, interview, architect Pelli was asked by a *Herald* reporter if he took any responsibility for the project's running so far over budget and now pegged at $446.3 million. But Pelli was adamant: he was a designer, not a builder, and he had designed the project in accordance with guidelines established by the performing arts center and the county. As for the builders' contentions that inaccurate architectural drawings had caused most of the delays, Pelli responded, "The builder was just trying to build arguments to ask for more money from the county, and they were using every argument that they could."

In Pelli's eyes, the problem was the builders' lack of experience with such complicated structures. "We have had this experience before. They are invariably surprised at how much more complicated these buildings are than they had imagined. And once they are in that pickle, they will try to use every argument they can to try to be compensated for what they should have figured out earlier." In addition, Pelli explained, the county was somewhat complicit at every stage. When delays in construction were encountered, more time was wasted in trying to determine just how much the county was obligated to pay. Meantime, the clock would keep on ticking, and by the time an overrun was approved, the amount allocated was already insufficient. In the end, however, Pelli and his team were insistent that the project would rank among the finest in the world when completed.

"A lot more interesting and fun than Lincoln center," Pelli assured *Herald* columnist Fred Tasker during a January 11, 2006, VIP tour of the main halls. "The best thing is, we made no compromises," added Sherwood Weiser, Performing Arts Center Foundation Chairperson, "in design, acoustics, architecture. This will rank with the best in the world." As for the oft-maligned 120-foot-high Sears Tower (officially renamed the Art Deco Tower), Pelli would tell Tasker, "At the beginning, we thought it to be best for the Sears Tower to disappear. But I must say, I have grown to like it, to enjoy the juxtaposition, to have designed around it and have it become an element in the new plaza."

It is unclear whether Pelli had ever heard of Steve Clark's often voiced suggestions to Parker Thomson during the height of debate on the tower: "Parker, you just say the word, and I'll go over there and hop on a bulldozer some night, and by morning there won't be any tower to worry about." But Mitch Hirsch, design principal in charge of the project for Pelli's firm, provided further insight for the tower's value to the architects during an interview in 2017. "We always thought it was doable," he says of the tower's inclusion into the plans. "But as we began to fine-tune the design, the structure became interesting and useful to us as a centering element for the plaza. The plaza wraps around the tower in an integral way, and the café's being there helps involve pedestrians. The structure is from a different era than the great halls, but somehow it complements them."

Asked recently if he was being truthful when he told Tasker he had actually grown fond of the tower, Pelli himself was unequivocal: "Yes," he said, during a May 2017 interview. "I have come to like the vertical element in the composition. The Sears Tower is not a great, or a good, design, but it adds to the forms of the center. And it connects it to the past. It makes it richer.

At about the same time that Pelli was touring the nearly finished halls with Fred Tasker in 2006, reports surfaced that the Concert Association of Florida, one of the four remaining performing groups expected to be among the resident companies once the center opened, had been in talks with the performing arts center regarding the possibility of a merger between the two entities. The Concert Association, its finances troubled over the past several years, was proposing to turn over the management of its business affairs to the performing arts center, while maintaining its own creative board and programming autonomy, but the talks stalled, leaving the future of South Florida's principal booking agent for visiting dance and classical music presentations in doubt. The association's director, Judy Drucker, was nearing retirement at seventy, and there was no heir apparent in the wings for the organization. While Drucker's stature in the arts community was formidable, and folding in the Concert Association would have given the performing arts center enhanced booking expertise, the prospect of taking on that company's substantial debt was an obstacle.

Meanwhile, Weiser and others at the trust foundation were in the home stretch of fund-raising activities, with about $60 million of its $80-million-plus target achieved. The principal focus of the foundation was now on finding a donor who would contribute $20 million for overall naming rights to the center. There were still lesser opportunities for philanthropists, including naming rights to the plaza connecting the two main halls ($5 million) and the pedestrian bridge spanning Biscayne Boulevard ($2.5 million). But foundation leaders had narrowed their focus to four individuals and four corporations who had expressed an interest in naming rights to the performing arts center, and Sherwood Weiser was hopeful that a decision would be forthcoming by May 1, 2006.

Concerns turned somewhat more prosaic later in the spring, when Florida's Department of Transportation sent workers to the stretch of Biscayne Boulevard between the concert and opera halls to make what it considered a necessary modification to that section of architect Pelli's plaza. Because Biscayne Boulevard was a federal highway, the Department of Transportation said, rules dictated that the north-south lines— even as they passed through the plaza connecting the two main halls— would have to be divided by a bold, double yellow stripe. In addition, all lanes would have to be clearly marked by the type of white striping familiar to motorists. The fact that the solid plastic stripes did not exactly blend with Pelli's pavers was precisely the point, transportation officials said. Without the clear striping, motorists might get confused, it was said, and there could be all manner of sideswipes and head-on collisions where opera- and concert-goers were meant to tread.

Pelli spokesperson Roberto Espejo lamented the step, pointing out that his company had originally proposed integrating some form of lane markings into the paving design itself, but that had been rejected by the Department of Transporation as insufficient. "Just getting the pavers [on the street itself] was a big win for us," Espejo told reporters on March 22. Opined Frank Rollason, executive director of the Omni Redevelopment Agency, "I guess we in this county are too stupid to drive a block without a stripe."

At about the same time, announcement of a number of bookings for the upcoming season at the performing arts center gave some sense of what was in store for South Florida audiences. Though struggling,

Drucker's Concert Association announced ten acts for the center, including appearances by violinist Itzhak Perlman and the Boston Pops Esplanade Orchestra. Among those whom the performing arts center itself had booked were Woody Allen and his New Orleans Jazz Band and Grammy Award–winning singer Dianne Reeves.

In all, the center planned upwards of ninety events in the halls. It was Hardy's intention for the center to present about 40 percent of the events at the complex and the resident companies to present about 25 percent, with outside commercial producers, including Broadway Across America, accounting for the other 35 percent. Already set for the latter series were runs for *Wicked* and *Light in the Piazza*, among others.

It also seemed as though the much-ballyhooed ripple effect of the performing arts center's construction for the neighborhood was finally coming to fruition. A *Herald* story of April 30, 2006, counted twenty-two major residential and commercial projects under construction, approved, or proposed for the forty-square-block area bounded by I-395 on the south, Biscayne Bay to the east, Northeast Twentieth Street on the north, and the FEC railroad tracks on the west, the bounds of the Omni Community Redevelopment District. That number did not include a number of high-rise condominium projects planned for the west side of Biscayne Boulevard just south of I-395. There was concern that all this activity had been undertaken without the formulation of a cohesive master plan for the district, but it also seemed that the imminent arrival of the performing arts center had stirred considerable commercial interest in an area long deemed moribund.

Backers' spirits were soon enough leavened, however, when Assistant County Manager Bill Johnson appeared before county commissioners a few months before the opening. On Wednesday, May 10, 2006, Johnson announced that the cost of the project would regrettably be rising once again, "by a few million." Though Johnson did not clarify what "a few" meant, a memo from Johnson's boss, George Burgess, explained that the $10 million fund set aside for change orders from the additional $34.4 million granted the project by commissioners the previous September was nearly exhausted. Under questioning by commissioners, Johnson delivered the sobering news that the final cost of the project might not be known until the building was completed and all the claims from subcontractors had been submitted.

While Johnson's announcement occasioned some grumblings, the time was long past for any serious posturing. With a targeted completion date fewer than three months away and an opening set for October, the collective response was one of resigned determination. The end was very clearly in sight. Furthermore, some long-delayed public recognition finally came that May for the individual who had shepherded the project essentially from its very conception, when Miami-Dade College announced that it would award an honorary degree to Trust Chairman Parker D. Thomson. "Very nice of them," Thomson recalls. "It was the only honorary degree I ever got."

In late June came more heartening news when the Florida Department of Transportation finally decided that the yellow and white striping that had been laid across the intricate brickwork connecting the performing arts center's opera and concert halls could be taken off. In place of the striping—composed, thankfully, of heavy-duty plastic, not paint—a network of highly reflective yellow and white pavement markers would distinguish the lanes. For an agency generally seen as having about the same flexibility as the Internal Revenue Service, the decision seemed a monumental reversal.

News of one other vehicular-related matter was addressed when Performing Arts Center Executive Director Hardy announced in July that agreement had been reached with several parking lots in the area surrounding the center to guarantee about twenty-five hundred spaces each evening at a cost to patrons of fifteen dollars for self-parking and twenty dollars for valet parking. Though a sold-out show at both venues would theoretically mean forty-eight hundred attendees, Hardy believed the number of secured spaces was sufficient to handle the crowds. As he told the *Herald* on July 5, there was always the option of taking a cab or Metrorail, with its newly rechristened Omni–Performing Arts Center Station only a block north.

On July 19, 2006, long-awaited word came from the Performing Arts Center Foundation when Chairperson Sherwood Weiser announced that the Carnival Corporation was increasing its gift from $10 million to

$20 million, thus acquiring naming rights to the entire complex, which would be known as the Carnival Center for the Performing Arts. Additionally, Weiser said, the John S. and James L. Knight Foundation would be increasing its grant from $3 million to $10 million, and as a result would have the naming rights to the concert hall. The additional $17 million in gifts brought the foundation total essentially to its goal of $83.7 million.

While it was indeed welcome news to the performing arts center, the gifts also reawakened in some the old fears that the center would siphon away dollars from the philanthropic community that had previously supported the artistic companies meant to take residence in the center. "It's bad in the sense that some of the money that would have gone to us is going there," Mike Eidson, board chair of the Miami City Ballet, told a *Herald* reporter. "But it will be a beautiful place to perform," Eidson allowed. "We will be able to bring in a bigger audience that will make bigger donations." Indeed, as the story noted, the Miami City Ballet had already attracted a new sponsor, New York's U.S. Trust, because of the enhanced profile provided by its association with the new Miami performing arts center. "We would not have gotten that gift if we were not going [to the center]," said Eidson.

19

· · · · · · · ·

With the Carnival Center finally named and construction virtually completed, the center—without Ron Austin having been hurled out of Bill Johnson's office to the pavement—in fact received its temporary certificate of occupancy on August 4, 2006. An impossible dream had, some thirty-five years after the germ of its inception, become reality.

"It felt like giving birth," recalls Pelli associate Roberto Espejo. "I'd been threatened by subcontractors I don't know how many times, had a picture frame broken over my head in my office, had my tires slit, but, when we got that CO, I thought, 'I'd do it all again in a heartbeat.'" Finally, those who had dreamed of a performing arts center in Miami could at last turn their decades of apprehension into something more resembling anticipation.

"It means we're going to make the opening," Trust Chair Parker Thomson told reporters with characteristic understatement when inspectors signed off on the project. "It's been a long time coming. I'm thrilled." That the date for completion of construction had remained firm since County Manager George Burgess had gone to the commission for added funding in 2004 seemed little short of a miracle to some observers. But as Assistant County Manager Bill Johnson, long the commission's point man on construction, said, "We're beyond excited. We're ecstatic."

On August 18, 2006, the Cleveland Orchestra mounted the stage of the Knight Concert Hall for a series of rehearsals to help acoustics designer Russell Johnson fine-tune the intricate system he had put in place, including the acoustical canopy hovering above the stage, the reverberation panels in the walls that could open and close to suit the performances, and heavy draping that could be lowered or raised to dampen or amplify sound.

The aim was to avoid the auditory nightmare that had taken place at the 2001 opening of Philadelphia's Verizon Hall, where Johnson's firm Artec had also done the acoustical design. However, that opening—including the use of those sand-filled reverberation panels—had been forced upon the acousticians long before they had pronounced their work complete, and Johnson was confident that no such issues would mar the first notes savored by the public in the Knight Concert Hall. What the firm was aiming for, said Artec partner Tateo Nakajima in a *Herald* interview with Fred Tasker, was a sound "so complex and yet so clear that even when the music stops, everybody's holding their breath, and you still hear its reverberation in the air."

The preliminary acoustical work was capped on Sunday, August 20, when a crowd of about one thousand invited guests, including State Senator Gwen Margolis, took seats in the concert hall, their live bodies helping to "tune the house" as the orchestra rehearsed. The Cleveland Orchestra's musical director, Franz Welser-Most, told reporters the sound was as good as that of the orchestra's home, Severance Hall, adding, "I think it's going to be one of the great halls in the country." Trust Chair Parker Thomson chimed in, "It's only the first day, but I can't be anything but very hopeful. We're off to a great start."

The prospect of an opening was one thing, but as last-minute preparations continued, there were some concerns expressed over how the center, beleaguered by cost overruns, would be able to keep itself going. When a draft of the first year's operating budget predicted a shortfall of $2.7 million, Executive Director Hardy pared the figure down to about $550,000. But as he admitted to reporters on August 13, "We have no benchmarks. Nobody will really know what it costs to run this center until we start operating it."

Commercial acts booking the hall, Hardy said, would be paying about eight thousand dollars per night in rent, while resident companies would pay about three-quarters of that. Still, such fees would not cover costs without significant subsidies from some source. And while the Performing Arts Center Trust Foundation had intended to have a $21 million endowment in place by opening night—providing some $640,000 per year in earnings toward annual operating costs—the amount of private funds needed to match ever-escalating construction costs meant that only $5.4 million of that contingency fund was in place. But despite all that, Assistant County Manager Bill Johnson asserted that there was no chance the county was going to walk away from the performing arts center. The lights would stay on, and the shows would continue.

As anyone who has ever planned a wedding, a bar mitzvah, or a gala of any sort knows, there comes a time when all the fretting must simply be put aside and be replaced with a focus on that which elicited all the fuss in the first place. In this case, it was the grand opening of a community's monument to culture that had been more than twenty-five years in the making, and the chief concern of the center's artistic director, Justin Macdonnell, was that the opening weekend would mirror the same eclectic mix of attractive, substantial, and broad-based programming that would distinguish the performing arts center for all the years to come.

Set for the evening of Thursday, October 5, 2006, in the Knight Concert Hall was a concert featuring Miami icon Gloria Estefan, and to include appearances by Bernadette Peters and Andy Garcia, a program to be emceed by Quincy Jones and produced by Emilio Estefan. On Friday night the Knight stage was to be given over to classical presentations by the New World Symphony and the Concert Association of Florida, including the world premiere of an orchestral fanfare by Steven Mackey. Saturday night would mark the opening of the Sanford and Dolores Ziff Ballet Opera House, with the Florida Grand Opera performing the second act of *La Boheme* and the Miami City Ballet presenting the third act of Tchaikovsky's *The Sleeping Beauty*, with those two performances interspersed with presentations by Broadway legend Harvey Fierstein. On Sunday, the public would be invited to tour the center complex at no charge, while bands and performance groups offering everything from hip-hop to jazz to reggae dotted the theaterscape.

"It was such a great feeling of community accomplishment," says Roberto Espejo—who had during the construction of the complex instituted a popular monthly series of cultural concerts for the construction crews, called "Hardhat Concerts." Recalls Espejo of the lead-up to the opening, "One evening while we were getting the last things ready, one of the electricians, a Haitian guy, pulled up on the plaza in his van, with his wife and kids inside. They all got out, and he walked over to one of the electrical panels and starts fiddling around, and all of a sudden the lights go on everywhere, and the water starts running in the fountain, and the kids are like awestruck: 'Dad, did you do this?' they're asking. And the guy points at me and says, 'He designed it. I just did the work.' I felt pretty good."

As for the buildings themselves, all had finally taken shape. While some remained perplexed by the unconventional shape of Pelli's buildings—"mountains of the arts for a flat landscape," the architect described them—no one could argue the fact that he had avoided a traditional architectural bugaboo by creating a virtually "backless" design. Most such structures are designed as rectangular boxes, and while they might have a striking front side with a gleaming entrance, the side walls were typically blank monoliths, with rear sides resembling warehouse loading docks. Pelli, however, had situated the two buildings diagonally on their sites and had wrapped the sides of both buildings with attractive paving and pedestrian-friendly colonnades.

Additionally, he had clipped the corners off the back-side loading areas, enhancing those utilitarian areas with pavers and planters. Both buildings receded from their bases as they gained in height, not only creating the "mountain" effect that Pelli prized, but also alleviating the sense of looming mass a pedestrian approaching such a sizable complex might experience. One need only take a walking tour from the Cultural Arts Complex to the Arsht Center to experience the difference.

The $4.2 million investment by the county's Art in Public Places Trust had also paid its dividends. The plaza connecting the two halls was enlivened by the fountains, pavers, and stone benches designed by Anna Valentina Murch; and sculptor Gary Moore's installation of the *Pharaoh's Dance* plaza—inspired by the music of Miles Davis and placed at the southwest corner of the opera house—had drawn notice from arts critics at the *New York Times*, where it was described as "An Egyptian Oasis in Miami." Murch's fountain, by the way, had been long championed by Parker Thomson, not always a fan of often ill-maintained county fountains. "The thing about this one is it looks good even when there's no water in it," Thomson said of Murch's design.

Inside, most everyone was agreed that no vestige of "value engineering" was apparent. The soaring glass lobby walls of both entrances were inviting from outside and expansive from within, and the detailed epoxy-covered terrazzo floors and etched glass-panel stair railings installed by Miami artist Jose Bedia were a rich complement to the lobby of the opera house. The auditorium of the opera house had been designed in the classic horseshoe shape found in many European forebears, though Pelli had purposefully understated the use of wood trim and fabric in order to drive attention toward the drama on stage—once Robert Zakanitch's intricately embroidered Hibiscus Curtain, also funded by the Art in Public Places program, had been raised, that is.

The theater of the symphony hall—the only dedicated concert hall ever built in South Florida, it should be noted—was far more dramatic, with some likening an entrance into the auditorium to that of walking into a giant, intricately fashioned wooden box. Even the massive reverberation doors, forming a kind of hall within a hall, had been dressed in delicate fabric and wood lattice to make them seem almost delicate in nature. And the 250-seat black-box theater, determinedly utilitarian in most respects, was enlivened by the installation of Cuban master Cundo Bermudez's colorful *Ways of Performing* floor-to-ceiling mural just outside its entrance.

The grand opening was in fact preceded by a "soft" opening of the Ziff Ballet Opera House on Tuesday evening, September 26, 2006, when Miami-area theater lovers attended a presentation of the Tony Award–winning musical *The Light in the Piazza*. While the 2,400-seat house was nearly full, fears of traffic gridlock and parking problems did not materialize, and audience members proclaimed themselves more than satisfied with the experience. "It's stunning," architecture student Cesar Rodriguez-Campo told the *Herald* as he left the performance. "And I have to say I'm proud that two of Cuba's most important artists [muralist Bermudez and terrazzo/railings designer Bedia] are represented in the new center. That says a lot about Miami recognizing its own."

As to what the placement of this set of cultural jewels would mean to Miami's future, no one could be sure, but as October 5 neared, hopes were certainly high. As Miami-Dade Cultural Affairs Council Director Michael Spring put it to the *Herald*'s Tasker, "I don't think it's fair to say we're going to be the next Paris, because Paris has a few hundred years on us. But I think we can set our aspirations to be a twenty-first-century cultural capital."

As the curtain was readied to go up on that appointed Thursday, the *Herald*'s Fabiola Santiago interviewed Trust Chair Parker Thomson, who had been at the helm of the Performing Arts Center Trust since its inception in 1991. "One of the first things we did when we created the trust was deal with the concern that it would kill all the other performing arts venues," Thomson said. "We explained to people that that is not the way it works. You build and it raises the water for all the boats," he continued, pointing out that along with monies approved to build the performing arts center had come $25 million to refurbish downtown's venerable Gusman Theater and the Colony Theater on Miami Beach's Lincoln Road, among other outlying venues.

Thomson also scoffed at the notion that the creation of a performing arts center was an elitist undertaking. "Performance art is an arena that brings people together," he said. And as to the lack of a dedicated parking garage attached to the center, a feature axed early on for budgetary reasons, Thomson was philosophic. "Sometimes things turn out for the best. Parking garages are the ugliest buildings I have ever seen."

There was an "only-in-Miami" moment outside the complex on opening night, when a sizable contingent of Miami policemen staged a raucous protest over pay and working conditions from behind barricades erected to keep them at bay, prompting Parker Thomson to turn to Michael Spring to say, "You know, it really is a miracle this got done." But by most accounts, the evening was little short of triumphant. A sold-out crowd that had paid five hundred dollars per seat watched Miami Heat stars Dwyane Wade, Alonzo Mourning, and Shaquille O'Neal come—basketballs thumping—across the stage of the Knight Concert Hall just as orchestra conductor Jose Antonio Molina raised his baton, and Gloria Estefan roused the crowd with her typical energetic renditions of Latin-inspired pop. Bernadette Peters was in high-vamp form, delivering vocals while draped across a shimmering grand piano, and Andy Garcia, Albita, Arturo Sandoval, and others had some concert-goers dancing in the aisles to an over-the-top rendition of "Guantanamera."

One *Herald* critic complained that the sound seemed better tuned to the smaller and individual acts than for the full orchestra numbers but lauded the three-hour-plus show for its diversity and energy. Longtime performing arts center supporters were unqualified in their enthusiasm, however. Cuban-born Andy Garcia, whose family brought him to Miami when he was five, told the audience, "I'm proud to say we finally have a center that can compete with any house in the world." Lin Arison, widow of Carnival founder Ted Arison, flew from her home in Israel to attend. "This is a once-in-a-lifetime experience," she told reporters. "Ted would have been proud."

Untiring fund-raising chief Sherwood Weiser called the event, attended by such notables as Governor Jeb Bush, Miami Heat Coach Pat Riley, University of Miami President Donna Shalala, and even Jackie Gleason's widow, Marilyn, "a magnificent night for the community. It defines the future of Miami." And Parker Thomson added, "Does anybody need more?" When a reporter pressed Thomson to say just how long he had been working on the project, his wife, Vann, intervened to say, "It feels like a hundred years."

Critical reaction to the sound of Friday night's presentations by Michael Tilson Thomas, conducting the New World Symphony, and Russian violinist Maxim Vengerov, presented by the Concert Association of Florida, was far more laudatory, with the *Herald* calling the evening "an acoustic triumph." Reaction to the debut of the Ziff Opera House on Saturday night was more about the spectacle surrounding the event than details of the performances by the Florida Grand Opera, Miami City Ballet, and actor Harvey Fierstein. The eighteen hundred patrons who paid one thousand dollars per ticket were treated to pre-performance cocktails and hors d'oeuvres in the lobby, then to an after-party in a big-band-themed tent designed by Barton G. and erected in a parking lot just across the street from the theater.

The centerpiece for Sunday's public celebration of the center's opening was the newly christened Parker and Vann Thomson Plaza for the Arts connecting the two main halls. Seven stages were erected about the vast fountain-featured open space for "Target GlobalBeat," which brought together such diverse musical styles as rhythm and blues, hip-hop, tango, calypso, reggae, *son Cubano*, and more—even fiddler James Kelly, who had recently been named Irish television's "musician of the year." Those interviewed by reporters lauded the center and its concept, though some echoed the complaints of the previous evenings' paying crowds that parking was a headache. Still, having a performing arts center in downtown Miami was long overdue, said South Dade resident Bill Rutan. "I'm tired of going to Broward."

In a lengthy, well-reasoned review of October 8, 2006, *Herald* architecture critic Beth Dunlop proclaimed the Carnival Center "an extraordinary gift to the community, an elegant and sophisticated home for the arts." She termed the architecture "pleasing" from within and "perplexing" from without, opining that the look of the complex was far more dazzling while lit up by night than it was by day. Still, said Dunlop, perhaps the visual appeal of the exterior might grow on one, much as a modern symphony might: difficult at first, then ever more seductive, more melodic, more embracing.

Dunlop found the interior of the Knight Concert Hall to be "exquisite, restrained and dignified," lauding the huge modernist chandelier as a "pièce de résistance," part art and part illumination. She also found the "festoon lights" outlining balcony edges, stair strings, and columns a seductive and spectacular touch. The interior of the opera house was also "simple and elegant" in Dunlop's view, though she reported that some who had sat high in the fourth tier of the hall experienced a hint of vertigo looking down at the stage. However, she said, the view southward toward the Port of Miami and Biscayne Bay from the balcony outside those higher tiers of the Ziff was nothing short of glorious.

Dunlop was not so sure that the expense of the stone façades was warranted, saying that one had to stand close to appreciate the textures that distinguished the paler hues of granite from concrete. Overall, Dunlop's assessment was more than positive, though she concluded by hoping that the grander dreams of the center's patrons would in fact come to fruition: that lovers of culture at all levels of income and from diverse backgrounds would fill the seats and that the presence of the center would be a beacon drawing businesses, cafés, and restaurants whose patrons would one day fill the nearby streets.

Whatever one might proclaim regarding the architecture, the acoustics, the interiors, the sprawling plaza, and the carefully wrought colonnades, however, the undeniable truth was this: an idea spawned in 1979 and seemingly beset by every conceivable obstacle of political and financial type had finally materialized into a reality. The impossible performing arts center in Miami had at last come to be.

20

. . . .

Though patrons and supporters who attended the 2006 opening events at the Carnival Center came away in large part excited and enthralled, there were some signs, even during the gala week, that the honeymoon for Miami's performing arts center might not be too lengthy or completely untroubled. Ticket sales for the Gloria Estefan concert that opened the 2,200-seat Knight Concert Hall totaled 1,755. Sales for the New World Symphony performance the following evening came to 1,433. On October 7, opening night at the Ziff Opera House brought 1,855 to that 2,400-seat hall. Sunday's multivenue, multifaceted all-day open house at the center was by far the best attended, with almost 14,000 patrons counted by center staff. Though the lack of any sellout could be attributed to ticket prices ranging from $250–1,000 for the evening performances, the numbers nonetheless suggested hard work ahead for the center's programmers and marketing staff.

In the ensuing months, there were other issues to contend with, including long waits for valet-parked cars, the lack of a sufficient number of ushers, and a number of falls taken by patrons in both major halls that required the installation of additional lighting strips and other precautions. The most troublesome issue, however, remained that of ticket sales. A *Herald* story of January 28, 2007, nearly three months and one hundred performances after the center's opening, reported that operations were already nearly $1 million behind projections. While the offerings of the Miami City Ballet, the New World Symphony, and the Florida Grand Opera exceeded expectations, with the latter two selling at more than 90 percent of capacity, overall ticket sales were at 59 percent, or about 5 percent below the center's projections. Figures for the Concert Association of Florida were particularly disappointing, with sales and subscriptions somewhere around 50 percent of capacity for the group's three programs. Ticket sales for the Carnival Center's own presentation of the Merce Cunningham Dance Company, a group not well known to Miami audiences, were hovering at 12 percent.

A *New York Times* story of February 4, 2007, gave high marks to the center's design, proclaiming the center well-integrated with its surroundings and praising the courtyard as "handsome" and the connecting pedestrian bridge "elegant." The writer also found the acoustics of both halls more than serviceable, with those of the Ziff Opera Hall apparently superior. However, the story also lamented the 2003 demise of the Florida Philharmonic Orchestra and referred to lingering hard feelings by Philharmonic members feeling displaced by the Cleveland Orchestra. And it also offered a recap of the disappointing ticket-sales figures, opining that the latter might have something to do with the parking issues: "after the symphony concert [by the Cleveland Orchestra], a long line of patrons waited outside on the balmy night for valets."

There was further dour news later in February when Carnival Center Executive Director Hardy appeared before the county commission to report that additional claims by construction subcontractors had resulted in an additional $12.5 million in costs, bringing the total to just short of $473 million. Commissioners voted to cover the costs by authorizing a bank loan to be secured by future convention development tax monies, and also agreed to consider a similar request from the Performing Arts Center Foundation, which was seeking authorization for a $16 million loan of its own, in order to fulfill its promised share of the construction budget. Pledges were on the books that would cover the amount, but some would not mature for up to nine years, while the construction payments were already overdue. At the same time Hardy also announced that the operating budget for the following year had been increased to $27 million, up from the estimate of $22.5 million for year one.

By the end of the center's first year of operations, the financial situation had only become more daunting, closing with a $2.4 million deficit, much of which was attributable to losses on shows produced by the performing arts center itself, which averaged about 43 percent of capacity. Ultimately, the blame came to rest on Executive Director Hardy, whose original salary of $175,000 had risen—in accordance with his contract—to $326,255 over his tenure. In late October of 2007, the Performing Arts Center Trust, with new board chair Ricky Arriola replacing retired chief Parker Thomson, voted unanimously to fire Hardy and programming chief Justin Macdonnell. Hired to replace Hardy in the position of interim chief executive officer was Lawrence J. Wilker, former president of the Kennedy Center in Washington, D.C. Hopes were high that Wilker could reproduce his success at the Kennedy Center, where he had resigned in 2000 after a decade at the helm, doubling annual attendance to nearly two million, also doubling the number of performances to some thirty-three hundred and increasing annual giving from $13 million to $38 million. The $40,000 monthly salary of Wilker was to be covered by a donation from Adrienne Arsht, a member of the Performing Arts Center Foundation, and whose name arts supporters in South Florida were soon to become far more familiar with.

One of the issues that contributed to the first-year deficit was lackluster marketing. As Parker Thomson told a reporter for the *New York Times* for a December 29, 2007, story, "A lot of people don't even know there's a cultural center there."

Furthermore, beyond the immediate need to schedule programming that would increase attendance was the prospect of increasing the size of the trust endowment meant to cover future operating deficits. Though the endowment was to have reached $10.75 million by opening day and $16 million by its first anniversary, there was only $3.65 million in the fund at that time. Wilker spoke to the same *New York Times* reporter of the difficulty of making any center into a world-class facility instantaneously and of the need to increase the sense of community ownership of the center, perhaps through more significant donations from the Hispanic community. But as he cautioned, "This won't happen overnight."

Added Edward Villella, then seventy-one and still director of the Miami City Ballet, "All of us have to embrace this Carnival thing . . . our survival depends upon it. It will either help us or kill us."

*   *   *

Indeed, those were trying days for an enterprise that had been thirty-five years in the making and scarcely a year in operation. Significant problems abounded; leadership had shifted; and doubters were clamoring. Repeating an age-old refrain, County Commissioner Javier Souto groused while Director Hardy's raise was being debated in October, "I would raise the salary fifty cents so they can drink some coffee and wake up to how people feel. If there's a vote today in Miami-Dade County, this thing wouldn't pass."

Such was the atmosphere into which Mr. Wilker arrived late in 2007. "I had been friends with Woody Weiser for many years," Wilker recalls, "and I had actually served on a panel in Miami about twenty years before, when it was being debated just what the PAC ought to look like, but I didn't know many people in the city, and I hadn't kept up with what was going on down there. When Woody called me up to ask if I would come down and lend a hand for about six months to try and get things back on track, I had just divested myself of some theaters I was involved in operating, and so I said, 'Sure.'"

As Wilker told the reporter for the *Times,* after he had taken the position, he saw programming as the key issue to turn around the center's fortunes. "The building was there," he says. "The issue was how to get people from the community to experience it." And though Wilker didn't know much about Miami, he immediately set about making connections with community leaders, talking about the kinds of programs that would draw that extremely diverse populace to the place. "We established the Gospel Sunday concert series," Wilker says, "along with Family Day programming and put on a wide array of Latino musical presentations."

Asked recently if he feels there was a turning point in his efforts, Wilker points to a set of bilingual concerts by diva Celia Cruz presented that spring. "I had to appear before the county commission to keep the members updated on our progress," Wilker recalls. "Right after the Celia Cruz concert, as I walked into the chambers, one of the council members rushed up and gave me a hug. That's when I began to think I was doing something right." When the center was able to successfully stage a two-month run of Doug Berky's improvisational production *No Show* that summer, another myth—that Miami audiences would not support theatrical programming out of season—was also dispelled.

Perhaps the most stirring moment of Wilker's tenure came less than two weeks following that glum year-end wrap-up in the *New York Times,* however, when that very newspaper published the somewhat astonishing news under the understated headline, "Gift for Miami Arts." The reference was to the announcement of Thursday, January 10, 2008, that changed everything. Adrienne Arsht—former chairwoman of Miami's TotalBank, which sold to a competitor earlier in 2007 for $300 million—had donated $30 million to the Performing Arts Center Trust.

The announcement of Arsht's gift came as quite the surprise to county commissioners, who learned of the arrangement only hours before the announcement. In fact, the formal documents were not signed until all parties arrived for the news conference. However, Weiser and performing arts center leaders had been working to bring the donation in for a number of weeks. In December, when they sent word to Carnival that they would like to arrange a meeting of some importance, Carnival Chief Operating Officer Howard Frank told reporters the company had no clue what was impending. "We joked," Frank said, "what is it going to cost us now?"

One key to the arrangement was a long-standing relationship between Ms. Arsht and Woody and Judy Weiser. Arsht, board member of both the Lincoln and Kennedy Centers and the widow of Myer "Mike" Feldman, wealthy Washington, D.C., attorney and former advisor to Presidents Kennedy and Johnson, had become acquainted with the Weisers in the early 1990s through a mutual interest in the American Ballet Theatre. Arsht often visited Miami when the American Ballet Theatre appeared at Judy Drucker–sponsored performances and learned of hopes for a Miami performing arts center from the Weisers during the early days of its planning. In 1996, Feldman turned over control of Miami's TotalBank to Arsht, who moved to the city and became involved with the work of the Performing Arts Center Trust, and in fact had already donated $250,000 for the Anna Murch–designed fountains in the center's plaza. "Adrienne had been involved with the project from early on," Parker Thomson says. "She was as interested as anyone in seeing the center shine."

As a result of her work with the Lincoln and Kennedy Centers, Arsht was well aware of the great difficulties involved in operating such sizable cultural centers. "You've got a huge set of buildings owned by the government, funded partly by private funds and partly by tax monies, with a governing board appointed by politicians . . . it's just a recipe for disaster," Arsht says. It was her suggestion that Lawrence Wilker might be able to right the ship at the Carnival Center, though even she sensed that time was running out.

"I sold TotalBank in July of 2007," Arsht recalls, "and in November, as Hardy was leaving and Larry was coming in, I had gone to Spain to meet with the new owners. I already had it in my mind that the center was about two months short of closing, so I made a transatlantic call to Woody Weiser."

Arsht's question to Weiser was simple: "What's it going to take to save the place?"

"Thirty-five million," was Weiser's response, using a figure that Parker Thomson had said the naming rights to the center might fetch.

"That's too much," Arsht told Weiser. "I'll give you thirty."

"I'll have to check with Carnival," Weiser told her, but it was no secret that much of the enthusiasm for that organization's support of the center had always come from the deceased Ted Arison. In short order, the Carnival Corporation agreed to relinquish its naming rights, allowing the complex to be renamed the Adrienne Arsht Center for the Performing Arts of Miami-Dade County. The monies were to come in three installments, $13 million at once, $7 million additional in 2009, and the remaining $10 million in 2010. The funds would allow repayment of a $14 million bank loan taken out in 2007 to cover a shortfall in the trust's share of construction costs, make up the lingering deficit in operating costs, and provide a sufficient endowment for future working capital.

As Carnival's Howard Frank told a *Herald* reporter at the time the announcement was finally made public in February of 2008, "How do we not do this? This is a great thing for the community and a great thing for the performing arts center." Under the new terms, the company's gift to the center would revert to a total of $10 million, and it would retain naming rights to the "black-box" theater, the former Sears Tower, and the pedestrian bridge (though plaques at either end of the structure today commemorate long-standing bridge champion Stuart Blumberg's fight to make it a reality).

As it turns out, there had been one glitch that turned up the very morning that the announcement was to be made. "Greenberg Traurig [a prominent Miami law firm] was representing me, and all of this had been going on in secrecy for various reasons for nearly two months," Arsht recalls. "As I was getting ready to go downtown for the announcement, the lawyers called and told me they couldn't find the actual agreement that would allow the county to rename the center. We're advising you not to make this announcement and not to sign anything," they said. "If you go ahead, you'll be doing it on your own, without our counsel."

To Arsht, that advice was a waste of lawyerly breath. "The train has left the station," she told her attorneys, and a few hours later she went public with her gift.

Certainly, the infusion of cash from Ms. Arsht was a godsend to the struggling center's balance sheet, but just as important was the message that Arsht's donation sent to the public and political communities of Miami. "It is impossible to overstate the difference that Adrienne Arsht made in stabilizing the center," says Lawrence Wilker. "Without her, I am not sure the place would still be operating today."

Both Michael Spring and Parker Thomson agree. Almost in unison during a recent conversation, they called Arsht's gift "the tipping point."

"I am not sure the center would have closed in two months without the gift," Arsht says today, "but I do know that at long last the performing arts center was no longer a live electrical wire that the commissioners had to worry about any longer."

Certainly, Arsht's generosity was a resounding stamp of approval for a project that had taken its share of lumps since the 2001 groundbreaking and before, and of further note was the fact that the gift had come from an individual who had called South Florida home for scarcely more than a decade. County Mayor Carlos Alvarez formally praised Arsht's generosity before commissioners (two of whom rose to offer proposals to her), though he took the opportunity to remind those in attendance that the performing arts center had always been intended as a public-private enterprise and that he would like to see more individuals following her lead.

For his part, new Center CEO Wilker added, "I hope that people will see the center in a new light." And Arsht, who had fought to carve out a place for herself in the largely male-driven centers of influence in Miami, had a direct challenge for her adopted community. "It is for you that this is being done," she told the *Herald*. "Now it's your responsibility to take it forward."

Indeed, the center did begin to move forward. Interim CEO Wilker appeared before county commissioners on April 14, 2008, to present an interim financial report with welcome news: operations from October through February of the second year of operations showed a $1.5 million surplus. Part of the surplus derived from a $622,000 operations grant from the State of Florida, but another $800,000 came from an increase from the Arsht-infused Performing Arts Center Foundation. Wilker and his staff had also managed to trim about $700,000 from salaries, utilities, and other expenses and had also increased average attendance at center-sponsored events from the opening year's 41 percent to more than 80 percent.

Wilker, who had agreed to extend his tenure through the end of the calendar year (with Ms. Arsht agreeing to pick up the donor's portion of the tab), also instituted a full summer programming slate and announced that his other programming efforts had resulted in $3.5 million in ticket sales and $1 million in profit, welcome news to commissioners. In December of 2008, Wilker retired and was replaced by M. John Richard, chief operating officer at the New Jersey Performing Arts Center in Newark, where he had served for twenty years. In terms of scope, Richard's experience was comparable to what he would face in Miami. The Newark center was costing about $30 million per year to operate, while the Miami center budget was nearly $27 million. In addition, Richard had faced similar political pressures in Newark: a significant proportion of the largely Hispanic and African American inner-city residents had complained from the beginning that a cultural center would benefit only the wealthy, while suburbanites regarded the prospect of going into downtown Newark after nightfall as a near-suicidal notion.

Richard, however, was confident. "My DNA is world-class, community-based organizations, and they don't have to be mutually exclusive categories," he said at the time of his appointment.

"I want this to be our CEO for the next five or ten years," added Trust Chair Ricky Arriola. As of this writing, some nine years later, Richard remained as Arsht CEO.

21

· · · · · · · · ·

The impact of the Arsht Center upon the South Florida community was predicted to be nigh onto transformational, both culturally and economically, though some scoffed that the mere presence of a pair of buildings dedicated to the presentation of theater and music could never effect significant change in such a large and diverse community. Posturing politicians were fond of lumping the prospect of a performing arts center supported by public funds in the same categories as subsidized sports arenas and theme parks built on public lands. And to be perfectly fair, there are still many taxpayers and citizens whose only acquaintance with the center is a passing glance at a pair of oddly shaped buildings as they walk past or zoom by on nearby I-395, which has yet to be buried or submerged or wished away. Grumbles persist over the Arsht Center's elevator speed, parking proximity, and valet efficiency. And to be sure, there remain pockets of undeveloped land close by Cesar Pelli's "mountains by the bay."

But the changes wrought on both the physical and cultural landscape of the community are demonstrable and significant. Auto dealership empire builder Ron Esserman, involved with fund-raising for the project from the beginning, does not hesitate in estimating the value of the 570,00-square-foot Arsht Center—its Knight Hall stage said to be the nation's second-largest—to the community at large. "It's the most important thing we've ever done," he says.

"The Arsht Center is a cultural crown jewel for Miami," says Cuban-born musician and producer Emilio Estefan, winner of nineteen Grammy Awards. "It symbolizes our diversity in music, theater, and dance, and it was an incredible honor for me to produce the inaugural show there." Former Pelli associate Roberto Espejo adds, "The center ignited a cultural revolution in a town that so desperately needed one. Cesar was right, and so was Parker Thomson. They're like the godfathers or the Pilgrims, in that the center gave birth to the concept that Miami was in fact a place for culture." Espejo speaks as a member of a Cuban emigrant family, though his father took the family to Galesburg, Illinois (for a medical residency), when they left their homeland. "My dad never got used to the fact there were no Cubans in Galesburg—he'd have been far more comfortable in Miami. And look around today: we have an acoustically perfect concert hall that adapts to any type of performance; we've got Museum Park [housing the acclaimed Perez Art Museum and Collection at the east end of the former Bicentennial Park] and so much more going on downtown these days."

One of the things "going on" referred to by Espejo is the Phillip and Patricia Frost Museum of Science, two blocks south of the Arsht on Biscayne Boulevard, on the opposite end of the Bicentennial Park site occupied by the Perez Art Museum. Though the Museum of Science project encountered its own financial ups and downs, the $305 million undertaking opened in 2017, at long last creating a triumvirate of cultural bastions deemed essential by supporters for cities aspiring to cultural prominence. Had the Arsht not paved the way, many feel, the art and science museums would not have come to be.

Eugenie Birch, codirector of the Penn Institute for Urban Research, has written extensively about the impact of "urban anchors," institutions that make urban life more attractive and that also attract economic development, often making the difference between oblivion and revival. "They contribute to urban reinvention and civic pride," Birch says, "and attract knowledge-industry workers and urban spenders. They often fill important vacuums when footloose industries leave a city." Universities, hospitals, and sports stadiums are the entities typically identified as anchors, Birch says, but her work has also focused on the impact of arts and cultural institutions such as the Art Institute of Chicago, Philadelphia's Kimmel Center, Atlanta's Woodruff Center, and the Arsht Center in Miami.

In a 2014 paper, "Arts and Culture Anchor Institutions as Urban Anchors," for the Penn Institute for Urban Research series of case studies, Birch points out that total property values for the Omni Redevelopment District increased from $247 million in 1998 to $1.4 billion in 2010, with corresponding tax revenues paid to the city and county climbing from $700,000 to $13.8 million. And between the time the first shovel of earth was turned on the project and her writing, thirty-five thousand new condominium units were open or under construction within a fifteen-block radius.

"It was difficult, trying to balance the needs and the desires of four distinct performing arts groups and a very diverse community, but I think we have left that legacy," adds Stuart Blumberg, referring to the motivation that first led him to seek appointment from Sherman Winn to the trust committee back in 1991. "Of course, I am proud that the [Blumberg] bridge is there, but I am also pleased that at a couple of points along the way, when critics were worried the monies would never materialize from the bed tax, and questions arose as to the feasibility of the project, I was able to point out that as much as an additional $117 million, and more, was actually rolling in. There could have been no better use for those monies."

By the end of 2015, the center had completed its eighth consecutive year in the black, with a $40-million-plus budget, 162 employees, and 508 events drawing more than four hundred thousand people to performances in the three main theaters—the Ziff Opera Hall, the Knight Concert Hall, and the 300-seat Carnival Studio Theater. Performances also take place in the Peacock Rehearsal Studio and Education Center, a 35,000-square-foot space with seating for as many as 270, and at times on the spacious Parker and Vann Thomson Plaza for the Arts, bracketed by the Carnival Pedestrian Bridge to the north and the Carnival (Sears) Tower to the south.

At the time of this writing, the main floor of the tower now houses the ultra-urbane Café at Books and Books, opened by popular Miami bookseller Mitchell Kaplan late in 2014. On Monday nights noted Café Chef Alan Susser was offering up a popular farm-to-table meal with communal seating outdoors on the plaza. And on an upper level of the opera house is Brava by Brad Kilgore, an upscale one-hundred-seat restaurant with a view of the downtown skyline, where both ticket-holders and the general public can enjoy artistically presented cuisine on performance nights. Kilgore, a James Beard Award finalist, was dividing his time between the new venue and his noted restaurant Alter, located just fifteen blocks to the north in Wynwood.

Though the Florida Philharmonic had disbanded in 2003 and the long-troubled Concert Association of Florida collapsed into bankruptcy in 2009 following a forty-two-year run, the Cleveland Orchestra continued its annual three-week residency at the Arsht, and the New World Symphony (along with its attendant America's Orchestral Academy presentations), the Florida Grand Opera, and the Miami City Ballet continued as resident companies. The center was presenting a number of programs, including the popular Broadway in Miami Series, Jazz Roots, the Knight Masterworks Season, the Ziff Classical Music Series, the Ziff Dance Series, Theater Up Close, Live at Knight, Flamenco Festival, Free Gospel Sundays, the Carnival Theater–based Summer Shorts, and Weekend Family Fest. If that were not enough, every Monday found a farmers market set up on Thomson Plaza or on the entryway to the Ziff Opera House.

One of his initial challenges was to replace the programming vacuum left by the Concert Association's demise, Arsht Center CEO Richard said. "It meant coming up with another ten to twelve major performances a year. But we managed." At the time of this writing, the Arsht was responsible for about 80–85 percent of the productions that take place in the complex, with variety in programming the watchword. "In Spring of 2015, we hosted nineteen different high school graduation ceremonies in a ten-day period," Richard notes.

Richard was particularly proud of the forward-looking nature of the summer programming efforts of the center, pointing to such shows as 2013's *Light in the Holocaust*, produced in tandem with Ballet Austin. "I had to assure people that, yes, we could in fact sell tickets to a ballet about the Holocaust," he said, adding that the show took nearly six months to prepare for. "But the response of the community made the effort worthwhile," the CEO said. "We have carried over the show's message to our summer school's programming since. It's not only historically educational, but the kids are able to relate it to important contemporary issues they face, such as bullying."

The 2008 unveiling of Free Gospel Sundays was intended to reflect the interests of the African American community, Richard noted, adding that the center also took pride in presenting more Spanish and Spanish-English programming than any of its counterparts in the country. Perhaps the most gratifying success for Richard was the much-talked-about 2010 production of *Fuerza Bruta,* an immersive experience that brought patrons through a "turned-around" box office erected on the opera house loading dock, and from there into a backstage lounge designed by Barton G. From there, audience members made their way onto the main stage of the theater, where they joined with performers in creating "the play." For Richard it was all part of his overall mission. "Purveying the Arsht Center brand," as he put it.

Beyond what happens at the Arsht Center itself, evidence suggested by 2017 that its presence had spurred a demonstrable trend in development in the immediate area. The Downtown Development Authority's Robertson pointed to data showing a rise in total taxable property from $9.8 billion in 2010 to $16.7 billion in 2016. "It's hard to know how much of that increase is owing to the center," Robertson said, "but I think anyone would admit that a lot of it is."

On the heels of the center's opening came a series of massive condominium towers that transformed the skyline north of downtown. Among others, the 63-story, 510-unit 900 Biscayne was completed in 2008, along with the 67-story, 306-unit Marquis; the 60-story, 541-unit Marina Blue; and the 49-story, 849-unit Vizcayne. The year before saw the completion of the 50-story, 200-unit Ten Museum Park and the 60-story, 630-unit Opera Tower at Seventeenth and Biscayne. In 2014, fears about the center being overshadowed by surrounding development were reawakened when construction began on the Melody, a 36-story, 497-unit building directly across Fourteenth Street from the Arsht; in 2016, the same development group announced plans for a 760-unit sister property just to the west at Fourteenth and North Miami Avenue.

As for what the center's presence has done for land values in the Omni area, Peter Andolina, director of the Land and Development Site Group for Metro 1 Commercial, says that in 2004, he sold an eighty-thousand-square-foot tract of land at Twentieth and Biscayne for a bit less than $150 per square foot. "That tract would sell for more than $450 per square foot today," he says. "The 1400 Biscayne Boulevard building sold in 2003 for $2 million. The same property sold for over $50 million in 2014. Need I say more?" In Andolina's view, once the projects planned for vacant lots west of the center are completed (including Melody 2), it will solidify what is now being called the Arts and Entertainment District "as one of Miami's premier neighborhoods."

To address concerns about so much development taking place in the absence of thoughtful oversight, in 2011 the Town Square Neighborhood Development Corporation (TSNDC) was founded as a nonprofit independent entity to oversee the development of the emerging Arsht Center district. The volunteer board of TSNDC is led by Armando Codina, chairman of Codina Partners; former City of Miami Mayor Manny Diaz; Michael Eidson, partner of the South Florida law firm Colson Hicks Eidson; and—no surprise—Parker Thomson. The group immediately selected Cesar Pelli and PCP Architects to develop a master development plan for the area, with Mitch Hirsch—who served as design principal for the center project—in charge. TSNDC also instituted partnerships with neighboring communities to oversee development and redevelopment of the Arsht Center area, advocating for infrastructure development, examining future Arsht Center expansion needs, and developing the Arsht Center itself as a catalyst to improve the neighborhoods through cultural programming and entrepreneurial business ventures.

As an advisory board, the group lacks authority to countermand existing codes, Arsht Board Chair Alan Fein points out, and while plans for the still-vacant former *Miami Herald* site (the newspaper moved its offices to Doral in 2013, and its iconic building on Biscayne Bay was demolished) have been put on hold, the future is uncertain. "None of the land is in [our] control," Fein says. "All we can do is provide a beacon." But Mitch Hirsch contends that the very existence of a blue-ribbon board has had a positive effect. "It is amazing," he says, "how many people have sought out our advice before moving forward with projects of significance in the area."

The Arsht Center also developed a number of access-enhancement and educational programs for young people, in consultation with the Miami-Dade Public Schools, the Miami-Dade County Department of Cultural Affairs, the resident companies, and a number of community-based organizations. Ailey Camp, a six-week full-scholarship summer dance camp for high schoolers, debuted in 2009, as did the Learning Through the Arts program, providing exposure to live music, theater, and dance via the public school system's Passport to Culture initiative. *Rock Odyssey* is the flagship of the Learning Through the Arts program and brings twenty-five thousand fifth-graders to the center every year to enjoy a live rock-and-roll musical based on Homer's *Odyssey*, free of charge to students and schools. In November 2016, the Ailey Camp received a rare National Endowment for the Arts/White House Commendation, an achievement that benefactor Arsht calls "remarkable for a ten-year-old institution and reason enough by itself for the whole undertaking."

"I didn't really know what I was doing when I wrote that check back in 2008," says Arsht, "but the fact that we have become an integral part of this community is what makes it all worth it. When a TSA screener at the airport tells me, 'I know that name,' then I get goosebumps, *and* I want to make sure they come and they get good seats." One of her favorite stories involves meeting the young granddaughter of Marlins Special Advisor Tony Perez, the former Reds Hall of Famer, at a baseball game. "Oh, I know who you are," the child assured Arsht. "I went to see *The Nutcracker* at your building."

Indeed, there was evidence that the Arsht had come to embody the cultural spirit of Miami in the global way that those who fought for it had hoped. *Miami New Times* writer Hannah Sentenac wrote on August 8, 2014, that the Arsht Center, alongside the I-395 umbilical connecting the city with the beach, "is the perfect metaphor for Miami." The complex was poised there, she wrote, "in greeting like the steely exoskeleton of some futuristic beast."

Sentenac continued, "On one hand, its sloping domes, glassy facades, and steel-straddling pedestrian bridge echo modernity and progress. On the other the seemingly out of place Carnival Tower and its off-white art deco charm are a throwback to the past." Like the city itself, Sentenac asserted, the center's exterior may not echo everyone's taste, but it is her belief that indeed the center has come to mirror the essence of a place. "At night, the whole lights up like a glittering beehive or an alien spaceship. . . . Both Miami and the Arsht Center are sexy and singular; delicate and hard; strange and unforgettable," Sentenac wrote. "We are a city like no other—we are avant garde and contradictory and larger than life. And so is the Arsht. What better structure to speak for us, without saying a word."

Former Assistant County Manager Bill Johnson, now Florida's Secretary of Commerce, recalls that one of the considerations that drew him to work with Dade County in 1980 was his chance reading of a magazine article proclaiming that there would be just seven or eight "great world cities" to emerge in the twenty-first century and that "Miami/Coral Gables" would be one of those. "In fact, that has happened," Johnson says. "Miami has become a vibrant global city, and the Arsht Center is one of the city's most valuable assets in terms of the quality of life here. It is certainly one of the premier performing arts centers in the nation."

Nor should there be any apologies regarding cost or pace of development surrounding the center, says Adrienne Arsht. "Look at those magnificent buildings. There were no 'cost overruns,'" she insists. "You go for as much as you can get. It is a lot easier to ask for forgiveness than for permission."

And as for the impact of the center on the neighborhood, she points to the Lincoln and Kennedy Centers for comparison. "What has happened here in the ten years the center has been open has been far greater than the first decade in New York or Washington. But today property values adjacent to the Lincoln Center, where you couldn't give away land thirty years ago, is more valuable than on the East Side." In fact, financier Sandy Weil sold his apartment at 15 Central Park West in early 2015 for a record-breaking $88 million, later selling the "maid's quarters" in the same building for $4 million. In the eyes of most, the Arsht is responsible not only for the explosion in nearby condominium building but in a revitalization of the so-called Biscayne Corridor, all the way north to the hipster haven of galleries and shops and eateries of Wynwood, fifteen blocks up the signature boulevard.

"The Arsht has succeeded beyond our wildest dreams," architect Hirsch says. "Its programming has opened the doors up to everyone, and as for how it has transformed a neighborhood, all you have to do is look at that shot of the building site in 2002 and compare it with what stands today."

Though some might still express puzzlement about how the price tag for the center roughly tripled from the beginning, Johnson points out that no local taxpayer is out so much as a dollar. Furthermore, Johnson says, "There was never a hint of corruption, a payoff, or a bribe. It's an open question whether it could have been built if that price tag had been announced at the beginning, but it is a certainty that no one made a crooked penny out of this project."

PAC Builders project executive Jesus Vazquez goes even further, saying, "I still brag about that project every chance I get. I think the county got a bargain in the end. There is no telling what the cost of such a set of buildings would be today. It would be virtually impossible to duplicate them."

"There is nothing the Knight Concert Hall can't accomplish in terms of its acoustics," adds veteran arts complex consultant Ron Austin. "It's right there with Carnegie Hall and Boston Symphony Hall—it could host the Olympics of classical music." Indeed, to a layperson, the hall's acoustics might seem little short of astounding. During a recent visit, this writer stood at one side of the 150-foot-wide stage, while Jeremy Shubrook, the center's director of production, walked to the opposite side of the vast expanse and murmured a few phrases in a conversational tone with his back turned.

Each phrase was crystal clear to the listener, as if Shubrook stood only inches away. Similarly, one can stand at the stage's forefront—where a soloist might stand for a performance, say—then turn to speak in a conversational tone toward the screen 150 feet or more away, at the far back of the stage. One's words immediately surround and echo inside the head, as if amplified by an invisible source, a phenomenon of invaluable assistance to performers and musicians who need to hear the sounds they are producing.

Former interim Center CEO Wilker asserts that today's Arsht Center is proof that culture is undeniably "on the radar" in Miami. "The building is working, and no one is worried about it any longer," he says. "Going out at night in Miami is not just about going to dinner and to clubs." He is philosophic about the cost of maintaining the center, pointing out that no such center is self-supporting. "A performing arts center is, like a library or a museum, part of a community's resources—part of what makes a city great." As to the final price tag, Wilker shares Bill Johnson's feeling that $168 million was never a feasible number. "But now you have three great halls for artists and audiences, including a remarkably warm and inviting concert hall, and look at what the center has done for the area," he says.

"The creation of the center has broken the dam for the support of the arts in Miami," says Michael Spring. In 2013, the $140 million Perez Art Museum, buoyed by a $40 million gift from developer Jorge Perez and supplanting the Miami Art Museum in the virtually moribund Dade Cultural Center at 101 W. Flagler, opened on waterfront land at Bicentennial Park, just south of I-395. And 2017 marks the opening of the aforementioned $300-million-plus Frost Museum of Science, also on that bayside parcel.

As for I-395, it is the roadway most perplexing to city planners since George Merrick, designer and founder of Coral Gables, wrestled with what to do about U.S. 1, the federal highway that slashes across his masterpiece "City Beautiful." While nothing much was ever done about U.S. 1, in 2016 Florida's Department of Transportation issued calls for redesign proposals for I-395, including a "signature bridge" that would replace the present access to the MacArthur Causeway leading to Miami Beach. The Town Square group chaired by developer Codina quickly commissioned drawings for what was termed an "aspirational vision" to guide the Department of Transportation, one that depicted the new roadway and bridge as a breathtaking elevated structure that removes the pilings and massive berms blocking views of the water from the Arsht Center, and incorporating a park, plaza, and hardwood forest on the land to be reclaimed. The concept would allow for an unmatched downtown tapestry of parks, shops, sports arena, museums, and performance centers stretching all the way from Bayfront Park to the Omni.

Along with all the talk about what the Arsht Center has helped make happen in Miami, it may be worth a recap of the many problems that detractors worried the center would bring. A de-emphasis on satellite arts venues was predicted, but it would seem that such support has actually been strengthened. A state-of-the-art, $51 million, 961-seat South Miami-Dade Cultural Arts Center, designed by the hometown firm of Arquitectonica, passed over in the competition for the Arsht, now stands in Cutler Bay in far south Dade County, offering a diverse array of performances well matched to a smaller venue. And as for downtown's venerable Gusman, recipient of a $1.4 million renovation from bed tax funds, it continues to operate primarily as a rental venue presenting programming about seventy-five nights or so a year.

As for the demise of the Concert Association, given the considerable overlap with the Arsht in mission—bringing high-profile acts and theater to South Florida—it was probably a foregone conclusion that the former's days were numbered; though with the retirement of its founder imminent, the ultimate impact of its loss on the cultural scene is questionable. And as for the disbanding of the Florida Philharmonic, that institution had been struggling mightily for several years before the performing arts center had so much as broken ground. It is probably just as accurate to say that were it not for the Arsht and its arrangement with the Cleveland Symphony, there would be no civic orchestra presence in South Florida today. The New World Symphony has continued to thrive, it should be noted, presenting a number of concerts annually at the Arsht and, since 2011, at its own 756-seat New World Center headquarters on Miami Beach, where $25 million of the necessary $160 million in costs came from Miami-Dade County.

Still, some smaller arts groups continue to grouse that the Arsht has not followed through on its promise to nurture local artists and productions. Such groups complain that even reduced rental rates at the black-box theater are prohibitive and that productions that don't promise significant returns are not of interest to the center's management. It is an issue that confronts most performing arts centers of size, says M. K. Wegman, president of the National Performance Network, in a *Herald* interview of 2010. Wegman points out that despite the best intentions, keeping a large center going often turns out to be at odds with presenting work of interest to only small audiences. Longtime Arsht CEO Richard agrees that it is a difficult balancing act to encourage risky productions while keeping the tastes of audiences in mind. "We want to present what people want to see," he says. "We are motivated to bring new content . . . but we just can't throw things onstage and say, 'You ought to come see it.'"

In any case, at the end of a ten-year run of balancing, promoting, edifying, and entertaining, the Arsht Center in 2016 marked an anniversary that some in the community might be forgiven for taking for granted, particularly if they were among the nearly one-quarter million who had come to call Miami home after 2008, when the center's dust—literal and metaphorical—had finally settled and a nearly thirty-year-long struggle was concluded. "Well, of course we have a world-class performing arts center," they might say. "Who would expect anything less?"

Such a response would overlook a great deal of difficult history, however. As Bill Johnson points out, "I am a great believer in public-private partnerships, but I have to say that in this case, it is the private sector that steered this project to completion. It would never have happened without the vision and the leadership of Parker Thomson—a political genius, by the way—along with the efforts of Woody Weiser and others, including Michael Spring."

Lawrence Wilker echoes the sentiment regarding Thomson, saying simply, "Without Parker Thomson it wouldn't have happened." And Ron Austin chimes in, "Parker Thomson is without a doubt the hero of this story."

Says Michael Spring, "The part I played in the early days was extremely gratifying, even though my wife refers to the 1990s as our 'lost decade' in terms of our marriage. But working alongside Parker was like a composer getting to work with a master lyricist. Parker had the vision, and he stayed with it, no matter what. There was never a time when we thought we had finally turned a corner or could let our guard down. But if we spent a month gearing up for a meeting with commissioners, and things didn't go well, Parker would shrug and say, 'Michael, there will be another meeting soon.' Art Teele and Gwen Margolis [former commission chairs] were invaluable and so were [County Managers] Merrett Stierheim [whom Ms. Arsht describes as "impossible to turn down"] and George Burgess. But without Parker, it couldn't have happened. He was not just a 'volunteer'; he worked long and hard, and he has made Miami a better place. He's the father of our cultural scene."

For PCP's Mitch Hirsch, Thomson's patience is the quality that stands above all and is probably to account for a major turning point that allowed the project to transform from good to great. "When the client made the decision to restore a number of the original design elements— increasing the volume of the buildings, putting all the glass back into the façade 'lanterns,' and scrapping the stucco exteriors in favor of stone—that is when the buildings stopped being simply 'handsome' and became 'iconic,'" Hirsch says. "It doesn't always happen, but I have witnessed it often enough," Hirsch adds. "If Parker Thomson had gone on a crusade to browbeat everyone into restoring those items, he would have probably created a backlash. Instead, he just sat back and let everyone come to understand for themselves how important it was to do things right."

Of course, one of the most important figures in getting things right was the center's architect, Cesar Pelli, ninety at the time of this writing and still quite active in the affairs of Pelli Clarke Pelli Architects. Asked in May of 2017 to look back at his work and the early suggestion that architects present designs that were somehow the physical embodiment of a place, Pelli had this to say: "Miami is a vibrant, multicultural center, sometimes called the Capital of the Americas," he said. "We believed that the PAC would help to strengthen this achievement. And it has. We never tried to design a building that expressed Miami. But the Arsht Center fits very comfortably in the city. It feels natural there. And it is a great magnet."

For the University of Pennsylvania's Birch, the ultimate success of the Arsht Center does raise important questions that go beyond South Florida: Does the Arsht represent a new model in its success with innovative and culturally diverse programming that swims against the tide of cultural elitism? Or is the center's success—with $10 million of its income derived annually from tourism taxes—a function of Miami's unique makeup, its innovations impossible to replicate elsewhere? Says Birch, "Most important is what the Arsht Center has meant to Miami. It has transformed local and outsider opinions about the region and helped make Miami relevant in the performing arts world. [It] mirrors its city in being modern, hip, and cutting-edge. . . . Its diverse population makes fundraising and marketing a challenge, but the organization capitalizes on Miami's diversity by presenting an exciting and culturally relevant mix of programming."

To anyone with the slightest appreciation for the complex and complicated political and social history of South Florida as it has played out over the last half-century, the presence of the Arsht Center for the Performing Arts is little short of mind-boggling. As Arthur Teitelbaum, longtime southern area director of the Anti-Defamation League, once told Thomson, "In twenty-five to fifty years, every American community of any size will be as complex in its makeup as Miami. If you prove that this performing arts center can be built in such a fractious place as this, then you will have accomplished a very important thing."

An important thing indeed, brought about by the hard work and dedication of so many whose work is detailed within these pages—though most of them would add that without the unflappable stewardship of a lawyer from Boston named Thomson, who wanted to go somewhere he could make a difference, it might never have happened.

ACKNOWLEDGMENTS

I am greatly indebted to a number of individuals whose assistance was invaluable in making this book possible, most prominent among them being Parker Thomson, Stuart Blumberg, and Roberto Espejo. I would also like to extend sincere thanks to Michael Spring, John Richard, Valerie Riles, Jeremy Shubrook, Stanley Arkin, Ron Esserman, Bill Johnson, Ron Austin, Alyce Robertson, Jack Lowell, Jesus Vazquez, Lawrence Wilker, Chantal Honore, Mitch Hirsch, and Adrienne Arsht. I would also like to acknowledge the understanding and assistance of my more than patient wife, Kimberly, for her willingness to put up with the moods, absences, distractions, and requests for advice and aid attendant to a project that has consumed me for the better part of three years.

NOTE ON SOURCES

As this is not a work of traditional scholarship, I have not made use of traditional footnotes but instead have endeavored to indicate the sources of factual materials in the text itself, calling attention to news stories presenting singular information by date, publication, and author where noted, and to articles, books, and other printed materials by title, author, and date. The chief primary materials pertinent to this account are found in the minutes of the Miami-Dade County Department of Cultural Affairs, the Miami and Miami Beach city councils, and the Dade County/Miami-Dade County commission; the discussions and decisions of those bodies are referred to in the text by date. I have also made significant use of press accounts from the *Miami Herald*, the *Sun-Sentinel*, *Miami Today*, the *New York Times*, *Miami New Times*, and others. In most cases, news stories summarizing pertinent governmental actions were published the day following the meetings, sometimes with additional comment from individuals involved. Local news media also kept close tabs on the progress of the center, and regular columnists and beat writers offered regular summaries and assessments of the project's fits and starts. I have endeavored to provide citations within the text to individual authors and articles containing singular materials; if I have made errors or omissions in that regard, I offer sincere apologies.

In addition to printed materials, this account has been enriched by the recollections of a number of those involved in the effort to create a performing arts center from the earliest days of its conception. I am particularly indebted to Parker Thomson and Stuart Blumberg for their many hours of discussions regarding the undertaking, and for their guiding me to interviews with a number of others whose observations have been so valuable in helping not only to reconstruct a complex and lengthy process but to appreciate the impact and the magnitude of present-day activities at the Arsht. The latter group includes Michael Spring, director of the Miami-Dade County Department of Cultural Affairs; John Richard, president and CEO of the Adrienne Arsht Center for the Performing Arts of Dade County; Jeremy Shubrook, director of production at the Arsht; and also Stanley Arkin, Ron Esserman, Roberto Espejo, Bill Johnson, Ron Austin, Alyce Robertson, Jack Lowell, Jesus Vazquez, former Arsht CEO Lawrence Wilker, and, last but not least, Adrienne Arsht. My interactions with these individuals have taken the form of numerous in-person interviews, phone conversations, and e-mail exchanges over the past three years, and their contributions are annotated in the text.

I would also like to thank Mitch Hirsch, design principal in charge of the Arsht Center for Pelli Clarke Pelli Architects, for his look back at the challenges faced in bringing Cesar Pelli's vision into reality and for his assessment of the role of the Arsht in its contemporary setting. And I am also indebted to Cesar Pelli himself for taking the time to reflect upon the significance of his work with this project.

It may be worth mentioning that my overarching aim has been to assemble the above-mentioned materials, drawn from some forty-five years of South Florida history, into a cohesive narrative allowing readers to follow what happened, to appreciate the difficulty with which it was achieved, and to have some measure of the significance of that achievement. To the extent that this narrative becomes a compelling story more than a mere recitation of facts, the effort will not have been in vain.

INDEX

LES STANDIFORD is the author of twenty previous books and novels, including *Last Train to Paradise: Henry Flagler and the Spectacular Rise and Fall of the Railroad That Crossed an Ocean* as well as eight novels in the John Deal mystery series. His books have appeared on the *New York Times* Best Sellers list on multiple occasions, have been designated as a *New York Times* Editor's Choice, and have been selected as the "One Read" choice of more than a dozen public library systems. *Spill* and *The Man Who Invented Christmas* have been adapted into feature motion pictures, and he is the recipient of fellowships from the National Endowment for the Arts, the National Endowment for the Humanities, and the Florida Council for the Arts. He is founding director of the Creative Writing Program and professor of English at Florida International University in Miami. He lives in Pinecrest, Florida, with his wife, Kimberly, an artist and psychotherapist. They are the parents of three children: Jeremy, Hannah, and Alexander.